13-99

Online Journalism

106431

KU-052-027

Online Journalism

A Critical Primer

Jim Hall

Pluto  Press

LONDON • STERLING, VIRGINIA

First published 2001 by Pluto Press
345 Archway Road, London N6 5AA
and 22883 Quicksilver Drive, Sterling, VA 20166–2012, USA

www.plutobooks.com

British Library Cataloguing in Publication Data
A catalogue record for this book is available from the British Library

Library of Congress Cataloging-in-Publication Data

Hall, Jim, 1950–
    Online journalism : a critical primer / Jim Hall
      p. cm.
    Includes bibliographical references (p.)
    ISBN 0-7453-1193-8 – ISBN 0-7453-1192-X (pbk.)
    1. Electronic journals.   I. Title.
PN4833.H35 2001
025.06'0704–dc21
            00-009184

ISBN   0 7453 1193 8 hardback
ISBN   0 7453 1192 X paperback

10	09	08	07	06	05	04	03	02	01
10	9	8	7	6	5	4	3	2	1

Designed and produced for Pluto Press by
Chase Publishing Services, Fortescue, Sidmouth EX10 9QG
Typeset from disk by Gawcott Typesetting Services
Printed in the European Union by TJ International, Padstow, England

Contents

For millennia, every attempt at civilization foundered because nations lacked the most essential information. Now we lurch forward, overburdened by hordes of misinformation. Sometimes I think our future existence will hang on whether we can keep false information from proliferating too rapidly. If our power to verify the facts does not keep pace, then distortions of information will eventually choke us.

Norman Mailer
Harlot's Ghost
London: Abacus, 1992, p. 249

Introduction

This book relates the story of news journalism's encounter with the World Wide Web. It conspicuously avoids words such as 'cyberspace' and 'virtuality' and the arguments, which already look anachronistic, around their implicit techno-utopias and dystopias. The short history of the web has certainly seen enough utopian claims that corporate and political hierarchies could be tumbled by a technology they could no longer control and their power dispersed into every conceivable kind of community, and I have tried to reflect some of these. In contrast, the web is also the site of moves by media conglomerates vigorously gearing-up for global pre-eminence and a new kind of hegemony. The two trends do not entirely contradict each other. With regard to its determining effects on culture and society, the web itself remains neutral even while it becomes the conduit for new power configurations and relations predicated upon a new corporate ideology.

The tendency of information technology is inherently conservative rather than revolutionary; it cannot easily leapfrog its own technical and compatibility standards. The changes in journalism explored by this book, while closely associated with the Internet, are, accordingly, traced to other determinisms: the globalisation of ownership, the widespread deregulation of broadcast news media, entrepreneurial risk economies seeking private money and initiatives, the mobilisation of new power relationships with the fall of the Iron Curtain and a whole spectrum of changes in social and cultural mores from reading habits to new routes to identity and subjectivity. The journalisms enabled by the web are driven by an agenda-setting

radically different from the corporate and statal gatekeeping of the
age of mass media, through which the information society is articulating the values that will premise its emerging institutions.

To engage in the process, we need a post-utopian imagination
that embraces the complexity of human institutions and a critical
technical practice that embraces the coevolution of institutions
and technologies. Both the imagination and the practice can be
dimly seen taking form around us.[1]

That imagination, while it is now renewing much of the social,
cultural and economic, was earlier applied to the forms and practices
of journalism as it explored the potential of Tim Berner-Lee's invention, the World Wide Web.

By the beginning of the twenty-first century the web was serving
around 200 million regular users with more than 800 million
separate web pages. A publisher such as Reuters routinely served
27,000 pages of data every second of every day. The web continues
to grow at an exponential rate and news, after email and search
engines, is one of the primary drivers for that growth.[2] Web users
access news through devices that range from small hand-held
machines which are principally telephones using Wireless
Application Protocol technologies (WAP) to adapted television sets
and desktop computers connected to an array of peripherals that
include cameras, printers and scanners. CNN's *CustomNews* service is
delivered through a mobile pager network. A potentially infinite
number of channels is carried through this expanding array of technologies.

The web's is a much larger constituency than those which delivered earlier media audiences, even the continental audiences of
satellite TV, and much more difficult to segment. For all its global
range and its millions of users it refuses to fit neatly into the category
of mass media. For media producers and the advertisers who under-
write them new paradigms seeking junctions and commonalities of
geography, age, gender, income, race and niche interests are
required. How do they deliver news to an audience that is at once
local and global? The interactive nature of the medium also demands
new approaches and, for journalism, it has become clear that the
tried and tested top-down forms, developed over the past three

centuries around print, have been made obsolete by the new media and are increasingly irrelevant to the lives of many readers. There have even been suggestions that newspapers and magazines could be completely supplanted by Internet-based information delivery systems.

It is salutary to enquire whether journalism itself is equally obsolete. As the technology takes over the role of mediation with software such as search engines and content filters, are the mediators still required? This book suggests that they are, but many traditional journalistic values such as objectivity, impartiality, accountability, balance, fairness and trustworthiness have, for old media, become ciphers and urgently need to be reviewed in the light of a new medium that trails with it all the confusions, opportunity and excitement of film one hundred years ago and printing at the time of Caxton.

A textbook on online journalism rests on the assumption that the Internet is somehow different from other channels of news and information. It should try to span the positions of extreme technological determinism, which underplays the cultural, ideological and economic contexts of the Internet, and the social constructivism which insists that technology is no more than an effect of the tectonic forces which move and shape those contexts. Current thinking in the media industries and in education, both in Europe and in North America, spans the full spectrum of views on the issue. While the opening sections of the book will introduce both the practices and theories of journalism on the web it seems apposite to open with a consideration of some of those opinions.

However we construe the relationship between the Internet and traditional news organisations what is now undeniable is that this relationship is important. The news media were the third global professional sector, after the military complex and higher education and research, to go online. In a period of some 18 months in the mid-1990s most national newspaper titles in the world and many regional and local titles produced web editions or went online to some extent. In some cases the transition radically affected the ways in which they produced news and, in the case of the American magazine *Omnium*, even allowed it to cease print publication for a period while it was restructured and yet apparently to retain the bulk of its circulation. One of the determining questions which I kept returning to as this book developed asks whether online news is journalism as it has been understood historically merely repackaged or some radical emergent form. Can we understand it as journalism at all?

Stephen Miller, assistant technology editor at the *New York Times*, manages the training of *New York Times* reporters and editors in new technologies and computer-assisted reporting. He believes that '... the Internet has fundamentally changed the news business' and suggests that online technologies and readers offer reporters a new way of working.

> ... the opportunity to focus on information that you never got before. Suddenly you have a different brand of story, a more precise story. Suddenly there are better questions to ask. It's a new starting place. It does not replace shoe leather and traditional reporting ... but it is a very powerful and very effective technology.[3]

The Internet adds momentum to trends that first appeared with the massification of media to expand further the constituency of journalism. It becomes more than news-gathering, analysis and reportage. Journalism provides and structures the information that people need to understand themselves, to understand the world and to understand their place in the world. Such information extends beyond news; it includes ideas, stories and the dialogues in which readers can learn from each other. To look at journalism on the Internet only in the narrow context of what is traditionally constituted as news, as merely another means of delivering information gathered elsewhere, is to imagine it too narrowly. Comparative studies of print editions and their online adjuncts find a much expanded remit for online newsrooms.

In *The Universal Journalist* David Randall suggests that the central role of the journalist is to 'discover and publish information that takes the place of rumour and speculation.'[4] Convention, developed over the past century and a half, dictates that such discoveries be published in specific narrative forms. The print journalist is effectively a storyteller and the nature of the story demands the series of filters and blind entries determined by the conventional structure of the 'inverted pyramid' if it is to attain its end. Increasingly the online journalist abjures that historic role to act as guide and commentator to primary sources – the discoveries themselves. As readers become their own storytellers the role of 'gatekeeper' is largely passed from the journalist to them. The move changes the nature of the story. The change is as momentous as those which took place during the period in which the press, capitalised by advertising, took over the role of information gatekeeper from those nation states which developed into modern liberal democracies or from the church.

Steve Case, the co-founder, chairman and chief executive officer of America Online (AOL), the largest subscriber Internet Service Provider (ISP), says that his organisation doesn't even hire journalists because it views itself as a 'news-packaging' rather than a 'news-gathering' organisation. As we shall see, that distinction is crucial to the provision of news on the web. Yet when Diana, Princess of Wales, was killed in a car crash in Paris in 1997, AOL had more than 6 million visits to its front news page. The day after John F. Kennedy Jr's fatal plane crash in July 1999 AOL's consumers responded with one message related to the event every second.[5] That level of interest (both *MSNBC* and *Fox News* audiences were up by more than 600 per cent over the previous weekend) seems to demand something more than 'packaging'.

In drawing the distinction between AOL, as a packager or aggregator of news, and traditional news outlets such as newspapers and magazines which report news, develop news sources and write stories, Case highlights one of the emerging roles of the online journalist. While he explains why AOL does not hire journalists, he indicates that the online service does, however, employ individuals with 'media backgrounds' because it recognises that its product does require 'sophisticated judgement', as well as an in-depth knowledge of audience preferences and presentation options.

Journalists in every country are currently using the Internet to rethink their roles as well as the social, political and commercial functions of news and information. That role is, to extend Case's definition, much more than the optimum arrangement of text across a range of media. Reading the news is increasingly a fully interactive process and it is predicated upon a journalism that is capable of offering news as an array of sources and comment, in addition to a report or account, which is easily negotiated by many different kinds of readers. Such a shift demands in turn a reassessment of traditional ways of thinking about journalistic roles, practices and ethics.

Particularly important is the problem of how a participatory news affects the public sphere and politics and how journalists contribute to those discourses. The democratising tendencies of the Net, and we should by no means accept these as givens, seem to make possible a news which becomes a heteroglossia accommodating interventions from many different kinds of readers, journalists and sources.

Most computer users – and in the West that increasingly means all of us – now routinely use the Internet to source information; students and readers in most countries around the globe are familiar with electronic journals and text databases, and regular Internet users access a range of web-based documents, from online newspapers and magazines to webzines and sites promoting entities from corporations to primary schools and villages to contemporary city states such as Singapore. These forms are all radically different in conception, design, content and delivery, yet online journalism employs them all and, indeed, helps to create them.

Online journalism is all of these things and more. It is also the industry that is experiencing the full and unmediated impact of converging media forms. It is this aspect of journalism that interests me – how the standards and practices that are applied in the media industries of the twentieth century are rethought to work at the place where television, radio and the new media forms of the Internet collide. Many of the obsolete accretions of traditional news culture are being rapidly discarded to create radical new forms for the twenty-first century. These new information forms will affect every aspect of our lives and many believe that their potential is, on balance, benign. Tim Berners-Lee has said that what is at stake is ultimately a 'more powerful democracy and whole new forms of government, but at the same time for each person ... self-expression and potential to grow. The richness of the information space should put back into our world even what broadcast television has, some say, taken out'.[6]

On a more cautionary note, and one which rather places the whole Internet adventure in perspective, at the end of the last century, at a moment when many in the West saw the web and its emergent media forms including its journalisms achieving a kind of maturity, cohesiveness and ubiquity, more than half of the world's population had yet to make its first phone call.[7]

The opening section of the book examines the emerging practices and conventions of online journalism, its technologies and some crucial ways in which the discourse of news is altered by its becoming interactive. Chapter 1 considers the Internet's rapidly expanding audiences and the arrival of the information society. New media's potential for inexpensive one-to-one, one-to-many and many-to-many reciprocal communications carries far-reaching and disruptive implications for traditional news producers and journalism. News now arrives in personalised packages and it has taken the global news corporations some time to realise that consumers have adopted new patterns of consumption which call for new forms such as aggregations of information and portals. Portals contain outlines of generic, personalised and news-related content, usually linked to the providers of such information.

While the potential of the new media is explored for workable commercial models there is scope for large investments and larger losses. As the web attains the status of a mass medium of global scale and range, albeit one based on a new, or at least different, paradigm, the struggle for consumers becomes increasingly frantic. Mark Poster has observed that the paradigm shift for the medium is to be found in the difficulty of understanding it through a broadcast model of communication. As we have seen it is equally effective as a narrowcast and even, as in the activity of flaming, a many-to-one, medium.

The nature of news and the values that guarantee it are not the eternal verities that liberal ideologies might have us believe. Newsworthiness is a negotiated construct. As its forms and contexts change, journalists are having to reassess the rules that they work by. The web encourages news consumers to negotiate breaking stories as they develop – news becomes a dynamic form and its values, such as truth and utility, have to be re-evaluated by readers. Immediacy and interactivity have radical implications for the way we consume news. Chapter 2 retells the story of the Columbine School killings in Denver as it unfolded on the web in May 1999 as a platform for these values. In a medium which makes the complexity of even the everyday manifest how do we begin to understand the extraordinary?

This book claims no pretensions to being either an HTML primer or a web design handbook, for which, in any case, I have neither the knowledge nor background to be able to do more than sketch. It would be difficult, however, to come to any understanding of how online journalism works without some consideration of its machinery and the aesthetic and technical parameters which constrain it. Chapter 3 discusses Hypertext Markup Language (HTML) and some of the software that is routinely used in online newsrooms to produce hypertext along with its new grammars and emergent narrative forms. It goes on to consider the profession of online journalist and the roles of editors and reporters in the virtual newsroom. I am far from convinced that these roles are substantively different from those of their colleagues in the broadcast and print newsrooms which are, in any case, already making way for their multimedia successors.

The second section begins with a study of the 1999 war in Kosovo as it was reported on the web, often in advance of TV and print media and probably from a wider range of sources than any war in history. In applying a range of theoretical positions to online representations of the war it begins to look very different from that in Bosnia and the earlier wars of the Yugoslavian succession. Patently, the medium has a determining effect upon the message and its advocates.

The next chapters examine online news as operating within a series of overlapping economies: moral, fiscal, political and regulatory, cultural and ideological. Chapter 5 tells the story of Matt Drudge's scooping of *Newsweek* magazine's 'Monicagate' exclusive. Drudge, the *bête noire* of online journalism, takes a heterodox approach to journalism based in part on a root and branch re-examination of its ethical standards, occasionally by the radical expedient of jettisoning them wholesale. It is by no means a simple 'tabloidisation' and tries to take account of the new economy of news that the web proposes. Drudge is one of the first representatives of a journalism which attempts to meet fully the logic of disintermediation, the process through which news consumers lose the filters and gatekeepers which sanction and promote preferred readings of the news. It insists that readers make up their own minds and, occasionally, provides them with the information and the tools to do so. The emerging ethic is one that values depth, context, immediacy and appropriateness over claims for objectivity, which while they are scrupulous about 'truth' and 'fairness' have no way of differentiating spin and media events, including political summits and celebrity weddings, from spontaneous occurrences. Among the other conundrums spawned by the web is, for journalism, a crisis of legitimacy of monumental proportions.

The initial chapters of the book might suggest an understanding of changes in global media that are largely technologically determined. Chapter 6 tries to mitigate any such misapprehension with an account of the development of online news in its commercial context. It examines a traditional, still highly profitable, media sector seizing the opportunity to discard its heaviest overheads, inked wood pulp and its distribution. The news industry is capitalised by the global advertising industry, itself testing the possibilities of a direct investment in a medium that places no spatial, temporal or demographic constraints upon its endeavours to communicate with consumers. The chapter examines the nature of virtual markets and considers how contemporary media producers discount income for credibility with advertisers while titles experiment with new retail models and products such as subscription, micropayment and sales from the archives to develop the revenue streams that will eventually lead to profits.

Chapter 7 examines a corporate political sphere that has been shaken and unnerved by a media which, freed, at least temporarily, from the corporations which are complicit with the West's political and economic elites, no longer keeps to the rules and seems to resist the very notion of hierarchy and order. The liberal democracies, burdened with the ethic, however compromised, of 'free speech' and a penchant for deregulation, remain baffled with their new media domain and try to terrorise their subjects from effectively using it with dire warnings of outrage and tsunamis of pornography. Other polities resort to coercion and blatant censorship. The Kosovo War in 1999 gave instances of a state simultaneously trying to shut down its dissident web media while exploiting exactly the same methods and technologies that its dissidents were using to undercut NATO and the West.

The chapter deviates slightly from the subjects of news and journalism to consider the possibilities for surveillance and the loss of privacy which come about with the web. For instance, knowing what the teenage gunmen of Columbine School were reading in the weeks prior to their attack on the school seems to tell news readers much about their state of mind. Yet are we so sanguine in the knowledge that the media corporations, and who knows else, can so easily track our own media consumption?

Finally, the issues of copyright and the ownership of intellectual property seem quite straightforward to most producers and consumers of media in the West. In the developing world the same issues are viewed in a very different light and are seen as yet another device instigated by the West (or perhaps, we should now be thinking, by the North) to keep its economic grip on the planet as a whole. The notion of a World Information Order seems clearly predicated upon such a hierarchy and geared specifically to sedimenting it in place. The countries of the South are clearly aware of the problem and are actively seeking another model.

The final chapter opens with the 'communities of interest', 'affinity niches' and other manifestations of the local which are articulated through the web. Such locales, of course, by no means always map directly on to more anachronistic notions of community and in many cases specifically recognise that they are held together only by information of one kind or another. The institutions organised around the discourse of journalism can be understood as one such community. Clearly, such communities are directly related to identity and subjectivity and are, at the same time, a response to the corporate globalisation project. Globality can separate existing communities and identities from their defining relationships and their traditions and practices. Some perish in the process, new ones emerge and others, including journalism, are reconstituted to meet the new conditions.

Notes on Usage

Strictly speaking, the World Wide Web (WWW) is part of the Internet or Net and I have tried to avoid conflating them. The Internet developed from the ARPANet (Advanced Research Projects Agency) commissioned by the US Department of Defense in 1969 for research into networking mainly military data. The story of how, as the Cold War approached absolute zero, the Pentagon was seeking a bomb-proof communications system is now legend. By 1971 a group of North American governmental and academic institutions were networked and by 1973 it had expanded to include European hosts or connected computers. By 1992 it connected 890,000 hosts and comprised such technologies as encrypted person-to-person electronic mail, Internet Relay Chat (IRC), video conferencing, mail-based distribution lists and Usenet groups. Current development of the Net includes Internet2 with the massively expanded bandwidth that will allow full multimedia on demand. In 1992 the web arrived with the release of the World Wide Web by CERN (Conseil Européen Pour La Recherche Nucléaire). The WWW software was originally developed by Tim Berners-Lee to facilitate real-time collaboration between scientists around the world working in the field of high-energy physics. It rapidly expanded to become the main trunk of the Internet with many millions of users. The web gave users the protocols to access WWW pages and seemed to provide a new public sphere which in the succeeding years continues to grow exponentially.[8] It is able to access and browse hypertext-formatted texts and to provide a gateway to other methods of information transfer such as File Transport Protocol (FTP). The system comprises clients (browser-editor software or computers used to access information) and servers (software or computers that manage information) along with the software that defines Uniform Resource Locators (URL), Hypertext Transfer Protocols (HTTP) and the structuration that makes texts readable by WWW clients, the Hypertext Markup Language (HTML) and its developments.

The nature of the web and the convergence of media forms leave me in something of a quandary with regard to notions of readership and audience. While both groups are clearly consumers I have loosely used 'audience' in the sociological sense and 'reading' to signify the act that occurs between the subject and the text. That act simultaneously produces meaning between reader and text and interpellates the reader into a subject position. My understanding of the more sociological (and social) construct of audience does not necessarily atomise it to a plurality of individual readings or readerships.

Finally, while many commentators capitalise the word 'web' I note that in its first decade or so the telegraph was also universally inscribed with an initial capital letter. As the technology naturalised it became just another common noun and I assume here a similar etymology around 'web'.

1
The Information Society

Michael Marien concluded the 1985 collection of essays, *The Information Revolution*, with 'Some Questions for the Information Society'. He considered the quality of communication in our era and the problem of information in a number of spheres including commerce, education, the family and politics, concluding that, 'Ideally, we need schemes such as the World Brain, proposed by H.G. Wells in 1938, to bring together the scattered mental wealth of the human race and make it universally accessible.'[1] Marien stressed his belief that not everyone would benefit from the revolution which was clearly already fomenting by 1985. His view of the information society implicitly underpins it with an emerging information colonialism. Also in 1985 Walter Wriston, the then head of Citicorp Bank, declared that 'the information standard has replaced the gold standard as the basis of world finance'.[2] Both views, expressed a decade before the Internet became a news medium in any real sense, should inform any reading of the web and its determining practices, including online news and journalism.

Ten years later, a more benign version of the information society was promulgated by Martin Bangemann, the member of the European Commission who drove so much of the legislation that deregulated broadcast media during the 1990s. Bangemann believed that the information society represented a net good, especially in terms of the employment that would flow from it and should become the motivating force behind all the EU's policies. Implicit in Bangemann's common-sense grasp of the information society is the suggestion that information, like water, flows easily and unimpeded from providers to be disseminated in an equitable way amongst receivers. The model is based on an over-simplistic communications theory, still dominant in both education and the industry itself, for which messages remain no more than packages of information enabled by particular technologies to pass from transmitters to receivers. It suggests that media institutions and technologies channel and filter information from the events and contingencies which animate the social sphere while the rest of us, their constituencies, are its unquestioning consumers. It comprises not only knowledge and data but also the thoughts, ideas, beliefs and values through which society understands itself and evolves.

Such an understanding lies uneasily between the Marxist view of the commodification of information and surveillance of its users which leads, not least, to widening gaps between the information-rich and information-poor, and the communitarian hopes which emphasise its democratising tendencies. While such an under-standing is clearly far from unproblematic, especially around issues of access and exclusion, the web reinforces and extends it on one hand with the proposal that news and other information can be personalised in a way that was unimaginable even two decades ago when deregulation and advances in media technology allowed providers and advertisers to segment radically the mass readerships and audiences of the mid-century. The web arrives with surveillance and feedback technologies, intimations of power and control, which enable advertisers and others to target consumers personally. Perhaps a more useful understanding of the streams of information which now galvanise the world is through Paul Virilio and McKenzie Wark's 'vector'. Information in this construction has no direction or fixed destination and no predetermined meaning. The vector comprises only force and, hence, effect.[3]

The understanding is broadened through the aspiration that a response to information – some form of personalised expression, intervention or feedback – is as important to the consumer as recep-tion. The Internet, originally designed as the most resilient two-way communications technology that humanity is currently capable of producing, can make our daily news a real-time interactive text. We still read all about it, as we have done for the past two centuries or so, but increasingly we tend also to respond by arranging textual elements to produce our own narrativisations or, using hypertext or email, to intervene in and extend the discourse. Such interventions by consumers have not always been welcome, or even possible, and, if they are to be at all meaningful, seem to signal moves towards a participatory democracy and more autonomous models of consumption based around communities.

Audiences and Producers in the Information Society

The large audiences that have resulted from globalisation of the traditional media corporations, especially of news-gathering and distribution, have attracted a series of mergers and buyouts in the closing decades of the century resulting in fewer, louder broadcast voices. It is the surviving brands, a global media rump dominated by about nine conglomerates such as AOL-Time Warner, Disney (including ABC), News International and, arguably, although its corporate structure is rather different and its capitalisation significantly less, the BBC, which have the resources to develop extensive holdings across the spectrum of media and to occupy maximum bandwidth in all of them. In the traditional media – television, radio and print journalism – they have attained what increasingly, as their business is developed through production partnerships and joint equity ventures with each other and their own subsidiaries, looks like a cartel. This method of reducing risk and locking out new competition is pervasive. McChesney and Herman suggest that 'each of the nine ... media giants has joint ventures with, on average, two-thirds of the other eight'. They are truly global in the sense that the world beyond their national boundaries is no longer discounted as a series of less profitable residual markets. Disney, for instance, now takes more than 50 per cent of its turnover from non-US markets.[4]

An important aside on this cartel, and one which has important implications for journalism, might be to emphasise that the holdings of the conglomerates are not limited to media companies. NBC, for instance, is owned by the conglomerate headed by General Electric, much of whose core business is armaments. In the representation of a news event such as the Kosovo War reporters for NBC are, on the face of it, heavily compromised. Recent history suggests that contemporary media conglomerates are increasingly ambivalent about the concept of 'glass walls'. The determining philosophies of these corporations serve the interests of the shareholders and the advertisers: they exist to make money.

Naturally, the conglomerates have attempted to replicate their success in traditional media on the web, but there, in an environment of potentially unlimited bandwidth, the monopoly is harder to defend and they are thrown back into a more competitive environment. They have to contend with an apparently unlimited choice and their voices, however loud, are forced, once more, to compete in a babble that has been all but squeezed from the traditional media. One of the purposes of this book is to explore the strategies and new forms that they, and their smaller, sometimes more lively, competitors, have evolved to maintain and develop audiences in a market, news and journalism on the web, where growth is presently exponential. One of the early hopes of the libertarian groups which helped to pioneer the Internet was that it would provide alternative voices to counter these concentrations of economic and political power. In terms of news this could mean the possibility of a more independent press which performs, for global audiences, a critical role in the development of social, political and cultural attitudes currently mediated by the media cartel.

At the time of writing, the volume of traffic on the Internet is doubling every 100 days. It can only be an estimate but between 10 and 14 million more computers join the network every year. US figures indicate that by the spring of 1999 around 20 per cent of Americans were receiving at least some of their daily news from the web.[5] Within five years more people in the developed world will get their news from the Internet rather than from a daily paper. And for those nine or ten global media companies who appeared to be on the verge of completely dominating world markets a mere decade ago, with a virtual monopoly (perhaps, more correctly, an oligopoly) on advertising space and the media that carried it, there has been the creeping realisation that shouting loudly, simply spending money to the axioms of received wisdom, no longer works as it did. This exponential rise in web traffic, while it drove the value of Internet companies sky-high (by 1999 Yahoo!, which began life as a web subject index or catalogue, was worth more than Boeing), was driven on the back of profit discounted until someone discovered the way to make money from this tidal wave of consumers. Yahoo!, one of the few companies to make a profit from the new media in its first decade, reported $86 million in revenues for the first three months of 1999. While that represented an increase by a factor of three on the previous year's total and a leap in profits by a factor of ten to $20.6 million for the quarter, it was derisory compared to corporations in other sectors with equivalent capitalisation. In the late 1990s it seemed that all of the global media conglomerates were content to continue making substantial investments to establish their presence on the new medium while awaiting its potential to mature. *Discovery Channel Online*, for instance, spent more than $8 million setting up its website for an advertising revenue of about one quarter of investment over the first two years.

The confusion might seem to be shared by readers who are overwhelmed by choice. In a medium which encourages such a massive proliferation of voices how do readers select those which offer trustworthy news? Can the same criteria they once used to select their daily paper or broadcast news apply? Will the news industry itself remain viable when, as in the case of the attempt to impeach the president of the United States, everyone can read the Starr Report for themselves and click directly to an unlimited choice of comment upon it? Much of that comment will be produced by readers very like themselves. What role is there now for the journalist? When a news event of note occurs, global or local, people email each other. They recommend websites related to the event, often the primary sources, websites which are only rarely those of the large media corporations.

The NATO war in Kosovo in 1999 led to an estimated 30–40 per cent gain in traffic for Western news sites, especially the brand name websites such as *BBC News Online*, but many readers, millions, were constructing their own story of the war, at least in part, from sites in Serbia and the Balkans as well as the UK Ministry of Defence, NATO and the refugee aid organisations. This has dramatic implications for news management by military and government institutions. Many people at work and at home take their news, as it breaks, from sites operating in the background as they work or play on their PCs, televisions and telephones. During times of crisis we might expect significant increases in such behaviour.

Finally, there is the issue of bandwidth itself. While the Internet enables an effectively unlimited number of channels the capacity of some of those channels, especially the premium content providers, BBC, CNN and *Go*, etc., to supply more and more information, including such memory-hungry media as video, to consumers is ultimately limited by the capacity of the networks. A news service based on video and sound requires consumption of information at megabits per second and, while capacity has risen at the same rate as processing power (indeed the technologies are closely linked) and prices have dropped, the web's natural operational level constantly seems to lie just beyond the limits of its capacity. In an information society we can expect bandwidth to take on the importance borne by oil in the second half of the twentieth century. It will both fuel the economy and set its limits. Those states or corporations in the position to turn it on and off will have a stranglehold on the global economy and will become the Gulf States of the twenty-first century.

New Models of News and Readership

Nicholas Negroponte suggests that intelligent multimedia computers, able to 'read' effectively on our behalf, will filter, sort, prioritise, and manage our daily intake of information. Part of that intake will come, along with the advertising that pays for it, from local and global news providers. Those media, the *Guardian's* *newsUnlimited* for instance, will, however, only forward those elements of the news which it knows we might be interested in. To this core of news will be added a range of stories (again with advertisments and other subsidiary information) which the computer has sent out agents to collect. These might come from anywhere on the web's billion or so pages and from media titles that we have never even heard of.

The millions of 'channels' that the Internet potentially offers thus provide opportunities for readers which were largely unforeseen by the global media corporations. Consumers can tailor their news precisely to their own interests. Cricket fans can access reports on games from around the world, as well as profiles of players, scorecards, both historical and contemporary, and gossip. This news package might come from a range of locations or all from one aggregating website (*cricinfo.com*). A cricket fan who is also a financial analyst could easily combine a diet of sports news with regular updates on the state of the market (in any country), corporate reports and commentary. The news package will come from a mixture of agencies, brand name newsites (*BBC News Online, MSNBC*) and special interest newsgroups or bulletin boards.

The information which comprises the news package could be delivered though a range of text, image and audio files to a screen or, increasingly, to a telephone. Negroponte describes such packages as being 'mediumless'. In the instance of the telephone the application is hardly orginal: it was used by the Telefon Hirmando company in Hungary to transmit news reports to public audiences during the first decade of the twentieth century.[6]

The medium is not the message in a digital world. It is an embodiment of it. A message might have several embodiments automatically derivable from the same data. In the future, the broadcaster will send out one stream of bits, like the weather for example, which can be converted by the receiver in many different ways. The same bits can be looked at by the viewer from many perspectives.[7]

Increasingly, news and information are distributed through personal communications networks (PCNs) comprising phones, networked devices such as Palm Pilots and, of course, even bleepers. It could take the form of a customised newspaper, perhaps to be actually printed in the office or at home or could be distributed to a portable electronic display like the flat panel that is used by the Japanese daily *Mainichi Shimbun*. More usually, it will be consumed through a variety of media and, most importantly, the mix will be constantly changing. During the period following Princess Diana's death in 1997 many people with access to the Internet followed the story through a range of news organisations in Britain, France and the US using sites that they would not normally have accessed. During the war in Kosovo Yugoslav newsites were searched out and regularly accessed by many who in other circumstances would not even have known of their existence.

The concept of this personalised news package was first seriously explored by the MIT Media Lab and Apple Computer in the mid-1980s. The system was called *Fishwrap* in reference to the old newsroom aphorism, 'Today's news wraps tomorrow's fish.' The system was predicated on the notion that most consumers feel a need for an overview of the world in general, especially their own part of it, but will also have special interests, so the resulting package of information would be tailored specifically to the individual consumer. It would thus offer a range of current general news items, both global and regional, and of course there is no reason why immigrants of Welsh extraction living in Canada or New Zealand might not keep abreast of events in Wales, as well as a range of other personal topics. My system might be constantly scanning the Internet for references to 'trout fishing', 'Martin Amis', 'Manchester United' and 'eczema' and delivering the results bundled with synopses of the *Irish Times*, *Herald Tribune* and the *Leicester Mercury*. *Fishwrap* recognised that readers construct a picture of the world and their image of themselves from a whole range of subjects and texts which the notion of 'news' frames or authenticates as being appropriate. The idea of the *Daily Me*,[8] popularised in Negroponte's 1995 book, *Being Digital*, foregrounding the issue of individual consumer identity over every other community, even one as specific as the smallest local weekly, say, the Cornish *Falmouth* (population 17,000) *Packet*, was thus established.

> … What if a newspaper company were willing to put its entire staff at your beck and call for one edition? It would mix headline news with less important stories relating to acquaintances, people you will see tomorrow, and places you are just about to go or have just come from. It would report on companies you know. In fact, under these conditions you might be willing to pay the Boston *Globe* a lot more for ten pages than for a hundred pages, if you could be confident that it was delivering you the right subset of information. You would consume every bit (so to speak). Call it the *Daily Me*.[9]

MyCNN.com offers a 'Create Your Own Newspaper' service based on readers' personal interests and details. In practice most consumers arrive at a more informal method of sourcing their daily news on the web but the general principle, of a balkanisation of the news through the provision of niche information, applies. Many readers will log on through a brand-name portal which they know will give them an easily digested overview of the news, perhaps in the simple bullet points of the aggregate, and allow them to click on to subjects of current interest. It makes something like the clippings services used by journalists for the past century or so available to readers. During the day, as they return to the portal site, *CNN Interactive* or *newsUnlimited*, it will have updated the day's stories from wire services and so on. Walter Bender refers to *Fishwrap* as a 'lightweight' newspaper and I think that the concept of 'lite' news is useful here. It does not refer to the seriousness or depth of the product so much as to its mode of consumption.

This ease of consumption – a kind of literary grazing or browsing which occasionally brings particular items into close focus and then returns to the overview – when linked to the fragmentation of readerships, has far-reaching implications for news providers. In cities as disparate as Leicester in the UK and in New Jersey, newspapers were experimenting during the mid-1990s with special editions targeted at sectors of their constituency. Thus the *Jersey Journal's India Journal* could be accessed and printed on demand in drugstores and other outlets throughout Jersey City. Like the *Leicester Mercury Asia Edition* it covered the major news stories but gave equivalent space to stories from the Asian community in the city and in other North American cities as well as coverage of the Indian subcontinent. The *Asia Edition* of the *Mercury* was relaunched in partnership with *Asian-Online* in 1999 as *Leicestershire Asian-Online*, publishing material from the general print edition with extra web-only copy. The site is run in parallel with a local Asian radio station on the Internet, and material from *Leicestershire Asian-Online* is also mirrored to a local RSL (Restricted Service Licence) television station as teletext. While news on the web allows everyone with access to a computer to take advantage of developments of the *Fishwrap* model it can also be easily repurposed for a range of other media.

Developments such as these, frequently allied to the more do-it-yourself model of web community publishing projects which enable local organisations and individuals to self-publish on news sites,[10] are rapidly spreading throughout the news industry and rather force a consideration of whether they can constitute communities. If they do, what is the relationship between those virtual communities with their flesh and blood analogues? Such a community could arise from individuals who live in the same geographic locale and in such a case would presumably operate over a range of overlapping locations between cyberspace, traditional media and face-to-face interaction. They could equally well comprise people who live on different continents and might share only the single defining characteristic of their community: Irish ancestors, stamp collecting, Californian wines or body piercing. That characteristic, then, inspires real-time electronic interactions between virtual co-presences and the relationships that develop from that sense of immanence or being there. Jonathan Steuer describes telepresence rather more succinctly as '... the extent to which one feels present in the mediated environment, rather than in the immediate physical environment. *Telepresence is defined as the experience of presence in an environment by means of a communication medium'.*[11] The environment or locale does not, of course, itself have to be, or even to represent, a physical one to meet the terms of Steuer's definition. That 'presence in an environment' might relate to the perception of 'natural' surroundings mediated by normal mental and sensory processes or virtual surroundings, perhaps a series of voices or texts, mediated by technology.

Web community publishing hosted on corporate news providers servers is often followed by editorial assistants in the newsroom. Where appropriate they will use that community information, after it has been verified and rewritten, as the basis for items in their own local editions, in print and online. Steve Outing makes the point that this approach allows local news to operate at a 'depth', reporting details about events such as school sports days, retirements and birthday parties, etc., which makes it instrumental in the day-to-day cohesion of the community and places existing local media at risk.

It's exactly that kind of community minutiae, which can be of great interest to members of a local community, that major metro dailies have not before been able to tackle. With a strong community publishing program, aided by a small staff of print editors to cull out interesting local news and contributions from staff reporters, the major daily can compete at the local-local level with suburban papers for whom that street-level news and information is their livelihood.[12]

The development of strategies such as web community publishing reinforces the tendency of consumers to set their browser to a default web page which they know will point them directly to the main items of news and information that they want to access every day. The notion of the portal site developed from an understanding of how consumers were using products like *Fishwrap*, other special editions and search engines. In many ways it makes lite news packages redundant. Portals, or gateways to the Internet, might be the front pages of global (Yahoo!, AOL), national (*newsUnlimited*, *Liberation*) or regional (*ThisisCornwall*) news provider websites. They provide links to news services, e-shopping, entertainment schedules and information from weather and tides to financial advice. Globally branded portals attract millions of visitors every day and, naturally, the advertising that goes with such volumes of traffic. However, portals are just as likely to be corporate or even an individual's home pages. Personalised portal pages offering a range of regularly used links and perhaps components from other websites such as news tickers or 'InfoFlashes' and in some cases coupled with the use of intelligent agents will culminate in a news package that is fully personalised and totally specific. The personal home page is here transformed into a dynamic news source which could feature the latest news, financial information, weather forecasts, sports news and horoscopes. The ability of consumers to filter out so completely what for them is bad news clearly has significant cultural implications.

Portals might look like simple indexes in the case of news aggregators such as UK provider Metaplus (*metaplus.com*) or can take quite complex magazine formats providing a large range of services. Yahoo! for instance, in addition to news, games, stock market quotes, city guides and other maps, provides web users with free home pages through its subsidiary GeoCities, phone directories through Four11, Internet shopping through ViaWeb, free email services through RocketMail, promotions through Yoyodyne Entertainment, online calendars through WebCal and online chat software through iChat. The portal company also operates a partnership arrangement with Rupert Murdoch's *Fox* broadcasting network. The whole range of *Fox* products are promoted through Yahoo! which in turn is featured in regular advertisements in *Fox* programming. Disney employs the same strategy in featuring the logo of its *Go* portal on all of its TV output including the ABC network. Each new addition to Yahoo!'s portfolio and to *Go*'s exposure strengthens their ability to attract new users and the advertising which follows them. Portals also offer a range of search engines and provide summaries of the pages that they link to. There is, of course, no reason why anyone should not regularly use a good personalised portal page that they come across, or construct for themselves, in preference to one of the corporate brands.

The portals that are used are those which are built around an organising principle, whether that be the news, local, regional or global, or their owner's personal interests. Time Warner's experience with the now defunct *Pathfinder* portal seems to indicate that the universal portal is not able to attract traffic. The company's individual brands (and portal items) were much more popular and consumers clicked directly to them. Even the most successful portals, and other interstitial sites such as search engines, are very poor advertising platforms. Consumers tend to ignore tangential information while they are en route to a destination and such sites attract very low rates; typically less than $2 for every thousand page views (CPM).

Intelligent software agents are the final element in the expanded *Fishwrap* model. They scour the web (and, in some instances, other networks) finding articles and snippets of interest from a massive range of sources including news sites, bulletin boards, databases, individuals' home pages, etc. The information is emailed back and its acceptance or rejection by the consumer is used by the agent to refine further its search, hence its intelligence. The learning ability of the agent also allows it to avoid duplicating information and even, to a certain extent, to place it in context. Access to my diary and a knowledge of my interest in ecclesiastical architecture could deliver features on Gaudi prior to the week when I plan to be in Barcelona. The agent will assess both the level of detail and the general content of information, taking the consumer's own knowledge and needs into account as well as setting it in the context in which it will be read. Competing with this level of specificity is proving daunting to the global news brands who increasingly meet resistance from consumers no longer demanding pre-packaged news and opinion pushed at them. In contrast, the *Daily Me,* a composite of portal, intelligent agents and one or two emailed titles, is a pull model of news consumption.

Obviously such advanced structures of news and consumption cannot be free-standing, much as the global news producers would have us believe that they are. They exist within economies, both political and commercial. In most liberal democracies they are capitalised by advertising. Systems that can segment, even atomise, markets as comprehensively as the one outlined are clearly going to be very attractive to advertisers. Advertising on the web tends to be integrated with other media, routinely achieved through the clumsy expedient of merely including website addresses on TV and print display ads. More creatively, there are advertisments which offer interactive versions of their TV narratives. Adverts on news platforms can also offer real-time information and, of course, link readers directly to the websites of producers and suppliers. In order to maximise the usefulness of such systems and allow web advertising to dovetail seamlessly into them they require the development of three instruments:

1. Methods of describing news content generated by and for the Internet. Advertisers will wish to know how it is consumed and, where possible, by whom.
2. Methods of modelling the consumers of such content. While the *Daily Me* model of completely atomised readerships might not be very useful to most above-the-line models of advertising, fragmented readerships like those offered by *Asian-Online* are clearly invaluable.
3. Interface technologies such as browsers and other software to facilitate the transferring of information. Interstitial locations such as portals and aggregators were immediately grasped by advertisers for their banner ads and other links.[13]

Such instruments determine both the relationship of advertisers to news providers and, to a significant extent, the form of news sites. I will consider them in more depth in Chapter 3. These new departures for news and journalism on the Internet also suggest changed relationships between news organisations, journalists and their readers. The insistence upon reciprocal links between news providers and readers determines a news which is more specific and hence more relevant. In order to achieve this, news providers will require comprehensive background knowledge about their client communities, however those communities are segmented: geographically, professionally or by interest, age or ethnicity. Others, the aggregators, will provide the overview. For the first ... 'The future of the industry is as much about description, observation and interpretation as it is about gathering news.'[14] Readers are increasingly interested in the histories and structural machinery of their own communities or locales. They want the gossip and the scandal that act as the social glue of those communities but they also want to know how they fit into them.

A New Medium

In the decades after the First World War the news industry saw newspapers being displaced by radio as the medium that audiences turned to for breaking news, especially in times of crisis. The wireless now seems a crucial element of so many accounts of society during the Second World War. Radio's brief ascendancy came to an end when it was supplanted by television in the 1950s. Again, a series of world crises from the Vietnam War to Chernobyl and the Gulf War are inextricably linked with the history of television. In 1999, during the Kosovo crisis, it is clear that such a displacement has occurred once more and readers are turning to the Internet for a news experience that has the immediacy of broadcast forms as well as more depth – it allows them to scan a range of primary sources for themselves. There is also significantly more breadth in the comment that is available. Readers seem to turn to the web for a range of reasons: to find information that is unavailable elsewhere and, during wars, that clearly becomes important; for convenience, in many cases the Internet is already on their desk at work or at home; and for the ability to search for news on a specific subject and filter out the full view.

This is not to propose the imminent disappearance of printed newspapers. While they survived both radio and television, earlier commentators had also prophesied the death of newspapers at the hand of telegraphy and photography. In the event each introduction was accommodated to enrich the older form and its owners.

Contemporary consumers have information in the guise of news swamping them from a variety of media. They will continue to read newspapers and watch TV for the overview but increasingly they turn to the web for what is important to them. The roots of the online news industry might be traced to the then US Senator Al Gore writing in the *Washington Post* on 15 July 1990.

> Just as the interstate highway system made sense for a post-war America with lots of new automobiles clogging crooked two-lane roads, a nationwide network of information superhighways now is needed to move the vast quantities of data that are creating a kind of information gridlock.[15]

Within twelve months of Gore's clarion call new media sites appeared, first in North America from organisations such as CNN and the *Chicago Tribune*, but rapidly expanded through sites around the world. By the end of 1992, 150 newspapers in North America offered full-text versions of their print editions through Internet vendors such as *Nexis*. In January 1993 the first graphical web browser, *Mosaic*, was launched. The launch was a defining moment. Prior to *Mosaic* the Internet had to be navigated by a cumbersome system of keyed command lines that effectively excluded all but computer professionals and enthusiasts. The graphical browser brought 'point and click' navigation to the Internet. It was followed with web search engines (the first ones were called Spiders) which allow users to search the now rapidly growing web for files containing key words and phrases.

At the beginning of 1994, most web users were academics and computer enthusiasts but developments such as graphical browsers and search engines were making the web more user-friendly every day. The year 1994 saw the first major European newspapers arrive online with the *Daily Telegraph*, the *Financial Times* and the *Irish Times* sites. By this time many newspapers and other news providers such as radio, television and news agencies were developing browsable websites. While many radio stations offered playlists, programming and news and weather over their websites it was not long before radio stations worldwide were also broadcasting over the Internet in real time. These were rapidly followed by new broadcasting organisations set up to take advantage of the new carrier, *Internet Television Network* and *C/net Radio*. The same year saw Yahoo! (Yet Another Hierarchical Officious Oracle!) start life as an Internet index and the arrival of *HotWired*, *Wired Magazine*'s mould-making website. The development of news publishing on the web – there were more than a thousand newspaper titles online by early 1996 – follows the broadening of the medium's limited constituency to include, first, corporate and education workers and then, as the web was rethought as a consumer medium, the general public.

The real potential of the web as a disseminator of news became apparent in April 1995 with the Oklahoma City bombing. Resources on the web included statements from the White House, photographs of the damage, the names of victims, eyewitness accounts and updated reports about the disaster from local news providers. Very rapidly after the blast, ISPs and other news services provided maps, links to news agency reports and graphics depicting the type of bombs used and their effects. All of this comprised a range and a depth of comment and information on the disaster that no single news provider or medium had ever been able to assemble so rapidly before. Many providers of news, particularly, although not exclusively, those with their roots in traditional media, did not at first grasp the significance of this potential.

Shovelware and 'Getting' the Web

Printed periodicals ... came onto the Web by the thousands. Many of these simply sprayed all or parts of their printed editions onto the Web with a few Net-native distractions to liven them up. Newspapers seemed to be particularly averse to the old *Wired* – No shovelware! – edict. This leads Andrew [Anker of *HotWired*] to view most newspaper sites as 'wonderful archives; there's nothing more than that to it' ... newspaper publishers embraced the web more than any other group.[16]

The development of news on the web followed two paths. One was employed largely by an old media, both print and broadcast, which did not really seem to understand the principles of interactive media and Net culture or even how contemporary media corporations profit from their media assets – very few magazines and fewer newspapers show a profit before their advertising revenues. The traditional press tried to apply old models of the market to the web. These were models which, while they had been well proven and had produced some of the most profitable businesses in Europe and North America, by no means always worked, as is evidenced by the high failure rate for new print publishing ventures. Their primary model of journalism reconstructed stories from mostly undisclosed sources for a readership that was expected to accept them unquestioningly.

These providers took yesterday's print news and transcribed it wholesale for their online editions. The short-sighted terror for editors of scooping their own print edition with their online news, coupled with owners' attempts to minimise a risky outlay in a new medium, was often cited as the rationale for the strategy. While the question of whether the new media should be allowed to cannibalise print is worth serious consideration, the argument generally ignores the possibility that such restraint allows other titles or other media to scoop them. This stale and often pinched content, the result of a completely inadequate repurposing process, was also determined by the constraints of web design during its fledgling years and the limitations on legibility imposed by a comparatively low resolution medium when compared to paper.

The result rapidly acquired the pejorative name of 'shovelware' and was largely ignored by web users, except in those cases where a mass of information was rapidly accumulated as a useful archive. Those archives were rapidly extended as newspapers saw ways of profiting from them as products in their own right. Shovelled print content, however, tended to be separated from its ancillary elements: headlines, photos, diagrams, quotes, side panels, even the columnar structure itself – all the conventions developed over several centuries to make newspapers readable. What was left was a bald and unprepossessing literary text which threw many of the shortcomings of traditional journalism into sharp relief. The limited, and limiting, scope of shovelware forced its early abandonment by most news providers.

Those titles which saw a real future on the web looked for other models which attempted to understand and capitalise upon the possibilities of the new medium and were in tune with its developing culture. They explored ways of exploiting the interactivity between reader, text and author, which hypertext offered. In Europe titles such as the *Irish Times* and the *Guardian* began to place original reporting on the web in 1994, in some cases even seeing web material subsequently finding its way to print editions. They also looked for innovative ways of employing the new medium; in 1996 the *Irish Times* tried distributing the whole daily edition by email. In March 1998 they launched the Irish portal site *Ireland.com* which expanded the newspaper site to include a wide range of Irish-related information and services. *The Economist* emails a business newsletter to readers every week and one on politics. Email editions, possibly in HTML format, are important as an alternative method of distribution to the web and one which can target a clearly defined readership very exactly. As a distribution system it is replacing the restricted circulation lists employed by the trade press and specialist titles in sectors such as finance and software development.

Titles such as the *Guardian*'s *newsUnlimited*, MSNBC and *CNN Interactive* were soon drawing millions of visitors each month. By the close of 1999, *newsUnlimited*, launched in January, was drawing around 80,000 readers each day, nearly a quarter of its parent's print circulation.[17] Other new ventures such as *Salon*, founded in 1994 by David Talbot and other journalists shaken out of the *San Francisco Examiner* during a labour dispute, and Microsoft's *Slate* provided news services from online platforms alone. *newsUnlimited* was an example of a paper with a strong print reputation rebranding itself for the web. This recognition of the particular demands of web audiences was far from typical in 1999, with many providers still shovelling print content on to the new medium.

Slate, launched in February 1995, makes an interesting case study in how not to produce news on the web. With all the financial and technical resources of the world's most successful IT corporation behind it, *Slate* should have been a sure-fire certainty, yet it broke what were emerging as the first two principles of online journalism.

First, it attempted to get readers to pay for subscriptions. In an environment in which 'information overload' hardly begins to describe most users' experience, it seems unlikely that they will actually pay for more unless it meets a very specific demand. There are commercial models which do seem to make sense for news on the web but subscription is not one them. Second, *Slate* employed a journalism that was wildly anachronistic. It launched with serious magazine-length features and a hierarchical management model of editor, subs and beat journalists. They sat on top of a structure which represented readers through what was essentially a letters page and which had already been long superseded by Microsoft's own technology. By 1995, when *Slate* was launched, it was already clear that effective online journalism encouraged its readers to intervene at every level and at every stage of its content's development – it is interactive.

When they came to design their online editions, providers like *newsUnlimited* and the *Wall Street Journal Interactive Edition* (*WSJIE*) were careful not merely to shovel the paper online. *newsUnlimited* comprises a network of sites including news, jobs, cricket, arts, media and football. The *WSJIE* offers a news wire, news briefings, *Dow Jones News Retrieval* and the *Asian Wall Street Journal*. In both cases the whole enlarges upon, and is complementary to, the print edition.

Microsoft was not the only global media corporation to expend time and money on anachronistic projects for which there was simply no market. Traditional journalistic practices are not directly transferable between media, as companies such as News Corporation, MCI and Time Warner with their *Pathfinder* project have found to their cost. These companies attempted to substitute multimedia (in some cases, expensive and innovatory), heavily linked over-populated screens and menu-driven options for the instant interactivity that the web had promised. Even the fundamental principles such as how readership is constituted and how circulations are counted (does a click on to a site constitute a read or is it more akin to a glance at the supermarket magazine rack?) have to be reconsidered. The problem is partly clarified with the term 'page impression' or 'page view'. Most pages comprise a series of files including text, audio, graphics and perhaps video or other media. A page impression describes a download of a complete page by a reader. A 'hit' is the request for a file from a web server.

The classic exemplar of a successful web start-up is probably *HotWired*, but there are others which will succeed commercially as well as journalistically; *Salon, Suck* and *Feed* have all developed strong personalities and large readerships around cultural and social issues and, of course, there also exist many more specialised web journals such as *ZDNet, Slashdot* and *Cnet* covering technology and the Internet itself. Every other sphere of human interest reveals similar start-ups across a huge quality continuum.

HotWired and *Salon* offer good examples of how the Internet has affected journalism. Their content has a direct relevance to their readers and they are clearly and immediately accessible. The result is a journalism that is often more accountable than its print predecessors. It uses the medium's interactive capabilities to include readers and to determine the shape and content of the publication.

This transparency does not necessarily imply a difference in editorial standards between online and print news. Since 1994 we have seen a series of panics, usually simmered in the traditional media, around web content and procedures. It is accused of harbouring salacious tabloid sites and pornography, conspiracy theorists and extremists. However, attempts to demonise the Internet have no more foundation than medieval rants against the printing press, which has been producing similar terrors since its inception. Old media has its paparazzi, its cameras mounted on police chase vehicles, its top-shelf glossies and its too-near-the-knuckle talk shows. Clearly a title like the *Telegraph* in the UK is going to apply the same rigour to its website as it does to its daily edition, as is the *National Enquirer* or the BBC's *999*. What such panics might more profitably propose is that some of the web's start-ups will give their more established rivals pause to reconsider their approach. Some of journalism's timeless truths might turn out to have passed their sell-by dates. The democratising of journalism is long overdue.

Content Providers and Aggregators

News services on the Internet can be usefully divided into aggregators and content providers. There are organisations that undertake both functions, possibly compromising themselves in the process. The aggregators provide links, headers and overview editorial comment to the sites which provide the actual coverage of the news. The structure of the Internet and its usage make aggregator sites very important since they act as indexes to the vast field of online news. Clearly their pages are dictated by what is being covered by the content providers. The larger aggregators compile their pages from thousands of news sources, often searching out material from non-traditional media sources. The best aggregators also use local and regional press and broadcast news to focus on stories. The Columbine High School killings in 1999 saw local sources such as the *Rocky Mountain News* <InsideDenver.com> and the *Denver Post Online* being cited by aggregators around the world. Consumers could also read responses to the tragedy from Colorado community websites, global newscasters such as CNN and the BBC, the National Rifle Association, the local radio station KMGH and, of course, the school itself.

Since the role of news aggregators is primarily editorial, the set of links that they provide to a story usually aims to provide a holistic view, in which the traditional news values are not necessarily paramount. The range of views on display will assist readers to make up their own mind. Jon Brooks and Kim Colwell, the co-editors of *Full Coverage*, Yahoo!'s news aggregator and archival service, suggest priorities which play to the full strengths of the web.

... we are concerned with trying to cover as many facets of a story as possible. We strive to present material from a variety of perspectives and then let the user decide as to its usefulness. One of the great strengths of online news is how much information you can put at the disposal of your readers, so the editorial content can be much more broad-based and reflective of alternative points of views or trends ... We use whatever we feel will contribute to a user's understanding of the story.[18]

Clearly some of these sources will not begin to meet the traditional journalistic values of impartiality, objectivity and even truth. *Full Coverage* itself is independent of newspapers and wire services and does not have prior agreements to link to any particular material. Not all aggregators are so non-partisan. Excite, one of the more successful news portals and search engines, also supplies a full cable service to 72 million homes around the world through Excite@Home.

By 1999 many of the regional and national news providers on the web were linking to news agencies for breaking news and sources to important stories. Sites with constituencies as different as *newsUnlimited* and the *Drudge Report* offered their readers links to Reuters, PA, AP and Agence France-Presse. As long as companies and their news workers in the various parts of the news industry retained their traditional roles, there seemed to be no problem with this arrangement but with the appearance of browser phones and WAP technologies in 2000, Reuters rapidly restructured to directly supply the new market. It had served niche consumer markets such as the European business community for more than a decade but in 2000 it created the Reuters portal site and went into direct competition with its own customers. Other global agencies rapidly followed putting more pressure on the old print brands to differentiate themselves vigorously from the growing competition.

Satellite news channels, along with talk radio and cable TV had already combined to produce a 24-hour news cycle before the Internet became a mass medium or its news providers had appeared. Round-the-clock news meant that the spin doctors who now front government and corporate organisations could no longer slate political announcements, air strikes and sports events to dovetail with media schedules. The arrival of news on the web also seemed to compromise the position of journalists with its implicit insistence that consumers be offered the full provenance of their news.

Caveat emptor rapidly becomes the primary guiding principle of the web user. One of the side-effects of the new medium is a more media-wise, certainly more sophisticated, readership. It is very aware that not all news providers are trustworthy and perhaps that suspicion is now spreading to all providers and all media. Consumers learn to become critical of the source of their news and information in an environment where schoolchildren, extremists of every denomination and global news organisations are all using the same production systems and design principles. For the generation after DTP, slick and expensive-looking production values are no longer the exclusive domain of the professional media industries.

With such an apparently arbitrary selection of news sources, enabling readers to mix primary sources with commentary and opinion, Internet technologies seem to promise a revolutionising of the collecting, processing, disseminating and presenting of news, as well as, of course, the advertising that has traditionally paid for it in most economies. Marshall McLuhan's great hope for the photo-copier was that it would make everyone a publisher; however, while the copier radically affected the way we deal with information and even took on a major political role in the opposition to some totalitarian regimes, that revolution was to be eclipsed a few years after his death by the word processor, PC and laser printer. The same technology also revolutionised publishing and news, making many traditional functions obsolete and speeding up the whole process from researching, producing and sending copy to print, to distribution. While media corporations thrived in a climate of ever-cheaper production costs and more effective news-gathering and dissemination it was still difficult for the disempowered to communicate information to mass audiences. Of course, McLuhan's hope was for self-publishers who could also distribute. The most advanced photo-copiers, word processors and printers were unable to achieve that but it is precisely what the Internet seems to do best.

New Audiences

As the web's audiences increase and broaden so its coverage becomes more general. It has become a mass medium drawing the content that we have come to expect of a mass medium. Until 1997, by which time 23 per cent of American adults were online, the news which drew most traffic was news about the technology itself.[19] There remains a lot of technical news, much of it having earlier migrated, apparently permanently, from print publishing. Two years later, by which time 41 per cent of Americans were connected, weather reports and forecasts were the main attraction, with shopping channels beginning to draw large readerships as well. In 1998, for the first time, there were more new women web users than men. The Pew Research figures for that year suggest that during the Christmas period 32 per cent of American Internet users made an online purchase, up from 8 per cent in 1995. The mainstream audience brought mainstream interests with it. Tabloid news, foregrounding scandal, entertainment news, weather and subjects such as cookery and community news have grown much faster than economic and political coverage. As the web audience grows, a smaller proportion use it to seek electoral or financial news while the accessing of TV and other entertainment schedules continues to grow at an exponential rate.[20] This is as we might expect from a medium undergoing rapid massification.

The 1998 Pew Research Center Report (albeit taken from a comparatively small sample – 3,184 adults) brings few surprises in this context. As suggested above it finds a consistent high growth in news consumption on the web, but with quite dramatic variations in consumption from month to month ranging between 37 per cent of users using news sites at least once a week in November to 64 per cent in December. Clearly, these differences will be accounted for by a range of factors, not least the differences in news events from week to week. Wars and disasters have produced readership surges since long before the Crimean War.

The report finds that only 11 per cent of consumers admit to using traditional news sources less frequently, although a similar proportion of the most recent news consumers on the web seem not to have been regular consumers of news at all before they went online. The news medium that this group of news consumers drops first seems to be television. Internet users tend to seek the kind of information that is featured by television news on the web. Weather, movies and local information (sought by 39 per cent of users), stock market prices and sports scores (38 per cent) and news headlines (28 per cent) are amongst the most often accessed features of web news sites. What is clear is that online consumers still tend to take their news from a range of media and forms. More than 40 per cent of the Pew Center's respondents indicated that they use the Internet to give them more background and depth on stories that they have first become aware of in the press or from broadcast news. This is now changing as consumers keep a portal or aggregator page on their screens keeping them informed of breaking news as they work. The smaller online audiences prior to 1996 tended to come from social groups which were more likely to be interested in news anyway and indeed, even in 1998, Pew discovered that online consumers were more likely to take a daily newspaper than the national average.

In America the broadcast news corporations websites are more popular than newspaper sites. While Pew does not consider the European situation, the same preference holds for the *BBC News Online* site in the UK. In the US the preference is explained by the fact that broadcast news sites attract national audiences and, historically, there are no national newspapers in North America. Most online newspaper sites attract a predominantly regional or even local readership. In the period between 1996 and 1998 the *MSNBC* website experienced the greatest increase in traffic, probably growing at about the same rate as traffic on *BBC News Online*.

The 1998 Pew survey suggests that nearly half of online news consumers felt that news organisations on the web were as accurate as more traditional media and were more likely to give the larger picture. At the same time, fewer web users considered news as a priority in their list of demands. Probably the key finding of Pew in 1998 was that the audience of the web was a mass audience, no longer with a predominance of college-trained, more affluent, perhaps even male, consumers. The newer web users came from socio-economic groups which were traditionally heavier-than-average television watchers and from a younger constituency than earlier users. Both of these groups hitherto relied primarily on TV rather than the press for their news and tended to be more interested in the headlines than in documentary and comment.

Conclusion

In 1997 James Fallows, the executive editor of *US News & World Report*, contemplated the qualities of news and journalism on the Internet with John McChesney of *Hotwired*.

McChesney: You've been a strong advocate of something called civic journalism ... [does] the Internet make this a more probable ... kind of journalism?

Fallows: I would define civic journalism as journalism which is useful to people in the largest sense. It gives them a picture of their communities, of their country, of the world, the political system, the economic system, which makes them feel they understand the forces acting upon them, as opposed to just being mere spectators in some kind of political food fight, which is what a lot of our journalism does. I think the Internet can be an important step in this direction, because by definition, getting involved in the Internet requires some active volition on the part of the user. You can't be a passive Internet user the same way as you can be a passive receiver of TV news.[21]

While there is clearly some degree of idealism behind Fallows' conception of journalism on the Internet it is perhaps not entirely unfounded. The systemic effects of the Internet are immense for everyone on the planet, including, as the global economy becomes the fief of the information-rich, those who will always be its largest class, the excluded. These effects propose transformations in the ways that we think about identity, freedom, democracy and the information society itself. One of the crucial sites for debate around those issues will be news and journalism. As governments, corporations, political interest groups and lobbyists (including media organisations) swamp the Internet with information and communications about every aspect of society and its regulation, journalism's contribution to democracy is crucial.

Online journalism doesn't only make news and comment available on the Internet, it directs consumers towards that sea of information from governmental, quasi-governmental and corporate agencies and provides the navigation charts. Such material is at once the journalists' sources and the context for developing many of the stories that touch consumers most closely. Branded news websites tie national and international news with more local material. Search software and hierarchical indexes provide a more complete editorial service than traditional news media were able to aspire to. Sending readers to sources is always risk-prone and strategies must be developed to ensure that they return and that sources are not encouraged to editorialise for themselves.

In addition to a wide range of services, from archives to games, news providers also offer interaction through discussion on major stories and local topics. Where such interaction is hosted effectively the possibility of participating in the development of the story can draw readers back to news sites. Consumers develop a different, in many ways more demanding, set of expectations around news providers on the web than of their daily paper or broadcast news provider. Those expectations surround the larger range of services and, most importantly, interactivity or participation and the sense of community that derives from it. The website becomes an important node in the community network rather than merely providing commentary upon it.

Such a development distances online news most distinctly from its traditional predecessors and, in many cases, owners. Where opinion and comment was previously retained within the purview of the editor or, less likely in an era of global conglomerates with massive diversities of interest, even the owner, the interactive opinion section, whichever way it is presented, in an online news environment can be driven by readers. Open discussion of issues will often direct the meaning of the story and attempt, contrary to the gist of most print editorials, to refuse it any definitive closure. This shift has a significant democratising potential capable of radically altering the relationships of readers and reader-communities with the media. It is the reason why many branded online providers offer news in multimedia formats which are as far from being interactive as their newspaper precursors. They neither provide links to their own sources and to other views of the story nor do they offer their readers effective ways of responding or intervening.

The very real nature of this democratising potential can be illustrated by the SangKancil mailing list on Malaysia.Net <www.malaysia.net/lists/sangkancil> which is hosted by a Malaysian-owned ISP in Australia. Stories which it is no longer possible to publish in Malaysia or Singapore are used to generate a very active, unfettered and wide-ranging discussion, most of which emanates from inside Malaysia and which includes postings from government officials. The SangKancil list is an excellent example of what the web's abolition of national frontiers can deliver and points to the effects that it can have on individual polities.[22] The clampdown on newspapers and broadcast media in neighbouring Indonesia during 1996 drove political activism in that country on to the web. While there were only about 20,000 web users in Indonesia at the time, they tended to be middle-class and politically informed with an influence that ran far beyond the immediate group. According to *Human Rights Watch/Asia* the government was routinely intercepting email by 1996 although they had no intention, at that time, of formally regulating the Internet.

Other examples of effective cross-border interventions are legion: the use of the web by the Zapatistas in the Chiapas uprising against the North American Free Trade Area agreement in Mexico in the mid-1990s or the publication of features 'whited out' from the heavily censored press of Egypt on newspaper websites based outside the country. The *Middle East Times'* server, for instance, is located in Cyprus. There are many other examples of the web being used by journalists opposed to repressive regimes. In 1996 the Zambian government seized an edition of the daily *The Post* to keep secret the plan to hold a referendum on a draft constitution. The suppressed edition was posted on the web for several days, giving at least some citizens the chance to consider the implications of the referendum and publicise it before it was held. Of course, such an intervention assumes that citizens have access, however restricted, to the Internet.

Most countries in the Middle East allow their citizens unrestricted Internet access; however Iraq, Iran and Saudi Arabia are less sanguine about its social and political effects. Saudi Arabia has developed a system through which thousands of sites are blacklisted and blocked. This form of censorship is technically difficult, if not impossible, to enforce and, of course, the blacklist is, of necessity, growing as fast as the Internet itself. Iran's users, some of whom are monitored by their ISPs, promise that they 'will not contact stations against Islamic regulations'.[23]

While the Internet throws the regimes of many political hues on the defensive it is, of course, a mistake to link such democratising influences to the technology itself. It can just as easily be used to disseminate the oppositional propaganda of racist[24] or fundamentalist extremisms such as *Al Gamaa Al Islamiyya*, Egypt's most violent Islamic group. The website *Al Murabeton*[25] (A Glittering Hope Facing Darkness) is published from a US ISP in Denmark. As is evidenced by the extensive use of the web by both NATO and Serbia during the Kosovo crisis in 1999, the web also serves the whole continuum of militaristic ideologies equally effectively.

This range of constituencies and potential is predicated on the size of the web's user base which, while not universal – there are entire populations excluded from it now and for the foreseeable future – is global. It also provides an effective and inexpensive carrier for the whole range of communication modes: one-to-one, one-to-many, many-to-many and even many-to-one. In 1993, in a move that was rapidly followed by politicians in accountable polities around the world, Bill Clinton was one of the first statesmen to make public a personal email address <president@whitehouse.gov>.

In addition to a potential for interactivity, the Internet brings with it other characteristics which, while they distinguish it from traditional news media, can be understood alongside the values and conventions that have come to define print and broadcast news. As is clear from the considerations of the next chapter, these signifiers – a capacity for real-time news or shifted time (shared, to a point, with television), the inclusion of multimedia elements, the direct referencing of sources and the possibility of interactivity for readers – seem to change the discourse of news fundamentally and irreversibly.

2
The Nature of News

News is one of the defining institutions of the information society. Its credibility derives from a set of values which are as much constructs of the media industries as are genre, style and form. The claims of the news media to values that guarantee impartiality, objectivity and, not least, veracity appear to be somehow self-evident and natural but they are, of course, both historical and cultural. They are determined by the social and cultural demands of the moment, by technology, and by the institutions they serve. In the eighteenth century any proposal of the virtues of objectivity would have been regarded as quite perverse by journalists and their readers. Writers such as Addison, Steele, Johnson, Swift and their less well-known brethren in Grub Street were read precisely for their views and opinions. Objectivity was an invention of the nineteenth-century press; one of the instruments of an emerging middle class which was flexing muscles that had already been proven in the economic sphere and impatient to take what it considered to be its rightful place in the public domain. Objectivity and impartiality were to stamp the news with a view of the world that was deterministic, bourgeois and limited to a very clearly defined set of boundaries. It was a view proposed by sociology and supported by science.

The underlying problems with the three central values of the bourgeois news media, truth, impartiality and objectivity, were ignored or repressed in the West for more than a century. Those problems or limitations are fundamental to the very nature of media and stem in part from the fact that messages transmitted through intermediary technologies are necessarily mediated. This means that information is compressed, changed or even corrupted as it is passed from sender to receiver. This corruption can be understood as a bandwidth problem; when we address each other directly, what Levi-Strauss called 'authentic communication', even in the most formal circumstances we employ a wide range of carriers: voice, vocabulary, volume, inflection, gesture, facial expression, clothing and other external artefacts including environment, even smell and texture on occasion. When we employ technological media as carriers they are able to transmit only parts, and sometimes very limited parts, of the whole communication. Radio and telephone, for instance, completely eliminate all cues that are not aural. Text eliminates an even wider bandwidth, leaving a signal that is heavily impoverished.

Interactive media, operated to their strengths, while they cannot produce that authentic multifaceted signal, can produce a richer one than all forms of traditional media. I am suspicious of the wilder claims of cyberculture for an expansion or simulation of Lévi-Strauss's authenticity.[1] What is certain is that media producers become blind to the limitations of their own media. When BBC Television News brings the latest headlines about the war in Kosovo, it can offer an overview of the war so far and bring special reports from Belgrade, from NATO headquarters in Brussels and from the refugee camps. It might even offer some opinion on the future conduct of the war. Until the arrival of full news services on the Internet that was about as comprehensive, as authentic, as news got.

Multimedia online news on the other hand can webcast those special reports, with transcripts, for consumption while they are taking place or later, at the readers' convenience. It can provide maps and diagrams which will allow readers to build geographies and histories of the crisis as it changes. It can allow citizens to have their say, both in terms of online polls and by responding by email either to the news provider or to the Ministry of Defence, the Pentagon (or both) or political representatives. They will have available to them, in some cases directly linked to their news site, the view from Belgrade, government and opposition, as well as accounts from private citizens who are living through the war and from anti-war groups within the NATO countries. They will also have immediate access to the war as it is being reported in other countries. While paper and videotape both allow consumers to timeshift, and there are always readers' letters, there is none of the potential for interactivity that networked multimedia journalism seems to propose and little of the breadth of sources. Multimedia production also brings financial benefits in the partnerships and mergers between different media companies which allow providers such as NBC News to deliver news over three media: broadcast TV, cable and, through *MSNBC*, the web.

Thus in the age of online journalism we might add interactivity to the short list of journalistic core values. It is determined partly by the technological aspects of the medium, by its availability, but, more importantly, by changes in society including a levelling of its structural hierarchies and with the way in which we understand text. In using hypertext, or linked elements of text or information, the relationship between reader and author undergoes a shift that inverts traditional understandings of the construction of meaning and reshapes some of the values that underpin it.

Impartiality and Objectivity

The very notion of objectivity suggests that journalists are able to operate somehow from a moral or intellectual high ground which provides a critical distance from the world of events and their repercussions. This spurious detachment is proposed as the result of the journalist's expensive education and professional training and is clearly intended to support the notions either that news can arrive unencumbered by values or that its values are those of progress, enlightenment and social good and are therefore beneficial. This had significant advantages to the media which served an emergent capitalism in the nineteenth century. It delivered a credibility that was not available to the discourses of public life as long as they remained immersed in that life, while at the same time ensuring that individual writers could never again take positions that ran counter to the views of their employers. By its very nature the objective report censored or erased the self that created it. News, apparently spontaneous and self-authored, became a self-determining construct; it was what appeared in the newspapers. Information from other sources, especially where the identity of the writer or other provenance is attached, must, the corollary goes, be assumed to be biased.

Its effect on the content of news can be even more deleterious since it forces a superficiality calculated not to detract from the effectiveness of the advertising alongside it and which, of course, pays for it.

Objectivity tended to keep news superficial because too deep a pursuit of a single subject might bore or offend some of the audience. It strained out interpretation and background despite the desperate need for them in a century wracked by political trauma. Recitations of facts about world wars, genocides, depressions, and nuclear proliferation are useful but inadequate; mere recitations imply that all facts are of equal value.[2]

John Hartley, in his *Understanding News*, has pointed out that amongst the implications of this is the consensus that those issues which are newsworthy are somehow naturally structured in a way that is neatly agonistic and confrontational. Clearly, most of the issues which dominate the global society of the twenty-first century, from firearms control to the Pacific Rim economic crisis, are much more complicated than that. John Naughton in his *Observer* feature of July 1998[3] makes the point that press opinion on the Pacific Rim economies swung dramatically that year from unmitigated admiration for the economic miracle to ridicule of the 'Eastern tigers ... toothless and mangy ... touting for IMF handouts'. Naughton procedes to offer Nouriel Roubini's *Asia Crisis Homepage*[4] as an example of how journalism on the web allows the space to accommodate such issues. The site offers links to hundreds of sources under 32 headings and while it will never offer the instant answers of much print editorialising it does allow productive access to an important world issue that is inherently chaotic and complex. Facile oversimplification renders it almost completely opaque.

The agonistic view of news proposes that there exist equal and opposing arguments around every issue of the moment which it is the job of the journalist to find and present. The argument rarely has more than two sides. One of those sides, usually the one aligned with the dominant culture, will, of course, when the appropriate evidence is laid before the readers or viewers, turn out to be the right one. That testimony is usually the citation of expert authorities, officially sanctioned and thus part of the establishment that they are validating.

The possibility that such authorities, perhaps the police spokesperson or a criminal psychiatrist in the case of the Columbine killings, have either a professional or personal interest in the outcome or meaning of the story is discounted. The literal facts that they offer, while they do provide a disciplined and ethical basis to the story, also limit it to the extent that it is rendered entirely banal, without either meaning or context. In this case, from the earliest reports, it was clear that the whole issue of American gun culture, central to any reasoned understanding of the tragedy, was off-limits. It would have remained so had the National Rifle Association's national convention not been planned for Denver within days of the killings and copycat attacks not occurred around the USA in the following weeks.

Views which are considered extreme by the existing dominant culture, even if they are legitimate, even the norm, in other cultures, are filtered out at the beginning of the process and remain unvoiced. The journalist, as representative of an objective and impartial news media, selects the evidence on behalf of the readership. Objectivity and impartiality are clearly, as Stuart Hall has described them, 'operational fictions' suited to 'push' media and to a particular economic and social system. They scientifically guarantee the logic of the journalism as unassailable and that integrity accrues to the system that produced it.

> We have ... some obligation to be impartial. We try to be objective ... but you can't make a good film which presents both points of view.[5]

While Jeremy Isaacs, at this time controller of features at Thames Television, asserts that reporting must have a point of view, he also reinforces the assumptions, first that objectivity is an attainable goal and also that, for most issues, there are only two points of view, the miners and the government, the Brits and the Argentinians, the Serbians and the rest of humanity, etc. On the briefest reflection this turns out to be wrong. In any news story, even one so apparently black and white as the Columbine School killings in Colorado in 1999, there is clearly an intricate complex of points of view and interests at stake – the families of the slain, the police, the National Rifle Association, the school, the families of the killers – and that hardly begins the list. Any serious analysis of an international situation like the war in Kosovo in the same year must take account of a myriad points of view – the very attempt to reduce the situation to a simple conflict between NATO and Serbia must clearly be spurious to even the most unsophisticated news consumer.

Pierre Bourdieu, writing in 1977 (*Outline of a Theory of Practice*) suggests that objectivity is related to the process of mediation rather than to the contingent world; that it allows, even insists upon, readers or viewers taking up positions by presenting the social world as a spectacle to which they are bound in a symbolic relationship. Thus objectivity, guaranteed by the reader's personal investment in the events related in the text, is a function of the act of reading or viewing; it serves to allow readers to deal with a complex and shifting world in a metaphoric or symbolic way. Without that objectivity the product of reading will become unfocused and unproductive for the reader.

While what Ben Bagdikian has ironically elevated to the 'doctrine of objectivity'[6] brought with it the undoubted benefit of tempering a press which, in the early nineteenth century was given to hyperbole or was even completely fictitious, it has limited advantages today and serves particular and private agendas. There are yawning problems with a system which completely excludes significant social forces from public discourse as it attempts to represent a complex and heterologic world for readers. There must be a better, let us say less tendentious, way of documenting events. Perhaps the Internet will lead us to it. By taking information from as many, and as wide a range, of sources as possible and perhaps even by abandoning an impossible objectivity for a reasoned subjectivity or reflexivity, readers will be able to make up their minds for themselves. It is clear from any tracking of a breaking news story on the Internet that the reader is never going to be able to identify and consume 'all' the information on the issue. There will always be that which remains unknown and, indeed, it is often that elision which allows space for critical thought. It is a perspective that John Merrill, long before the Internet made it a real possibility, described as a function of 'existential journalism'.

After Sartre, Merrill understood the proper roles of journalism as revealing to readers the 'developing patterns of the social world, and to disclose and judge social weaknesses'. This knowledge was intended to give the reader the capacity for action, for intervening in the community and thus 'to close the gap between knowledge and practice'. Camus attempted to short-circuit the process by helping readers to deal directly with the immediate demands of their contingent realities. 'Camus's confrontations are mainly with himself; he may have to struggle against others, but he does not "judge" them.'[7] Merril suggests that such a journalism demands 'honest' writers and a press that is willing to credit its readers with intelligence.

Truth

The news media's insistence upon objectivity suggests that there is an ultimate reality behind the events that it reports. Despite the prevarications of government, enemies of state and class, and other disseminators of disinformation, the truth, it is assumed, will eventually out. Much more than merely the current consensus, structured through the shifting relations between power, ideology and the structures of the media industries, consumers of news assume that, behind the appearances, this truth is tangible and monolithic. Jean Baudrillard, in a series of essays and monographs culminating in his *The Gulf War Did Not Take Place* (1991), argues that consumers must abandon this obsession with the ethereal grail of 'truth' before they can escape the machinations of opinion managers and manipulators and begin to comprehend the complexity of the world.

Some of the truths that the media fostered about the Gulf War included the proposals that modern warfare can be conducted without loss of life, that the war was entirely provoked and initiated by the Iraqis under Saddam Hussein, that Iraq could be policed, and the Kurds and Marsh People protected, from the air. In retrospect, it is easy enough to point to the flaws in these rickety assertions; they turn out to be uninformed proposals at best and plain wrong in some cases. A mass media, which assented to being managed by the military establishments of the Western powers and their allies, accepted and disseminated these proposals as truths. In Kosovo, part of a wired European state, the same establishment attempted to propose a similar array of truths. The Internet, developed in the decade that separated the two wars, made such truths untenable to those who took their news from it and, of course, difficult to defend even in the traditional media. By 1999 it was much more difficult for governments to sustain the strategy that had worked so successfully during the Falklands campaign in 1982. In his account of reporting that war Phillip Knightley proposes a fundamental criticism of the strategy.

> In Argentina during the war the newspapers printed what they were told to print; disobedience was punished by closure. But a democratic government cannot be as crude as that. It never goes in for summary repression or direct control; it nullifies rather than conceals undesirable news; it controls emphasis rather than facts; it balances bad news with good; it lies directly only when it is certain that the lie will not be found out during the course of the war.[8]

The House of Commons Defence Committee report of 1982 includes a BBC statement which more or less accuses the Ministry of Defence of the manipulation of news. It is no longer enough for contemporary war planners to control troops and ordinance, they must control the representation of war as well. It is clear that it is increasingly difficult for governments to maintain a totalitarian hold on their media, securing control of channels of information and news by coercion alone. In polities as diverse as Singapore, China and Mexico the Internet has made this all but impossible. The only possibility for such a strategy would be in a situation like that adopted by the Taliban in Afghanistan, of complete economic and technological stagnation. Sohaila Danish, writing in an anti-Taliban website hosted outside Afghanistan, describes the fundamentalist regime's approach to the web. 'All communications infrastructure installations and equipment, like all other infrastructure, have either been destroyed or sold off in the Pakistani flea markets.'[9] The strategy is hardly seen as an option for most states in the twenty-first century. As we shall see, in addition to rendering the coercion of news producers more difficult, the development of news on the Internet also mitigates very powerfully against the second of Knightley's strategies retaining any effectiveness at all. In an open economy, to adapt a financial metaphor, it becomes much more difficult for bad news to drive out good.

Interactivity[10]

Jonathan Steuer defines interactivity as '... the extent to which users can participate in modifying the form and content of a mediated environment in real time'.[11] A broad understanding of Steuer's definition might suggest that all textual materials, particularly journalistic genres, are, in some sense, interactive. Few readers follow text in a rigid linear progression. Newspaper narratives, for example, are rather constructed through a process that darts for information between a whole series of graphical and semantic entry points: from headlines, to photographs and images, sub-headings and other openings in the main galleys, side panels and then perhaps to the conclusion and back to the main image. Such a reading is quite clearly 'interactive' within Steuer's definition. The same process can be seen in the consumption of more literary texts as readers refer back and forth to corroborate or expand on their understanding of the emerging story. They might also leave the primary text to refer to dictionaries, other textbooks and, of course, other individuals, both readers of the text at issue and non-readers. All forms of text are interactive in this sense; it is a function of narrativity itself and derives from modes of consumption rather than from the ways in which the content has been structured.

Multimedia, and more traditional text, is not, however, necessarily interactive in that second sense. The button that intimates 'Click here to go to the next screen' is only as interactive as the convention that instructs us to turn the page to find the continuation of the text. The text becomes more interactive as readers are enabled (and encouraged) to restructure it to their own ends using a range of hierarchical entry points. Hypertext links allow readers to produce individual narratives which can resegment the primary text and may include or conjoin other texts or sets of texts to produce new texts. A thoughtfully crafted set of links, appropriately described, will set a news piece in context as well as guiding its readers through it. Many otherwise excellent news sites completely fail that last test of interactivity by producing hermetically sealed packages of information which implicitly refuse, to return to Steuer's definition, to allow the reader to 'participate'.

The *Guardian's newsUnlimited* site moved from the sealed to a more open model in mid-1999, to immediate effect. When the Royal

Society entered the debate on genetically modified foods in the UK with a paper attempting to demolish earlier research flagging its dangers, *newsUnlimited* was able to link directly to evidence arguing both sides of the debate from its features on the issue. Readers, with comparatively little effort, were encouraged to become informed readers, able to reach more independent conclusions on a complex issue which affected them intimately. With such an insight into the underlying discourse of GMF they would have been largely unsurprised when the following day brought yet another report which seemed to replicate the damaging conclusions that the Royal Society had been attempting to quash.

James Fallows sees this move as being pivotal in the development of news as discourse, demanding new roles from its practitioners and incorporating new modalities.

> ... the Internet is by definition a more 'small-d' democratic medium than most other news media are. It gives people a variety of voices and vehicles that they can seek, and at its best, it removes the one-way-ness of traditional news and you can build in natural ... discussion forums. When I was working at *The Atlantic* [*Monthly*], I guess for the last three or four years before I left ... I spent a lot of time on our Web site just being part of discussion with readers. [12]

Steuer stresses that 'the apparent presence of others in virtual worlds should enhance the experience of telepresence',[13] and indeed such a forum, conducted in a bulletin board through text or teleconferencing through video, amounts to a sharing of the mediated environment or virtual space and determines the users' relationship to that space. Interactivity shifts the consumption of news into the social sphere. Steuer sees the factors that contribute to interactivity in such spaces as including the *speed* 'at which input can be assimilated into the mediated environment', the 'number of possibilities for action at any given time' or *range,* and *mapping,* which refers to the 'ability of a system to map its controls to changes in the mediated environment in a natural and predictable manner'[14] and finally the *engagement* with which readers participate. Engaged readers will bring more to the forum and construct news stories with more depth than casual browsers. That commitment will be a variable that is, to a great extent, generated by the issues that affect them most closely.

In following – perhaps we should now think of it, more correctly, as constructing – a news story, speed is clearly going to be crucial. The actions of the reader should alter the mediated environment in real time and where a dialogue with other consumers is taking place the media should intervene with minimum time lags between turn-taking. Thus, in text-driven arenas text input should appear no slower than normal keyboard speed. Steuer makes the point that the closer the approximation to real time the interaction is, as, for example, in a telephone conversation, the more 'vivid' or rich is the impact. In the reading of hypertext, linked lexias (self-contained units of signification) should appear immediately; elements which are slow or erratic to load make interactive media feel provisional or even incoherent.

The range of interactivity relates to the number of changes that the consumer can effect in the mediated environment. Steuer suggests that these include 'temporal ordering ... spatial organization (where objects appear), intensity (loudness of sounds, brightness of images ...), and frequency characteristics (timbre, color).'[15] For online news, then, while a high degree of temporal and spatial ordering is in the hands of consumers who can jump to different parts of the text at any time and reorder it to their own preferences, the full range of interactivity seems to depend on both the producer's use of hypertext and other programming devices, and on the consumer's facility with the browser. While all web users can, by definition, drive a browser, not everyone bothers to learn about all of the controls that their software offers.

'Mapping is ... a function of both the types of controllers used to interact with a mediated environment, and the ways in which the actions of these controllers are connected to actions within that environment.'[16] Steuer is referring here to the way in which aspects of the world outside the mediated environment can be employed as a metaphor for negotiating it. A good example is the Mac or Windows desktop and users' intuitive understandings and expectations of its topography. The link between the computer action and the command that initiates it can be simply mimetic as in the case of the echo of the Windows' cursor to movements on a touch pad. The user's physical actions initiate responses within the mediated environment. The examples above are mapped fairly closely to our experience of the contingent world and are easily learnt. This analogic approach also works in online news.

Readers approach news websites using their knowledge of the associated print edition although since most news sites aspire to be much more than just an online version of the printed newspaper or magazine, such a mapping strategy is of limited use and readers quickly discover new paradigms. The pages of news websites tend to be interlinked around themes or stories. The sports section is neither at the 'back' of the site nor is it at a deeper level than the lead story or international news. Readers of the *Guardian* will come to the *newsUnlimited* website with an expectation of sections on media, education, social welfare, etc. since, for some decades, these have been the daily inserts in the printed edition on Mondays, Tuesdays and Wednesdays respectively. Since the website is still largely driven by repurposed content, expectations fuelled by the print edition are met but readers soon learn that the online edition is structured in a very different way, not least since the current edition sits on top of an extensive archive of old material which can be drilled into with a single link.

Another level of interactivity which appears on the web is that between alliances of media titles. In 1996 *Newsweek*, ABC Television, the *National Journal* and the *Washington Post* set up a site called *Politics Now* specifically to cover the 1996 US presidential elections. While such alliances might be seen as a further example of the media establishment locking their market dominance in place they also have the potential of enabling a new kind of cross-media synergy on sustained and complex stories. Clearly in a protracted political campaign there are elements, such as the ubiquitous sound bite, that are perfectly suited to television while in-depth analysis of voter constituencies and intentions might be best served by print journalism. The use of databases (enabled by a journalism that employs some programming) characterises a specifically online journalism. Allowing readers direct access to databases of sports and political statistics radically changes their relationship with journalists. The interactive potential of such a site might be employed to enable voters to find out precisely how the tax proposals of candidates or parties would affect them personally just as it is used to set the current performance of their team in its detailed historical context.

The third level of interactivity, and possibly the most important in political terms, is the potentiality of the web to encourage communities of users, often from wide, even global, geographical areas, through chat rooms and bulletin boards. News providers of all kinds on the web use them to enable readers to mobilise around specific issues or stories. Levels of traffic over the chat rooms on Colorado news sites after the Columbine killings clearly reveals the desire of people to communicate directly with each other over the issues that concern them most deeply.

Ultimately, modes of user interactivity seem to reduce the amount of control retained by the news producer. That control, usually manifest in news filtering and agenda setting around what is seen to be in the public interest, now accrues largely to the consumer and this, more than its new media forms or the latest technology, is what makes the web unique as a news carrier and holds out the greatest promise for the future. News still reaches its consumers in mediated forms but that mediation is increasingly removed from the hands of (at least) local politicians and the corporations they legislate on behalf of, entailing the unlamented loss of so-called 'family values' and the blind spots that arise when news becomes a commodity.

Disintermediation

The roles that journalism assigned to itself in the mid-nineteenth century, on the strength of its newly acquired professionalism, as gatekeeper, agenda-setter and news filter, are all placed at risk when its primary sources become readily available to its audiences. The commentary, fact-checking and inflection that journalism places on such material remain available to readerships as secondary texts but the web itself has taken over the role of mediating those sources for audiences. It generally applies a lighter touch. This disintermediation effect also applies to retailers, legislators and book publishers; e-commerce allows the web to adopt the role of intermediary in business and politics as readily and effectively as it mediates news and information. Shopkeepers and middle-ranking party functionaries both lose their roles in the flattened hierarchical structures determined by the web.

The UK Department of Trade and Industry's 'Future Unit' report, 'Converging Technologies',[17] makes it clear that government, whose actions are traditionally heavily mediated by the press for its constituents, will play a leading role in the process of disintermediation as 'central and local government services are progressively made available' over the Internet. The report stresses 'profound implications' for intermediaries and mediators.

Journalists add cartographer to the role of news-worker but, in the universal library that is the web, they also become authenticators and designers for those who follow the maps they draw. Steve Case, the chief executive officer of AOL-Time Warner, uses the metaphor of 'clutter' to describe the context of online journalism. 'Many of you worry about the growth of what's called "clutter" on the Internet ... But what this "clutter" lacks is the basic value of analysis, perspective and insight ... The role of journalists – making sense of all this information – is very important.'[18] The maps contextualise and mediate the sources that they point to but the interpretation of sources becomes the responsibility of the readers themselves.

Immediacy

George Gerbner suggests that the Gulf War was a global media crisis calculated, or as he has it, orchestrated, to make instant history.[19] The commonplace view that history is written by the victors is here given a twist on behalf of the side that orchestrates that history. History is reduced to a rhetorical effect.

> As the technology of persuasion grows more complex, the art of telling stories in the wake of events grows both more complex and more instantaneous.[20]

Deprived of time to consider events as they unfold, audiences are forced into a 'conditioned reflex'. Gerbner suggests that in 1981 the allies were able to achieve this through a range of media devices. They could control real-time imagery, almost drip-feed it to the extent that events could be scheduled to meet North American or European prime-time news. Euphemisms were invented to mask the real horror, even the danger, of warfare; the oxymoron 'friendly fire' fastidiously conceals the bloody confusion of even the most technological warfare. Audiences are spuriously involved by the suggestion that they are witnessing spontaneous events (occasionally in real time). The complicity that is engendered through that involvement is reinforced by participants' accounts of the same event and the whole is 'quick frozen'. The account can, at best, be only partially true and yet it is increasingly placed on record as instant history. It concretises as fact as it is returned to, in its archival form, for a whole range of reasons including teaching, documentary and history itself.

Such accounts remain the crucial sources which subsequent historians, journalists, students and professional researchers will turn to first. They are to be found in the archives of the global news producers which will doubtless continue to disseminate histories which support the winner. My chapter on the reporting of the Kosovo crisis of 1999 suggests that it is more difficult to achieve a social sanction for such deterministic and instant histories in an information-rich environment like the web. The establishment of disinformation (official or otherwise) will get harder as realisation of the complexity of events is forced by the sheer range of sources on the web. Instant concretised history may well be one of the first casualties of the web.

The 24-hour news cycle that is commonplace on the web produces a culture of 'breaking news'. News appears online as it happens and the implications of this are that it is still undigested even by those presenting and commenting upon it. The web also gives consumers the opportunity to source their news, as it breaks, from local providers. In the case of the Columbine School killings in Littleton, Colorado, in 1999, versions of the story began to unfold while the situation was still going on. Broadcast news followed close behind but it would not appear in print for several hours. The first reports merely attempted to comprehend the situation and it would be some time before commentary sought to understand the event and begin to allocate the blame.

The web forces both audiences and journalists to rethink news to accommodate this idea of the 'first draft'. Some such drafts will be announcements of breaking stories that will be expanded in later versions. Others, such as local reports on traffic snarl-ups or stories which rapidly conclude, the bridge-jumper who changes his mind, will never merit a full-length piece. The danger for news values is that, in the view of journalists such as Matt Drudge, the publisher of the *Drudge Report,* such unconfirmed news inevitably includes gossip and if it is legitimate to post breaking news to the web it is just as legitimate, and more profitable, to post gossip. 'And his obsession is to get the hottest Washington and Hollywood gossip and deliver it to his network of readers as quickly as possible – before it's printed anywhere else.'[21]

Even for more conventional news stories the definitive interpretation would not appear for days or weeks after the event and, of course, one of the problems with such opinion pieces is that they arrive packaged with all the weight of traditional journalistic values. They propose a balanced, in-depth analysis of what might be a complex social and cultural crisis. They are rarely offered for what they are – opinion – and are used as a kind of banner pinned to the newspaper's masthead. Such journalism abandons the role of impartial informer and adopts the advocacy of a particular position. In the case of the Littleton killings there were clearly many other bodies from the NRA to TV viewers' groups who were more appropriately fitted and willing to use the story to create such political leverage.

The Columbine School Killings

Disasters and tragedies, while they can bring massive boosts to circulation, also bring with them new problems, opportunities and responsibilities to reporters and news providers. The reporting of the Columbine School killings makes an illuminating case study of how news is disseminated on the web, with some of its implications. As might have been anticipated the story of the killing spree at Columbine High School in Colorado produced large spikes in the flow of traffic across Denver's news sites and gave those organisations their first experience of a global audience.

In April 1999 two senior students, members of a small dissaffected group calling themselves the Trenchcoat Mafia, entered the High School in Littleton, Colorado, with guns, ammunition and explosives. Their subsequent attack left 15 people, mostly teenagers, dead and 24 injured. The event completely dominated the North American and the world's media for several days afterwards, taking the lead from the Kosovo crisis, which was becoming more entrenched and serious for European peace by the day, and diminishing it to a place in 'the rest of the news'. The web was not merely one of the channels used to report the event. A Gallup poll taken a week after the killings indicated that 80 per cent of Americans considered that the Internet was at least partly responsible for both the immediate tragedy and the general dissaffection of American youth.[22]

The reporting of such an event, which took several hours to run its course and continued to attract the world's attention for weeks afterwards, raises questions about newsroom practice and wider issues of morality. Many of the issues are similar to those faced by broadcast news producers every day but with the substantial difference that the web reporter's text will still be generally available to scrutiny the next day and, as part of the title's online archive, the next month and the next year. It will be available as part of the context for the next school killing and, intensely local, it is also available around the world. In this crucial aspect it transcends both the ubiquity of traditional print journalism and its ephemeral nature. It places a definitive stamp on the representation of events that neither print nor broadcast journalism can do, and without needing the subsequent authority of historians and other commentators. It also suggests that it arrives with an accountability which is at least equivalent to, and which accrues in part from, that which regulation and convention place on its predecessors.

This last factor, as is apparent in considering web news-makers like Matt Drudge, is rather more problematic. Communications technologies coupled with popular expectations around the immediacy of contemporary news reporting compromise that journalistic accountability in many ways. The *Boston Globe* reported that, as the siege at Columbine High School progressed, Denver's journalists found themselves being drawn into the event itself as the trapped students turned to them for help. Since it was clear that both the students and the killers were able to watch the event on televisions in every classroom in the school, any response to such appeals, beyond suggesting that the gunmen should give themselves up, had the potential of dramatically exacerbating the situation.

Reporting the story as it broke ... paved the way for mistakes. At one point, the exact location of a trapped student was broadcast, a dangerous move if the gunmen were watching the broadcast. Another time, [the] KUSA anchor ... urged students watching the broadcast to 'call the station ... to be put in touch with police'. Minutes later [the anchor] retracted the instructions, asking students not to call the station. 'Be quiet. Stay where you are.'[23]

In reporting this kind of event local journalists have to produce a lot of content very rapidly which brings with it a complex of issues beyond the need for accuracy in what might be a fast-changing situation. As crucially, in an online environment, news providers might have to contend with an audience that expands from a routinely stable, local one to a global one, in this case of many millions, over a period of a few hours. This quantum and rapid growth in traffic, which was sustained for several weeks, clearly has both technical and professional implications. How would Littleton's press' web servers cope with such an increased traffic and how did they feel about having their content aggregated for global readerships? Did their response to their temporary global audience swamp their commitment to their regular constituency? The factor that is new in this situation is that the local papers, in this case the *Rocky Mountain News* (owned by E.W. Scripps in Knoxville, Tennessee) and the *Denver Post,* suddenly become primary sources, along with the local websites of individuals, Columbine School itself and the North American agencies, for news consumers and fellow journalists around the world. For their local consumers they found themselves competing directly with broadcast news. What might, in less tragic circumstances, have also been a key primary source, the website of Eric Harris, one of the gunmen, was blocked by AOL, his ISP, a few days after the killings. The site, which implicated the web itself into the story, included:

> ... a lengthy discussion of pipe bomb construction, recipes for napalm and storage of explosives ... Another page included a reproduction of an image from a notebook. It shows several violent figures such as a sword-and-gun-wielding man standing atop a pile of burning skulls, another gunman firing two weapons into a bloody victim standing below him, and a horned creature with claw-like hands.[24]

Naturally Harris' interest in the Internet became part of the story, and while AOL's action in taking the site offline might be considered contentious in itself (an AOL spokesperson said that the site was removed in anticipation of a subpoena, although she was unable to be specific as to exactly where that would come from), the tragedy instigated a wave of copycat attacks and threats of attack across the

USA. By 12 May Excite.com was aggregating regular newswire reports like the following from Reuters and UPI.

Bomb Threats Targeted – Lawmakers are considering new legislation that would stiffen penalties against those who make school bomb threats. More than 40 bomb threats have been reported at North Carolina schools since the shootings at Columbine High School in Colorado last month.

Parents Are On Edge – An exploding bomb at an Omaha-area school is making many parents fearful about sending their youngsters to school. State law enforcement officials say they're working around-the-clock to arrest those who are responsible for placing the explosive device in a bathroom at Bryan High School yesterday ... or for calling in bomb threats.[25]

InsideDenver.com, the website of *Rocky Mountain News,* has its own staff and is run as a separate organisation from the parent newspaper. Robert Niles, the then executive producer, estimated traffic at between five and ten times the norm over the two weeks after the killings.[26] Such a volume caused problems for some of the software used by *InsideDenver.com* and substantially slowed down the site, hosted by the parent company. The management took the decision to take advertisements off the site and move it to its own server, providing extra bandwidth. By prioritising news publishing over advertising during the period of peak demand it was possible once more to serve pages rapidly to consumers. The decision does not entirely reflect the highest journalistic principles, although it is to be commended, since, if consumers cannot access the paper's site, to quote Robert Niles, 'You might as well not be writing anything.'[27]

Coverage of the unfolding tragedy was mainly repurposed from material prepared for the print edition. The site gave synopses of televised news conferences in the form of short bulleted pieces written by the online newsroom staff and provided audio and video clips. By transcribing material directly from broadcast media to the web *InsideDenver.com* was able to be first on the web (and hours ahead of print editions) with accurate information. Other news organisations were still waiting for their reporters to file their accounts of the news conference. Traffic on the 911 emergency channel was encoded as was *actualité* footage from KCNC, the local TV station, so the online newsroom was performing a kind of synoptic role that drew on the press, TV, radio, police scanners and other sources. The relationship between KCNC and *Rocky Mountain News* existed before the killings and is used to cross-promote the organisations even though they have different ownerships.

The important conclusion Robert Niles drew from the experience was that online newsrooms clearly cannot depend on their print newsrooms for coverage in reporting an event like the Columbine School killings. The print journalists have more than enough to contend with in getting their own edition out. Equally, it is clearly not adequate to shovel that edition online. For Denver, which within a week or so of the event was once more the main constituency of its local media, this was a moment of peak news consumption. Local readers would have been consuming print, broadcast and online bulletins avidly and would hardly have been satisfied with mere duplication of copy. The ideal solution here, applied by the *Chicago Tribune* in the USA and the *Guardian* in the UK, is for a breaking-news team to cover stories exclusively for online editions, allowing the routine running of the online newsroom to continue in the background. Perhaps such an answer is not so simple for news providers meeting the demands of smaller circulations on a commercial basis.

At the *Denver Post Online* the experience was broadly similar. The title is hosted by ISP InfiNet rather than being held on the newspaper's own servers so the problems of having to scale up rapidly to meet the extra traffic were avoided by Todd Engdahl, the editor. In the event InfiNet provided the same solution as Scripps by moving the site to a dedicated server the day after the killings as pages in heavy demand started to load more slowly. Engdahl managed the site with his usual staff of two online news producers and three interns from the journalism department of the University of Colorado. With such a small staff there was little that could be produced by way of web-specific reporting although reports were continually updated in the light of live news briefings from state and community officials and links to agency stories that the print edition did not have.

As the story developed, a whole range of links, which were either directly associated with it or would be called upon by the Littleton community in the aftermath, were added. Sites such as the Columbine High School itself, the Parents of Murdered Children support group in Denver and the Family Education Network on School Violence allowed readers to explore some of the issues that the shootings raised. Other sites such as the American Psychological Association, the White House Conference on School Safety, Report on School Violence and the Center on Juvenile and Criminal Justice, some of which addressed the tragedy directly, allowed readers to begin to comprehend it in a wider perspective. By expanding the story in this way and mobilising these organisations around the tragedy, the *Denver Post Online* directly intervened in community affairs. Both editors were clearly aware of their responsibilities to meet the rapidly changing information demands of a community which was numbed and distressed from grief and extreme emotional fatigue. While such interventions are not unheard of for traditional local media they are quite rare and in this instance newspapers and broadcast organisations could have done little more than referred to such organisations in passing with perhaps a contact telephone number.

Once more the bulk of the reporting of the story was repurposed from the paper's main newsroom. During the first few days reporters produced breaking-news stories for the website as well as print stories which would be published the following day. On the day of the shootings stories were produced throughout the day and into the evening. As the story developed many of these were short headline features placed on the website for no more than a few hours before they were updated.

Two more radical departures, both heavily subscribed, which appeared on the *Denver Post Online* site, were an online discussion forum about the shootings and a self-publishing area where readers could create their own memorial pages. Both print and online editions of the *Denver Post* received many messages of solicitude and polemics about issues such as gun control and youth crime. While the print edition was only able to print a small sample, Engdahl, who did not post the emails on the site while the story was running, was able to post them all later as staff resources allowed.

A month after the shootings the site was still drawing higher than normal traffic and had been widened to include an extended special report on teenagers, a 'Readers' Speakout on Youth Violence' area and an email form. There is also a multimedia section offering audio files of the 911 tapes, the Associated Press photo and video galleries of the tragedy, an interactive chronology of the tragedy and a photo gallery of other school shootings. While they do not purport to explain the killings the sites comprise a resource guide and an encounter arena for the grieving community. The sites act as a medium through which those who are affected, both directly and indirectly, can communicate with and support each other.

The volume of traffic that was attracted by the disaster also begs the question as to why consumers abandon their regular national news providers for the local perspective. The patterns of access suggest that it is not a casual readership but one which will follow the story through. Perhaps some of the answer lies in a readerly response to impartiality and objectivity. Readers will get a more authentic feel for the area and its people through the local media and since the reporters are also local the reporting tends to be both more informed and tactful. The reporters are often on first name terms with, and often get better access to, officials, at least in the early stages of an event like the Columbine killings. Finally – and this also relates to the fact that the reporters are part of the community – the story is more likely to be given a human context, with a view to causes and effects that will continue to unravel long after the national press corps have left town.

The experience of news sites that have had to report local disasters suggests a predictable pattern of traffic. While it can increase by factors of ten or more during the unfolding of the story, meeting a global audience's expectation that the local news sites will have the most comprehensive coverage, such stories regularly leave behind permanently increased levels of site traffic and the advertising that accompanies them.[28] Of course, every title will try to place its own inflection upon such a story to make it local. In this instance the international press, for whom by 21 April Columbine was the lead story, generally tried to apply a moral from the story to their own context with the headline: 'Could it happen here?' *Le Monde* linked the story to many of its primary sources in Colorado and to its own report on school security while *newsUnlimited* produced a web documentary on the killings with an investigation of whether the UK's stricter firearms regulations are more successful in protecting children from such outrages.

In later chapters I propose that online news forces quite radical changes around the conventions of journalistic ethics. The online reporting of the shootings at Columbine School, while it brought problems of its own, suggests that the web can bring new values to the reporting of events like this. Danny Schechter, writing on the *Common Dreams* website, suggests that, for much of the media, 'Both Columbine and Kosovo are treated as entertainments.'[29] He finds many parallels in the treatment of both events.

Both stories were personalised through human interest stories about the bravery of individuals, the tragedies of lost and dead children and the shocked communities who clearly thought that such barbarity could not be happening to them. The pathos obscures the issues that lie behind and set a context for the stories. The questions of what so alienates the youth of the most affluent nation on the planet and why the post-communist governments of Yugoslavia were apparently encouraged to commit suicide by the rest of Europe are lost in saturation coverage of private horror. Broadcast news employed similar ranges of images for both stories, in one case 'fires in the sky and lines of displaced people on the road or in camps' and in the other 'eye-in-the-sky' shots of the military-style SWAT squad police operation, and running, hysterical students and staff, to articulate what amounted to no more than a narrative of crime and punishment.

The online reporting of the shootings at Columbine High School, as we have seen, aspired to something more. The local online press were able to offer initiatives and information which directly intervened in the aftermath. The international press, particularly through their online editions, tried to understand the story through their own local situations. In both cases the emotional and visceral response to the story was moderated to allow the new journalism to examine its causes and possible impacts upon its contingent world.

3
From Photosetting to XML

The global media brands have perfected the presentation of news as a finished and seamless product, packaged with the advertising which capitalises it for instant and profitable consumption. While news on the web is forcing a reconsideration of journalistic genres and values, including a reassessment of that glossiness, it still adopts the 'characteristic organisation' described by Raymond Williams as 'sequence and flow'. It naturalises into the patterns of its consumers' daily lives. Online news is arranged across the screen to fulfil itself when we key in the URL (the Uniform Resource Locator – the distinctive address for the page that will find it as long as it remains available on the Internet) or link to the site. We immediately understand the format – itself an intrinsic part of the news – and for the most part there is no recognition of how it mediates events. The front page of a news site like *newsUnlimited* appears with overviews of the top ten or twenty stories of the day, including breaking news and updates, with links to articles and the other associated material which will allow the reader to negotiate it. Clearly, the production of such an elaborate media text demands a complex of technology, craft skills, professional knowledge and organisation. This chapter examines how these elements are brought together to present the news in a new and rapidly evolving medium.

Electronic publication should be significantly cheaper both to produce and to distribute for media producers. Any savings, however, remain speculative for most major producers as they make significant initial capital investments sometimes, apparently, with no immediate prospects of recouping them. The sheer scale of news provision on the web is such that sites such as *BBC News Online* and *CNN Interactive* produce many millions of page impressions (pages downloaded) each day. In 1998 *CNN Interactive* drew the largest amount of recorded traffic to date averaging 55 million page impressions per week and peaking at 76 million during the breaking of the President Clinton/Monica Lewinsky story.

At the other end of the scale the web provides access to publication for an explosion of independent and alternative voices in electronic zines and even radio. On the face of it *The Great Rivers Bluegrass Music Association* website <www.stringbendersbfg.com> competes on an equal basis with *CNN Interactive*. For those who do not necessarily need the massive volumes of traffic demanded by advertisers all that publication on the web requires is a computer, an ISP and something to say. There are web zines, many attracting very respectable readerships, on an eclectic, not to say encyclopaedic, range of subjects from poetry (*Zipzap Deep Style,* <www.dnai.com/~zipzap>) to aromatherapy (*Beyond the Rainbow,* <www,rainbowcrystal.com/oils/oils.html>), and slot-car racing and collecting (*HO-USA* on <pages.prodigy.com/housa>) to tea-tasting (*Only Gourmet,* <www.onlygourmet.com/ezine>). While this disparate range of interests is, to an extent, represented in print and mainstream broadcast media, there it is largely driven by the needs of advertisers in a range of clearly segmented markets. On the web it seems to derive much more directly from the interests of hobbyists and fans and is accordingly mobilised around communities rather than markets. What is certain is that electronic information is disseminated much more quickly than print. The information in most newspapers is already at least eight hours old before it is read by its first reader and for magazines that lag can be extended to a matter of weeks or even months. On the web the delay between production and dissemination is minimal.

Increasingly newspapers and magazines are moving away from 'shovelware' to websites that foreground original content (which will sometimes find its way to print in a kind of backwards shovel). This chapter examines the implications of that shift for readers, journalism and the meaning of news itself. The 5th Media in Cyberspace Conference reported in the *New York Times* in March 1999 indicated that, in a climate of generally eroding circulations, three-quarters of American newspapers surveyed claimed more than 5 per cent original content on their websites, a significant increase on the previous survey, and more than 95 per cent of respondents regarded the Internet as a resource second only to the telephone.[1] It offers journalists an extensive and growing set of tools for researching, gathering and verifying news.

Hypertext, New Ways of Writing and Narrative

The web enhances the discursiveness of print with the impact and immediacy of traditional broadcast media. One of the most productive differences between earlier texts in all media and those published electronically is the possibility of the instant link. It is the immediate linkage of documents or, more correctly, of specified elements within documents, which creates the possibility of hypertext and narratives which are in part determined by the reader. An analogy might be the tendency of oral storytellers in many cultures, depending on their audience, to follow a range of subsidiary plots in their narratives, periodically branching back to the main story. A hypertext might usefully be considered as a particular trajectory through a series of texts rather than merely the texts themselves.

Those texts, the matrix which contains the hypertext, can take a range of forms or combination of forms – video, typographic text and tables, audio, video, photographs and other images – which are linked one to another at one or more meaningful junctures. Such a convergence of forms demands journalists who can readily adapt to new roles and challenges. That convergence seems to supersede earlier news forms to the extent that Microsoft Network developers refer to their news sites as 'shows', partly in reference to the influence upon the form of TV rather than print news, but also, I suspect, to the constituency that they are aimed at.[2]

The individual elements of a hypertext can be thought of as the screen or page, although they can be smaller – an animation could comprise such an element – or larger, a video clip. George Landow, after Roland Barthes, describes such packages of information or units of reading as 'lexias'.[3] In news texts such elements of non-linear storytelling will comprise infographics, blocks of text and images as well as ancillary information such as character profiles, statistics and sets of links. The lexia is the basic self-contained unit of signification and should be structured to be read on its own. It comprises a meaningful textual fragment containing closure. Each page should comprise only one or two of these information packages and a limited number of buttons, pull-down menus or other devices to link to the other pages (any one of which might be the next page). The point of each lexia should be clear as should the function of every choice presented to the reader. This becomes crucial with the routine use of web search engines which can deliver readers, without preamble, straight into pages in the middle of stories. Such readers will not necessarily share the writer's agenda and for the page to be of use to them it will need to have a clear beginning and end as well as a range of navigational links to other parts of the story and its site. Of course, if they do find information that is useful to them they may well be inclined to explore other elements of the site. This can be encouraged by readily understood navigation instructions, perhaps utilising site maps or tables of content linked from every page. When their archives are taken into account the global news brands sites already comprise several hundred thousand pages, with up to 200 new pages being added daily, so effective navigation aids are essential. Many news sites have adopted the convention of listing the table of contents in a side bar known as the 'rail' on the left side of the screen. *newsUnlimited* uses this for breaking stories on their main pages. A further convention allows readers to link directly to any of the title's main sections from any page; *newsUnlimited* uses a series of fairly unobtrusive buttons at the top of each page.

When selected by the reader, the hyperlink, which can comprise a single word, phrase, image or part of an image, will replace the current lexia with a succeeding one that has been predetermined by the author. The target documents for hyperlinks can be within the same document, in another document stored on the same server, possibly by the same author, or on another server, by another author and possibly originated for another purpose entirely. In order to create a link to any document, anywhere, the journalist only has to know its URL.

In most news hypertexts few of those target choices will also have been written by that author so that, by the time the reader has linked from the second text, the narrative is also twice removed from the original author. A grasp of the diversity of alternative approaches to any subject, from a huge heterogeneity of readers, is crucial if the author is to intervene in any meaningful way in such a narrative system. Hypertext is used to produce a unique narrative in a process requiring such a degree of agency on the part of the reader that it can be usefully regarded as an interactive reading process. Janet Murray is careful to qualify the idea of user interactivity in digital environments as agency,[4] and, indeed, others talk of 'quasi-interactivity'.

Hypertext challenges both the way in which news texts are read and the traditional values which determine and constrain them. Thus, for example, in the entry page of the documentary feature produced on the Columbine killings by the *Guardian*'s *newsUnlimited* there are 36 possible links to allow the reader to continue further into the story; or perhaps we should say one of 36 possible stories and, of course, once the reader has clicked from the second page, either back to the entry page to select another of those 36 stories or on from within one of those stories to focus closer on some aspect that has been identified in the larger perspective, the number of possibilities for the subsequent development of the story could run into many thousands. The first page of the documentary is arranged to allow the reader enough information on each link, but no more, to make an informed choice. In this textual environment the meaning and the moment of closure are dictated by the reader alone.

Some links will retain the reader within the *Guardian*'s website but others, no less germaine to the story, for instance the one that links to the URL of Columbine High School, will bring up a page from a server on another continent. From there the reader might follow this story on the website of a local Denver broadcaster, KCNC. Of course, the KCNC website might equally have been the reader's entry point to the story, with the *newsUnlimited* documentary comprising one of a series of elements. While the web is able to contain hypertexts of dizzying complexity it is clearly counterproductive for editors merely to load every possible link on to a story page. Such a repudiation of structure, frequently encountered in the home pages of individuals ranting on their current hobbyhorse, merely produces a jumble or overload of information. It becomes difficult or even impossible for readers to identify significant narratives or to place them in relevant contexts.

Links radically affect the tone and meaning of a narrative. They can be used to explain or expand upon elements of the anchor text or to extend or redirect the narrative. Each one that is encountered by the reader forces a decision as to whether to follow the link or stay with the anchor text. The process insists that the reader thinks about the text in a way that print or broadcast texts do not. In creating their narratives readers will necessarily fragment the text and if the editor is to retain them it is important that there are links and structures in place which will consistently allow it to reconstitute to new formations. Where this is accomplished effectively, even where readers have linked away from the anchor text, having expanded the narrative, they will return to what for them is its primary text.

How the pieces of the story are connected together, and in what order, is fundamental in determining its meaning. Hypertext can make the reader instrumental, if not defining, in those decisions. It is crucial that editors have a clear notion of their audiences and are pursuing recognised objectives with both story and website. Lexias in a news context might comprise merely a sentence, or they might, less productively, be an article of several thousand words. They might contain no links at all, insisting that the reader moves either to the next page or the preceding one, in a substantially more constraining pattern than a magazine or newspaper, or they could contain many links. A reader who elects to click on a link near the beginning of a lexia will not read the rest of it, unless it is clicked back to later in the process. However the story is structured it is the role of the editor to guide the reader through it or at least part of it and to flag other parts of the narrative with markers, perhaps giving some indication of the provenance of sources. If the editorial grip is either too rigid or too permissive there is always a danger of losing the reader. The editor should be aware that at any juncture in the text the reader could decide to close the story and follow a different one. The way trajectories through the text are designed is crucial. This consideration is clearly determining in the convention of placing links in side bars or at the foot of pages rather than, as is still practised in more literary productions, embedding them in the text. *BBC News Online* embeds links to images and video but other links are kept at the foot of each column or placed in side panels.

A further major departure from traditional news narratives lies in the conclusion. The loss of linear structure allows no clear authorial thesis or summation. Closure is brought about by the reader for a range of reasons: either she now has the information she wants or there is a more interesting story to follow in another set of links.

As the inverted pyramid structure of the traditional print news story adds progressively further layers of detail to the bald headline that it commences with, a complementary flow opens the reading with a plurality of meaning(s) which are discounted until a single final truth is determined upon. The final all-encompassing version ties all the narrative elements together and comprises the definitive meaning or truth which explains the story. Even in instances where the story derives from a variety of sources, these will be given appropriate inflections to allow such a resolution. For lead stories, especially those concerning war, politics and morality, this truth will often be repeated and underpinned in the opinion/editorial section of the paper.

Online news stories are not so easily shoehorned into the inverted pyramid shape and their many strands might be more comfortably expressed as a net or matrix. This more complex narrative form achieves readerly gratification through 'patterns of exploration and discovery'[5] rather than any tendentious and partisan closure. Readers are able to become more roundly informed but they are less likely to meet the truths or sureties of traditional op/ed sections. Online journalism claims to do no more than bring some parts of the story together in what the reader strives to secure as a comprehensible structure. As is clear from the form itself, neither reader nor journalist can assume that all the parts are present or even available. The mystification that is routinely practised by traditional journalism on this account, through the spurious claim to comprehensive, even total, coverage, is not available to the online journalist.

Any understanding of the story which ensues is dependent on the narrative trajectory and context which the reader weaves around it. Janet Murray describes this as mapping the story. She points out the importance of an effective and informed navigation process and how association can completely change the meaning of each lexia through its juxtaposition with different information. She cites Lev Kuleshov's demonstration in the 1920s of how 'audiences will take the same footage of an actor's face as signifying appetite, grief, or affection depending on whether it is juxtaposed with images of a bowl of soup, a dead woman, or a little girl playing with a teddy bear'.[6] Along with the loss of control over the positioning or context of their writing, the lexias that precede or follow it, the journalist loses the ability to either resolve it or determine its meaning. While the online journalist will have tried to ensure appropriate associations in the links which extend the story, there are many opportunities for the reader to subvert those and force the lexia into a personal trajectory that is far removed from the journalist's intention or understanding of the story.

It becomes, therefore, an editorial imperative to consider the structure that would be most appropriate for the story. With the range of media and sources available to the online editor the templates produced by earlier news forms, such as the inverted pyramid, hardly seem adequate. In online journalism there is no reason why the form should not be determined by the content. Thom Lieb, in his website on *Editing for the Web*, suggests that a 'good starting point in determining structure is to think in terms of metaphors: could the information be best presented as a novel? a magazine? a series of "baseball" cards?'[7] The magazine and card formula are frequently used and I look forward to the next romance involving the British royal family presented as an online bodice-ripper.

A further device suggested by Lieb, which is employed by most producers of online news, is layering. The top level of the story gives readers the essentials with links down to lower levels which give background, ancillary information and a range of perspectives on the story. *newsUnlimited*'s reporting of the genetically modified food crisis in 1999 gave readers a range of scientific and ethical thinking on the subject, the government's view, links to Monsanto, the corporation which was lobbying to commence trialing of their products, and the viewpoint of the consumers.

> Layering can be applied even to breaking news [with] ... a structure in which a top layer provides the traditional who, what, when, where and why. The next layer would offer a historical context. Additional layers would offer analysis, expert commentary, and reader discussion and feedback. The limitless storage of computers allows Web producers to archive all previous material, making such layering an easy task to accomplish.[8]

In practice the top layer of a web news story might comprise the headline, a photograph and enough text to give readers a rough idea of the directions that the story might go in and links to take them there. Subsequent pages will expand on story elements that are layered 'above' them. Such a three-dimensional array of information, with links connecting the layers at different points and others pointing beyond the immediate structure to produce fresh readings, radically affects readers' expectations of news narratives. The journalist's ability to present a cogent argument around a limited range of facts is less important than the skills needed to create a rich and productive information environment.

Design and HTML

The design conventions of print journalism, from the spare utility of the seventeenth-century *Coranto*s to the trumpeting headlines and provocative front page imagery of the *Sun* or the cool iconoclasm of the *Guardian,* have taken 400 years and many twists and blind alleys to develop. Much early television programming comprised little more than radio announcers and performers reading from scripts and working to the microphone exactly as they had done for the medium they had learned their craft in. While the technology of television had been successfully launched the conventions that define the form were far from evident to either audiences or producers. They still had to develop new understandings of television's potential, its limitations and how to make meaning with it. The conventions and genres of radio, universally recognised and proven, were the obvious place to start from. Any conclusions about design or form with regard to journalism on the web, not yet a decade old and with its readership expanding and changing exponentially, must be considered as both tentative and very provisional. With that proviso, there do seem to be some generalisations which we might broach.

First, as in print or broadcast media, the site design reveals its unique individuality or identity with each page ideally marked by a coherent and consistent style. It has taken some of the world's best-known titles nearly a decade to discover that they do not need all the colours that HTML editors can offer and comprehensive application of all the latest plug-ins (usually delivering additional multimedia capabilities) to package news effectively. As with other media, consumers rapidly develop a sophisticated understanding of form and function and become dismissive of poorly or over-designed websites. A simple and clean design, employing basic graphic design principles brings its own credibility with it. Elements such as typography, colour and the employment of white space are all crucial. On the other hand new functionality is constantly being offered to web designers and some of it is very useful to news producers. It should not be ignored.

Information on the web, in news or any other genre, is broken into screen-sized chunks (lexia) and keywords, where they are used as links, are emphasised. Where information is supplied in the form of text the lexia is rarely more than 400 to 500 words long. Some genres of web document attempt to develop boldface keywords which are not links but rather act as headers for the lexia, making the subject clear. These can easily be confused with links and have not generally been adopted by news sites. A fairly typical indicator of the emergent nature of the conventions of the web was to be found in the tautological link that demanded that readers 'Click Here'. Since all browsers differentiate links by colour and underlining, the practice of highlighting regular text in colour is also redundant if not confusing. Equally, in a situation that is analogous to early television, many news providers do not employ the full range of multimedia. Consumers coming to a medium which can support video and audio will increasingly expect more than text and images.

The lexia or, in the case of audio files, an icon representing it, is displayed on the screen, arranged to the wishes of the journalist or producer, through HTML or a Hypertext Markup Language which is read by the browser software. It might be considered as a Page Description language, not unlike the code that drove phototypesetters. The language uses a fairly limited series of instuctions or tags to tell the browser how to display the text. Thus the instruction or tag <HTML> tells the browser that the following is an HTML file and </HTML> tells it that the end of the file has been reached. <i> will <i>italicise</i> and its pair, </i>, tells the browser to revert to the regular font. Similar tags will format text through the range of parameters that we have come to expect from word processors and, most importantly, enable the links or jumps to other files and other host computers. Clearly a complex layout such as the home screen of a major news site would require many, perhaps thousands, of such tags and be very time consuming, not to say boring, to accomplish. Hence the process of creating documents, or converting them to

HTML from other formats, has been automated. HTML editing software allows files in other formats, such as desktop publishing or word-processing, to become web readable at the stroke of a key.

Variants and developments of HTML such as XML and NewsML or NITF (News Industry Text Format)[9] are specifically geared to the creation, transfer and delivery of news forms and the data that they carry. XML is a data-structuring language which enables the production of documents in which the data is separated from its form or presentation. Information, including different file standards, can be shared between computer systems with less modification, and documents can employ data that is stored in different systems. These highly portable markup languages based on XML allow news organisations to share news, in all of its media forms and with all its features (graphics, photos, etc.), without the need to translate or edit files specifically for their own websites. Another development, WML (Wireless Markup Language) is used to format the bare-bones one-sentence news stories that are delivered to WAP phones. Like HTML these markup languages are open-standards-based and hence more likely to be taken up as the web standard for news producers. Reuters adopted NewsML in 1999 as part of the International Press Telecommunications Council programme aimed at agreeing a single XML-based format for managing news production.

Since they are open-standard, structures of HTML code cannot be copyrighted and, hence, by far the most usual way of learning markup languages is the borrowing of code from pages on the web. The 'Page Source' command under the 'View' menu on Netscape browsers, the 'Source' command under the 'View' menu on *Opera* and Microsoft Internet Explorer will reveal the code of most pages. That can easily be pasted into a text editor and amended to act as the basis for a new page. More ambitious novice HTML coders will go beyond this and start to alter the code to develop screen layouts of their own. While most producers and editors will not use HTML on a day-to-day basis, and most journalists will not use it at all, it can be a useful troubleshooting skill in understanding how HTML editing software performs its magic.

While many of the precepts of good graphic design seem to carry on to the web it must sometimes be hard for editors and producers to keep up with the endless stream of new functionality provided by software designers. One solution is to employ a modularity which allows new navigation structures, images and media technologies to be applied piecemeal. Modularity allows updates and content additions or changes to be made without disrupting the design itself. An excellent example of modular design is in the *newsUnlimited* website which retains its coherence from day to day and week to week while accommodating stories as diverse as royal weddings and mass graves in Kosovo. The structure also gives producers the opportunity to employ new media types and interactive forms. It can potentially also allow a media-rich version, which might take some time to download on to the consumer's screen, to be offered alongside one comprising much smaller files for faster viewing.

Download times can be crucial in retaining readers and each element of any page, graphics, audio, video, or new media forms such as Shockwave, etc. is called up separately to complete the basic page. The front page of an average news story could demand ten or twelve downloads from the news provider's server with large files such as video clips taking minutes rather than seconds to load. Where video or audio are routinely used, rather than being downloaded as rather cumbersome files they are 'streamed'. A plug-in player (a piece of software working within the browser) will start to play back the beginning of the clip while it is still receiving the rest of it. Providers such as *CNN Interactive* and *BBC News Online* now employ the technology routinely to offer not-quite broadcast-quality web TV. Clearly it would be inappropriate for a provider to offer a fully streamed service at the moment – TV does that rather better than the Internet can – but, as part of a multimedia news package, streamed video is crucial.

A range of new media forms are used on the web which cannot really be categorised in traditional terms. The programming language Java, for instance, is used to create small applications, called applets, that are run from inside a piece of HTML code. They are used to create many of the interactive and dynamic elements in web pages such as forms, games and scrolling information tickers. One development of Java, Castanet, is used to update automatically both 'push' and 'pull' media devices which can be accessed when the consumer's computer is offline. It also means that software such as browsers can be automatically updated whenever the computer is connected to the Internet. Shockwave is used to compress large multimedia files. The technology allows the kind of complex effects which are usually associated with console games and video animation to be used on the web.

Less dramatically, but as importantly for news providers, while images can be digitised in over a hundred different formats for various applications a quite limited range is employed by web documents. HTML can include GIF formatted images (generally used for quite simple graphics) and JPEGs which are used for photographs and more complex graphics. Most browsers also support a third format, PNG (Portable Network Graphics). Web graphics can be extended both by creating a sequence of GIF files to produce an animation and through the development of the image map. Any part of an image map can be clickable, taking readers to new pages. The device makes an excellent site navigation tool and is also routinely used to render maps and diagrams of all sorts information-rich.

Even the most basic news site will employ graphics, possibly as a 'splash page' to welcome readers to the site but also, on the first content page, to provide the sense of a rich or many-faceted text. Splash pages usually only feature some kind of graphic device (often an animated version of the corporate logo) which after a brief period automatically calls up the first page of the site.

The introduction of imagery in the nineteenth century was a defining moment for journalism. Newspapers used engravings before photographs and have employed photographic images ever since. Editors and readers recognise the importance of images in the production of news narratives. They are often used to anchor the series of contingent events which will comprise the story. The relationship becomes paramount with TV news and remains important for web production although here a balance has to be struck between loading times and impact. The most striking image will do little for the reader whose browser takes so long to load it that she moves on. Hence most news providers tend to employ small and/or low resolution (and hence low memory) photographs. Larger or more full-colour images can always be linked to separately. Another way of saving download time is to use the same images on several pages since once the reader's computer has the images in its own memory it will get them from there to set up the new page rather than requesting them from the news server again. This provides a visual feel to pages at little cost. There is a corollary of this use of images which seems to be that, once they have started to read the text, readers prefer a minimum of clutter such as graphics, quote panels, etc. These can be removed to side bars. Readers will also seek ways of skimming the text, either for an overview or to check that it is worth devoting more time to. Some news providers provide brief overviews and others use subheadings which are also employed as links from the top of the feature (and hence a kind of overview as well).

In the packaging of news stories for the web, editors and producers have to search out suitable sources and links. Some such links will derive from routine journalistic practice; for instance, in any account of the Columbine killings, on the web, television or print, information from the school itself and the local county was important. More detailed web searches would have revealed that the killers had websites and while editors might not have wished to include those in documentaries they clearly had the potential of being important to any understanding of the event. Searches would also have revealed reporting on previous similar events both in North America and elsewhere, initiatives on school violence, gun control, teenage cults, bomb-making and other terrorist activities, high-school culture and the regulation of firearms. In a medium as information-rich as the web any comprehensive account of a news issue will demand journalists who are skilled in searching very large bodies of data rapidly and effectively. Sites such as the *Spider's Apprentice, searchinsider.com* and *searchenginewatch.com* provide primers on web searching as well as information and rankings for the rapidly expanding range of search engines available to web users.

With 200 million pages to search, most search tools have their own strengths; some will search by keywords, either in the header or in the body of the text, others will specialise in searching multimedia documents. Search engines might search by geographical location, domain (.ac, .org, .com, etc.) or by news category. AltaVista's *Discovery* engine will include the files on the user's own computer, including emails, in the search. There are search engines which will search news providers and their archives or academic databases. As online news archives get rapidly larger most news providers offer search engines which have been specifically developed or adapted to search their own sites. There are also meta-searchers such as *Internets.com* and *Metacrawler* which will allow users to employ a range of search tools simultaneously.

The development of online archives was one of web news' early successes. For some sites more than 30 per cent of news stories looked at every day are in the archives. While some providers, such as *MSNBC*, employ the same URL for each day's front page, usually archiving that material under a new URL, others, for instance the *Irish Times,* leave old news online allowing readers and researchers to readily set the latest news in context. Such access to the archives enables journalists to assume informed readerships on subjects that would otherwise have become lost. The unfolding of the Littleton shootings was written in the context of earlier shootings and the lessons that editors had drawn from them as well as from the North American gun lobby and its critics. If another such outrage should occur there is a mass of material available on news sites both in Colorado and around the world on subjects as diverse as teenage disaffection, gun legislation and trauma counselling to help readers to place it in context and comprehend it. Those links enable readers to capitalise on the arguments, information and knowledge of the past and apply them to present crises in ways that, while they were theoretically possible, were previously heavily mediated by media professionals and difficult to effect before the web.

Before the web, newspaper archives were largely the musty domain of professional researchers and journalism students. Journalism was, by definition, current. The general accessibility of archives has radically extended the shelf life of journalism, with older stories now regularly cited to provide context for more current ones. With regard to how meaning is made of complex issues encountered in the news, this departure can be understood as a readiness by online news consumers to engage with the underlying issues and contexts of the news that was not apparent in, or even possible for, print consumers. One of the emergent qualities of online news, determined in part by the depth of readily accessible online archives, seems to be the possibility of understanding news stories as the manifest outcomes of larger economic, social and cultural issues rather than ephemeral and unconnected media spectacles.

It is, however, over-optimistic to view the Internet as a kind of contemporary Library of Alexandria. The average life of a web document is 75 days after which, unless it has been copied to the *Internet Archive* or another digital library such as the news titles' own archives, prospective readers will be returned the ubiquitous '404

Document not found' error message.[10] Much of the early development of the web, including the first attempts at online journalism,
was lost as old files were replaced by fresher ones on their host
servers.

Web archives and search engines employ software described vari-
ously as spiders, crawlers or robots which are programmed to seek
new sites by following links between documents. Ultimately they
will find and index or copy every page on the web. There are engines
which can search text, audio, image and video files as well as more
recently developed media such as Java, Javascript and Shockwave,
etc. New or updated pages are catalogued at the searcher's main site.
Obviously, the more pages an engine has indexed the more effective
it is likely to be and, equally obviously, as the web becomes the locus
for the world's information industries, which directory has the most
comprehensive index is commercially sensitive information.
Effective searches will probably employ both web directories (such as
Yahoo!) and search engines. Web directories are hierarchically
arranged subject catalogues organised around topics and sub-topics.
At the top level these will comprise headings such as Science, Health,
Business, News and Sport. Yahoo! employs 14 such categories. The
news indexes will be constantly updated and expanded in range and
organised across a range of sub-topics.

When searching for information on a breaking news story,
perhaps during the early days of the crisis in Kosovo, a directory
might have been very useful in keeping readers up with what the
major news providers were reporting but would have failed to pick
up some of the primary sources in the Balkans. A search engine such
as HotBot or Excite on the other hand, would seek out keywords and
concepts wherever they were and would have found the Balkan sites
rather more quickly, unfortunately in the middle of a mass of other,
often completely superfluous, information. All search engines allow
users to refine searches and one such sophistication found on several
engines allows users to assign relevance weightings to query terms.
Any journalist using the web, and that includes most of us now, is
increasingly handicapped without recourse to the most powerful and
effective search software and the skills to employ it.

There remain many unnerving aspects of browser technology and
HTML for journalists more used to working with the certainties of
print or the occasional hiccups and 'dead air' of broadcast media.

Not least of these is the problem that there is no way of knowing what the most carefully designed page will look like to the reader. HTML and its derivatives, which by no means all meet the same standards, are interpreted differently by different browsers, even Netscape and Internet Explorer. They also look different on every computer and that is before we account for the fact that users can all set both browsers and computers to their own sets of preferences over a huge range of variables. Since browsers are regularly augmented and improved, often automatically, pages can look quite different even if they are viewed on the same browser and computer before and after a browser update. It becomes crucial, therefore, for news producers to know what their output looks like on a extensive range of browsers and computers and to offer readers a range of viewing formats. Frames, for example, which allow pages to be segmented into a number of windows, are completely invisible to many pre-1996 browsers. In addition to offering fast-loading versions of their pages, many news providers also offer non-framed versions.

The Virtual Newsroom

While there are many news providers, the *Guardian* in the UK being a case in point, who, for a range of reasons, remove their online journalists from their print or broadcast newsrooms, in many instances the newsroom has now become an integrated multimedia affair. The multimedia desk, which allows web producers to work alongside print and broadcast journalists, while it can be an expensive option for owners and is often seen as a drain on resources that are already hard-pressed, ultimately allows them to compete effectively with broadcast news providers and the emerging super-aggregators. For broadcast journalists that convergence is not seen as such a threat since many multimedia newsrooms are set up on a model not far removed from television and radio. The 1999 'Media in Cyberspace' survey found that, certainly in the USA, there was a general trend towards integrated newsrooms.

There are, however, quite fundamental differences between online journalism and both print and some broadcast news media which have a direct impact on working practices. Many print journalists, for instance, work to the principle that news stories can attain a kind of completion. The assumption derives more from the nature of deadlines and the packaging and filing of news stories than to any intrinsic quality of events in the contingent world. The 24-hour news cycle and current modes of news consumption make any such assumption completely redundant. In integrated newsrooms the online editors will attend all editorial meetings and keep their teams informed about network plans for coverage. Such meetings are increasingly focused on breaking news and how stories are developing rather than on identifying the news of the day. Stories are posted to the website, with links from primary or associated sources and perhaps archive background, as they break and they will be continuously updated. Stories and elements that are not date-lined can be irritating for readers and, of course, news sites that are not updated continuously are likely to lose their readers rapidly. Kurt Greenbaum, editor of Fort Lauderdale's *Sun-Sentinel*, suggests that this comprises a change in culture and, indeed, a return to a news cycle which was closer to its readerships.

> Newspaper reporters today have grown up with the culture that at a certain time my story will be done … but 30 years ago, when papers had three or four editions a day, it was just expected that the story would be constantly updated and never really done. [11]

In a market where, as CNN's Will King says, 'It's always prime time somewhere', it makes no sense for online journalists to file to deadlines. While there might well be a surge in traffic at local mid-morning, depending on the structure of their day and the time zone they inhabit, readers will be continuously arriving on the website and, anyway, the story on the web, while it may eventually end up in the archives, is never 'done'. As new information becomes available it is used to update existing stories or break new ones. A site like *CNN Interactive* updates 24 hours a day and most national online titles also update important stories such as wars and national elections every ten minutes or so. Clearly this has more of an impact on some sectors, for instance the financial press, than on others, but most online news sites break stories as they appear, sometimes by merely linking directly to agencies and other sources but also by producing their own material. Elements such as regular columns and diaries will, of course, be updated to a scheduled frequency.

The issue of frequency can be defining for titles on the web, where large resources could theoretically enable 24-hour minute by minute updating. In practice, most providers develop a range of update frequencies for different types of content. Breaking stories, often merely linked from agencies, are updated as infomation becomes available. Regular columns are updated to a fixed cycle – daily, weekly or monthly – and a regular periodic update deals with all the title's content, disposing old material to the archive and replacing it with new along with links and other components. That comprehensive periodic update is what defines the title as a 24-hour news cycle provider such as *BBC News Online* or *CNN Interactive,* a daily such as *newsUnlimited,* a weekly, *The Economist,* or a biweekly or monthly, *Salon.*

Push media will keep the reader constantly updated for those who have direct Internet connections, or periodically to a customised schedule for consumers with dial up connections and mobile viewers. A news packaging service such as *Pointcast,* which in the UK is operated in association with BT, will let readers select their region (UK, USA, Europe, etc.) and areas of interest (industry, weather, UK News, sport, etc.) as well as providers (ITN, *The Economist,* CNN, *ZDnet,* etc.) and will then deliver the customised package via a news ticker at the base of the screen, a screen saver which delivers headlines and summaries while the computer is idle, or as a window, which can be accessed with its last update even when the computer is disconnected from its network. Since *Pointcast* is not a web service *per se* but rather draws upon other providers' web content, it functions perfectly well offline. Content is deleted from the reader's computer after several days unless it has been selected to be saved. Depending on the consumer's mix of channels push news services like *Pointcast* are good at delivering sports results, weather forecasts, entertainment reviews and schedules, breaking news and market reports. What push news is not so good at is depth of reporting. That deficiency can be compensated for by the headline emailing service provided by titles such as the *Wall Street Journal,* the *Irish Times* and the *Business Times* of Singapore. These can be used to alert readers to stories that they should be interested in and which they will then pursue on the title's website or print edition.

For a more specialised package of information, services such as *NewsTracker, Newshound* and *NewsPage Direct* search for daily news reports on subjects of the reader's choice from a much larger range of web publications or channels, which makes them more of a 'pull' form. *RealAudio Timecast* offers a similar service, with the difference that, as the name suggests, its customised package is selected from the daily schedules of web radio services. The news becomes audio background to other tasks that the listener is undertaking on the computer or is delivered as a telephone service. Some of these systems include a degree of intelligence in that they can follow the consumer's selection of what they deliver to find more of the same. As the number of pages on the web surpasses 800 million[12] it becomes progressively more difficult for consumers, especially new ones, to find the information they need. Increasingly sophisticated and specialised though they are, search engines can only skim the surface. Content providers accordingly move from 'pull' models of dissemination, in which consumers find them, to 'push' models, where they find consumers.

Ultimately, even the aggregators and packagers are dependent on the newsrooms of the content suppliers, local, regional, national and the global brands, for their news. The process that places that on the web is closely modelled on, and increasingly integrated with, the newsrooms of the traditional media.

News is gathered from agencies, news-gathering systems such as Basys and the organisation's own journalists, ready for an editorial conference where it is placed in a hierarchy determined by its perceived importance and any coverage that has already been planned by the organisation. As in broadcast newsrooms the important breaking stories tend to be ranked first followed by features. The global news brands will run three or four such conferences every day on a shift basis, while smaller organisations might only have them once a week. Editorial staff, producers and journalists decide presentation strategies for each story at these conferences.

Each story is developed by a team which includes journalists, producers and editors. The structure of the news delivery vehicle, the website, will be largely predetermined by the information architecture. That role is a macro-level one and does not necessarily determine the form of specific content. 'Information architects look at structuring a huge amount of information. It's not even so much about communication as it is about navigation and "information spaces" ... the methods used by information architects are quite different from editors' methods ... information architecture is where you do more usability testing and modeling.'[13] Generally the information template, which tries to account for all aspects of usability is specific to the title although a corporate information architect such as Northcliffe Electronic Publishing in the UK produces and manages a template to which all regional Associated Newspapers titles in the UK adhere.

For a local paper such as Northcliffe's *West Briton* in Cornwall, UK, the editorial team, working to that template and thus avoiding the need for technical support, might comprise only one or two staff. One implication for local weekly newspapers is that a website allows an inexpensively produced daily update and taster for the print edition. For the BBC or *MSNBC*, at the other extreme, editorial teams might entail ten or twenty people for an important story. The journalist will select material, including images, audio and primary text such as transcripts, briefings and reports from agencies and other sources that can be brought together to give a coherent account of the story. The producer will commission multimedia and reader-interactive elements such as bulletin boards and chat rooms and begin to consider how databases and primary sources might best be employed. An important editorial role at this point in the development of the story is the assembly and evaluation of appropriate links and other background information. The team is not seeking any fixed meaning or conclusion for the story, but rather a comprehensive account.

When the journalist has written the textual elements of the story and the material that connects other media components to it, these are checked by copy-editors for style, spelling and factual accuracy. The whole is then laid out, often but not necessarily, on paper. The layout then goes to the producer/editor who renders the story into the markup code which makes it web readable. At this point the story can be run on a server, all of its multimedia elements checked and, once more, checked for factual accuracy. The final stage of production entails ensuring that the document can run on a range of browsers. It will look different (sometimes substantially) on each one but as long as it meets the news provider's house standard on Netscape and Internet Explorer, which will deliver it to the vast proportion of its readers, and is readable on other browsers, it will be published on an external server. News on the web is the product of a hybrid process combining the dynamism of broadcast media with the rigour and tested effectiveness of newspaper publishing.

Even stories which do not include elements encouraging feedback can well generate them, often addressed directly to the journalist under whose byline the story appears. This material can be usefully posted on to the site and linked to the original story. There are many examples of stories which might otherwise have been moved to the archives being revived and radically extended by such readers' interventions.

This just-in-time assembly-line approach to news clearly has implications for the roles and autonomy of newsworkers. Jeremy Iggers describes the approach as a kind of 'maestro session, where all the elements of the story are initiated simultaneously'.[14] The news story becomes a package with all of the elements being brought together to produce an integrated and harmonious whole. The presentation of the story, including all its textual strands and its illustrations, is planned from the outset. 'The approach works best when the reporter is adducing evidence or anecdotes in support of a foregone conclusion.' [15] This attrition of content by form, in which the narrative is fragmented into many layers comprising shorter lexias, diagrams, side panels, time lines and bullet points, appeared first in newspapers but found its natural environment on the hyperlink-enabled web. While online news forms can very powerfully draw out the issues behind news events they can, as easily, become tiresomely self-referential, focused on the technology and on its surface and gloss. More than ever they demand a considered and appropriate use of technology.

The Online Journalist

> Responsibilities for this position include organising and producing interactive broadcasts and web coverage. Experience with web and multimedia production required as well as good writing and copy-editing skills. Some evening production required. Salary commensurate with experience.

This recruitment advert is fairly typical. Journalists joining multimedia newsrooms need to be broadly skilled and, especially for titles with global readerships, willing to accommodate a full 24-hour news cycle. They will be asked to write stories, produce photographs, audio and video and possibly even create web pages. Journalists working in online environments do so under a range of titles, although no longer, thankfully, as Webmaster or Guru. The multimedia format of online journalism is recognised in the role of producer. Producers will largely repurpose material from print and broadcasting. That is to say, in addition to processing it through software that renders it web readable they will also add the links and headers that make it readable as hypertext. While much of the producer's work will be around the creation of online features or documentaries, they are also regularly asked to provide interfaces which will allow consumers to make use of large databases, perhaps an archive or listings schedule, but also government, corporate and academic databases.

The *UpMyStreet* site <www.upmystreet.com>, which is based in the UK, allows consumers to cross reference a whole range of parliamentary and governmental information to profound effect. In addition to finding out the interests of their local Member of Parliament users can correlate data about industry in their constituency with schools or crime rates and their MP's extra-parliamentary interests. It is this kind of interaction, which insists upon the personal dimension of news, how it affects me and how I might intervene in it, wherein lies online journalism's greatest potential. In another aspect of that, potential producers will also be asked to develop online communities, particularly through web chat lines and other interactive features.

Resources such as chat lines hosted from the newsroom change our whole conception of what the journalist is. In the past, the newsroom's relationship with its audiences was very different from most other professional relationships.

> Unlike doctors or lawyers, journalists do not personally know their 'clients' nor do journalists interact directly with readers and viewers on a one-to-one basis. Indeed, what most journalists know about the audience, if they know anything, is likely to be 'the numbers', i.e. how many people read the newspaper or watch the newscast. Thus, journalists are not likely to have first-hand knowledge which would lead them to share news values with their audiences. [16]

Online journalism, on the contrary, will, of necessity share those values with their readers. The 'self-proclaimed expertise, criteria and norms' of the traditional press become an anachronism for audiences who are able to share the primary sources with the newsroom and react to it, often in the same space that is disseminating it.

This potential for interactivity also affects journalists writing material for the web. In print journalism the writer will wait several days for any response in the form of letters to the editor. For magazine journalism that might be weeks or months and for broadcast forms readers' feedback is even more erratic. Readers can respond to material on the web immediately, and regularly do. Where such responses are published this much more rapid feedback loop creates a sense of community, with the journalist or regular feature at the centre of it, which can be very productive. Such communities are at the heart of strategies around retaining and building readerships.

The attributes that produce effective journalism for print publishing and broadcasting, such as an eye for an interesting story and basic copy-editing skills, remain the foundations upon which the online journalist builds. The shift to non-linear narrative, in an ethos that resolutely stresses content over form, requires some adaptation and additions to those skills. The values that traditional forms of journalism stressed must be rethought and renegotiated online. The objectivity which characterises so much journalism in the West, at times reducing it to the anodyne, is being largely abandoned by online journalism, even where quite technical subjects are being addressed. Novel and more subjective voices are being given platforms by a new media whose audiences are not committed to it in the same way that print or broadcast audiences were in the past. In the era of unconstrained massification, that commitment may well have resulted from lack of choice as much as any brand loyalty.

In following the news on the web the reader can link from the BBC to CNN in a single move to follow the story and from there to the *Zambia Post*. In such a market, where suppliers can find themselves, far from competing, actually amalgamated at the hands of their readers to deliver their stories most appropriately, new devices are required to differentiate news providers from their competition. Distinctive journalistic voices have spilled over from the weekend editions of print news and magazines to the web to achieve just that.

When *newsUnlimited* was launched in 1998 it contained, for instance, a twice-daily column, 'Guardian Eye', written by Derek Brown. Brown's experience as a foreign correspondent and his idiosyncratic and witty commentary gave *newsUnlimited* a real edge on many other online news providers.

The critical thinking which will enable the journalist to structure information around organising principles geared to readerly interaction and the narratives which will produce it is crucial. Stories no longer have to be shoehorned into the headline, photograph and column format or thirty seconds of footage and a soundbite. There will be occasions when such approaches are appropriate and they make perfect sense on the web, but the online journalist also has the opportunity to employ a wide range of other forms which might better meet the demands of the story. An awareness of the images, graphics, audio and text that readers are likely to be drawn to as entry points in the story is clearly important. Online editors must also be able to deal with video and audio, and, because of the exigencies of rolling deadlines, at a speed that is more akin to broadcast newsrooms than print. The convention of indexed headline-type links not only offers a formation of stories or story elements but can also suggest in what order the parts of the story are to be read. Clearly this can be a much more erratic and wide-ranging process than it is for print news publishing and the journalist needs to be aware of an array of entry points to the story and multiple viewpoints within it.

The online news story will therefore comprise a much larger document, or set of documents, than its print or broadcast counterpart. It will offer clearly delineated points of entry to a broad spectrum of readers, each of whom comes with different demands upon the story. The announcements of cuts in primary education, for example, will be read very differently by educationalists, parents, taxpayers and those in parallel employment sectors. The story might begin with, and be about, savings and tax reductions serving politicians and taxpayers. For others it will mean impoverished provision and perhaps carry with it the threat of similar cuts in other areas. The story has radically different implications for these various readers, and online journalism, unlike earlier news media which tended to simplify and encase such events in a monolithic meaning, has the space to examine the whole range of positions and discourses which are implicated.

This discursiveness also insists that the journalist should supply depth to the story. It is no longer enough to merely cite the latest cut in education funding and top it off with a couple of sound bites defending and attacking it. Readers can now click through to other levels of the story which will report previous cutbacks and investments in education made by the present government and its predecessors. They can compare, for example, provision of primary education in the UK with that in other countries. They might even be given some assessment of how previous cuts have manifested, whether in larger class sizes, cancellation of building programmes or other services, and whether the changes in funding might be justified in terms of population growth or decline. Such stories might also be personalised with a profile of a teacher in jeopardy of redundancy or a child who now has to bus to school instead of walk. Issues such as this will also generate significant volumes of reader correspondence and the journalist can also usefully act as the moderator for such exchanges on the subject. While all of these devices are seen in traditional journalism they are very rarely used in concert; for online journalism they are routine.

Perhaps the major development in online journalism involves the direct incorporation of sources into stories. Where databases and transcripts have been used in preparing news, readers are given direct access to them. Using the *Upmystreet.com* model of extracting very local information from government databases and correlating it with other information, there is no reason why the journalist should not give readers the possibility of using published information to understand how cuts might affect them personally. How much exactly would a 5 per cent cut amount to for my local education authority? How many teachers' salaries is that? How many ancillary hours? Any ability to provide answers to such questions requires a new approach to journalism. Eric Meyer suggests that the key dimensions of online journalism are 'depth, breadth and interaction'[17] and that those three aspects of any reporting will serve readers more significantly than any formal aspects of the presentation of news. The principle that emerges from this understanding is that 'form should not drive content. Content should drive form'.[18]

Of course, the great benefit for journalists of any determining form, which arrives complete with its set of defining conventions, is brevity and the certainty that the story will be understood by its readers on the terms of the journalism that produces it. For the print journalist the story, with its accompanying images, can be word-processed to length and despatched to print. The broadcast journalist will compile a similar package, again to length, and deliver it to the newsroom. For the online journalist neither space nor time are a determining constraint in the same way and the prospect is altogether more daunting. The crucial skill lies in understanding how the stories (not story) will be told. Those multiple viewpoints and layers of information will be set against one another to gain an understanding of the issues and their contexts. Having gathered the raw information and decided how it might be presented the project becomes a team effort in which the producer, or production team, applies a range of technologies to the information to meet the form of its presentation. As this chapter indicates, at least three distinct roles are emerging in online newsrooms: those of journalist, producer and editor.

The questioning of the rules of traditional journalism does not mean that they should automatically be discarded. On the contrary, as readers become aware of the importance of verifying all information on the web, editorial rigour needs to be enhanced by journalists wishing to protect the integrity of their profession and the reputation of their title. Web publishing is not necessarily instant publishing. While its emphasis has changed, the editorial role of gatekeeper is still applied and a similar set of questions moderates the process. 'Is this reporting appropriate for the title?', whether that be *BBC News Online* or *The Onion*. 'Will our consumers wish to read this?' Information needs to be checked and rechecked. The axiom incidentally explains why this book is about 'online journalism' rather than the more general overview of online news. The journalist, more than the producer or the editor, is responsible for the content of news. I have tried to stress that online journalism is content driven, more so than other news forms, and it is that content, not the latest design fashion or media technology, that readers look for online. The axiom can lead journalism into novel and highly productive situations such as the *Financial Times*'s highly innovative Wimbledon coverage in 1999 or the *Washington Post*'s feature, 'Chapter One', which places the first chapter of newly published books online and links them to the paper's reviews. Both of these ideas are resolutely content driven and draw global audiences. On a smaller scale, public forums on neighbourhood issues or items such as regular 'shopping baskets' comparing the prices at local supermarkets can also be linked to online news in a way that attracts and retains both readers and advertisers.

While journalists might well understand the principles of audio, video, photography, Shockwave, Java and HTML in order to know which skills to call upon to most appropriately present the story, it is unlikely that they would be called upon to use them. Other considerations apart, the actual production of the story would simply take so long that it would be redundant by the time it was ready to file. What is important for the journalist is the ability to conceptualise a piece of journalism in multimedia and interactive terms.

A crucial part of that ability lies in understanding that the textual element of the journalism no longer, if it ever has since the introduction of the daguerrotype in in the mid-nineteenth century, carries the story. There will be some information for which it is the appropriate form, but, in order to make its effective contribution to the story, that needs to be organised alongside or in sequence with other pieces of information (lexias) for which different media forms are more appropriate. Such an understanding is fundamental even to print journalism, where the text is mobilised with, not by, accompanying photography, captions, headlines, and composition elements such as columns and panels. Where such elements become ornamentation, journalism is reduced to pastiche. The rule applies even more profoundly to multimedia journalism. The question of organising information in appropriate formal contexts lies at the centre of effective online journalism.

Such skills can be developed through the exercises that are used in visual media, film or video, such as story-boarding or diagrams, which explore how readers with a variety of interests might approach the story. Each lexia is entered on a critical path analysis chart and they are linked to each other along the paths which might be chosen by a range of readers. There will be some pieces of information that are essential to every reading, for instance, any account of the Columbine killings that left out the events in the school on 20 April would clearly limit any understanding of the tragedy, and others which, while they are not crucial, would make interesting asides to particular readings; perhaps the National Rifle Association early responses to the tragedy.

The ability to segment stories, either as a series of typographic elements or as images, gives the journalist useful insights into how to structure them as main bar and side bars over a series of screens, perhaps also with indications of how the various formal elements are to be employed as well. An understanding of how to reduce news stories to their constituent elements is, of course, also useful as newsroom teams are assigned to cover complex events.

Many web news providers have few or none of their own reporters. While a site such as the *Guardian's newsUnlimited* does retain one or two journalists who write daily material specifically for the site, most of what appears there is developed from content that has appeared in the print edition. *newsUnlimited* is able to add considerably to that material by adding links to its sources as well as to related archive material and to transcripts as well as alternative perspectives and developments from the story such as forums or web interviews. The resulting product, such as those which *newsUnlimited* describes as web documentaries, amounts to much more than its constituent parts. The texts and recordings supporting the journalist's claims place the reader in a very different relationship to the reporting than the one imposed by traditional journalism with all of its assumptions and opacities.

A fairly benign understanding of such developments is offered by the DTI's report on 'Converging Technologies'. Rather than online journalism displacing the traditional press it finds the two forms to be 'complementary. The print medium is used for a broad overview of events and the website is used to follow up breaking news, or the detail and background on specific items of interest'.[19] The report then comments upon the economic climate for this symbiotic relationship and there it is rather less sanguine.

Just as journalism has had to comprehend new skills and principles as it adapts to the depth and interactive nature of the web so its readers, pressed by the sheer volume of information overload, have adapted as well. Jacob Nielsen points out that people no longer read; they scan, making sense from a limited range of significant words and phrases rather than complete paragraphs.[20] Highlighted keywords, bulleted lists and significant sub-headings facilitate scanning. Reduced word counts and paragraphs limited to a single idea also help readers to negotiate text rapidly.

As with so many other cultural texts including literature, advertising and fine art, we can anticipate quite radical formal changes in journalism. Web-natural forms of news will appear. The technology of print encouraged the meaningful segmentation of information into easily portable units, typically books, magazines and newspapers. The web simultaneously reduces the size of communications, most emails are substantially shorter than most other epistolary forms, and increases it in the huge amounts of information contained in distributed databases. These new textual forms, including journalistic ones, some designed to interact with such databases, are emerging as the first web-natural texts.

4
Armageddon.com: Home Pages and Refugees

> Modern communications are making it easier for a journalist to
> pass his information, with or without approval, and making it
> more difficult for any authority to control the passage of infor-
> mation or even know that it is being passed.[1]

The UK Ministry of Defence, in its evidence to the Beach Committee
on censorship in the aftermath of the Falklands War, hinted, at least
in its tone, of a growing uncertainty around the assumption that the
reporting of the war, while integral to the information war, was
somehow separate from the events in the South Atlantic experienced
by the soldiers and sailors on both sides. Within two decades that
assumption had become completely untenable.

In 1999 the war in Kosovo was the first major international
conflict to be extensively reported and, arguably, fought on the
Internet. Propaganda, military and political analysis, appeals for aid,
government and military communications, diaries of soldiers and
the dispossessed, email interventions of a thousand different voices,
and reportage in video, text and photography all combined to give a
more comprehensive and confused account of war than any medium
before it. While the war was heavily reported, especially in Europe,
in newspapers and by broadcast media, that reporting often
presented, and regularly sampled, a discourse that had already been
explored on the web. The mass of information on the web, from
NATO and US State Department sites offering news of atrocities and
images of destruction to counter-claims by the government in

Belgrade numbering civilians killed and planes brought down, influenced much of what appeared in other media.

By the spring of 1999 and the commencement of NATO's air strikes there was already a wide range of historical, political, economic and social information about the Balkans on the Internet which determined an approach, both online and in traditional media, very different to the media coverage of earlier wars, including the civil war in Bosnia only a few years previously. The reporting of that war was summed up by Matt Welch writing in the *Online Journalism Review*.

> From 1992 to 1995, when residents of Sarajevo were shot crossing the street and bombed while standing in line for bread, reporting about their plight was funneled to the world's media giants through a clutch of correspondents and stringers holed up at the Sarajevo Holiday Inn. What a difference four years makes.[2]

The earlier Balkan wars of the 1990s received the same quality of media coverage as Korea, the Congo, Vietnam and the countless other conflagrations that marked not only the Cold War, but the latter half of the twentieth century itself. It was managed, more or less, and heavily partisan. Broadcast news of the NATO bombing of Serbia, which started on 24 March 1999, began very much like a rerun of the Gulf War a decade previously. Military spokespeople talked around bomb-sight video and aerial photos of the results of 'precision' bombing to an unquestioning cohort of largely hand-picked journalists. They, in turn, segmented the package into easily digested bites framed by images of distraught refugees and the comments of experts, usually older military men who had won their colours in past conflicts, for the world's news audiences.

On the Internet, even during the first days of the war, a very different kind of narrative was unfolding. There had been some indication of the potential brought by the Internet to such situations with the activities of the Association for Progressive Communications and PeaceNet in 1991. They were able to bypass the blanket censorship imposed on world media by the Pentagon and its allies to carry independent reports about the Gulf War and its effects and to report a widespread antipathy towards the war. At that time the 15,000 or so subscribers worldwide were hardly able to affect the outcome of the information war but the impact of public networked information systems was already clear.

At the opening of conventional hostilities both NATO and Serbia arrived very differently armed to fight the information war. The outcome of that war was to have implications for both sides as far-reaching as the bombing war. Not only was it to change Serbia politically – the bombs saw to its economic and environmental breakdown – but NATO too would never be viewed in the same way in the light of a series of all too questionable tactics, decisions and mistakes which proved impossible to conceal or even explain in a new, more open, information economy. The spotlight on NATO also raised, to an uncomfortable level, public questions about the organisation's function and its long-term strategies. Ambivalence about the war on the web went so far as to question whether it was deliberately provoked by NATO and the United States within the terms of the Rambouillet Agreement to justify its continued existence in the post-Cold War era. The issue was hotly debated on the web from a range of perspectives before, during and after the bombing.

News from Open Sources

From the first days of the war, reporters found themselves in the novel situation of sharing their sources with their readers. By March 1999 the Internet hosted a wide range of information and rhetoric offering the positions of many of those involved in the war as well as an encyclopaedic volume of general background on NATO, Kosovo and the Federal Republic of Yugoslavia. This information was consumed, debated, supplemented or attacked by Balkan and global audiences who responded to newsgroups, IRCs (Internet Relay Chatlines) and bulletin boards, some of which rapidly degenerated into bile-laden soapboxes while others carried cogent and considered comment or the terrifying accounts of those caught up in the war. The websites included the voices which had dominated the coverage of previous conflicts, such as NATO, the Pentagon and the UK Ministry of Defence, as well as others, hitherto excluded from such discourses, from inside and/or opposed to the Serbian establishment such as those of the Serbian ministries conducting the war, the Chinese-Yugoslavian press agency Tanjug, various Balkan non-governmental organisations, the website of the Orthodox Decani monastery, maintained by one of the monks, Father Sava Janjic, and the commentaries and diaries of private citizens. There were even web-cams, including one installed by B92, the independent Belgrade radio station, and producing live images of Belgrade throughout the war to prove to the outside world that there was an opposition to the regime that was willing, even during the darkest days, to take to the streets.

Hard as NATO spokespeople and Slobodan Milosevic tried to mythologise or simplify the war it was clear to those who followed it on the web that it could not be reduced to a bipolar confrontation of right and wrong, good and evil. That breadth of comment would, without the web, have remained invisible to both Western and Serb audiences. These sources offered a wide, albeit by no means comprehensive, spectrum of positions around the war and, since they were universally available, they both problematised and expanded the role of propagandists on both sides and threatened journalism itself with a degree of redundancy. The war made it clear to those who still remained blind to it that the role of the journalist was being inexorably forced into radical and permanent changes by the new medium.

There were further implications of the technology which enables this sharing of sources. In an information war which moves as fast as the events it recounts, journalists remain aware of what their rivals, including the global news agencies and newsrooms on the other side of the battle lines, are running and, to a large extent, what their sources are. In a networked medium it is pointless to duplicate others' reports since news providers can merely link to them. Five minutes with a search engine will give journalists a comprehensive view of the current state of the story. The sheer volume of information that is generated by such a crisis delivers a stream of new sources and perspectives with further searches.

That much of this discourse on the web was conducted in English seems to indicate that the debate was being played for global audiences, including the large Serbian diasporic community in North America, rather than for local Yugoslav constituencies. There were Balkan web users, albeit a limited number, certainly before the bombing, belonging to a small, mostly urban, socio-economic range. By 1999 about ten ISPs were seeking markets in the FRY and there was some public web access in Belgrade as well as restricted academic access at schools and universities. Many of the providers waived their fees during the period of the air strikes. If the demographics of early Internet take-up in the USA and Britain can be extrapolated to the Serbian population most users at that time were quite affluent and with liberal inclinations, although in a Balkan context that seems to imply no lessening of nationalistic fervour.

We get a flavour of this constituency from Veran Matic, editor-in-chief of the original Radio B92 in Belgrade. He saw B92, the independent radio station, as a 'self-defence project' for a quite privileged minority, many of whom would have been able to follow the radio station on to the web when it was eventually suppressed by the Milosevic regime. 'The most creative elements of the society had come to be associated with B92: artists, writers, theatre companies, the feminist movement, contemporary musicians – all of them found a creative outlet under the umbrella of B92.'[3] What is certain is that the war brought unprecedented numbers of consumers online in the Balkans. *BBC News Online* experienced five-fold increases in traffic from the Balkans and *CNN.com* achieved some of the heaviest traffic in its history with between five- and ten-fold increases in Balkan use.[4]

B92 escaped state control by operating for the first nine years of its existence on an unlicensed frequency. For nearly a decade prior to the Kosovo War, it had routinely reported political protest within the Yugoslav Republics. It was often jammed and its transmitter, limited by the Yugoslav Telecommunications Ministry to 300W, was so weak that it barely covered the centre of Belgrade although other independent Serbian radio stations regularly rebroadcast its programmes. As the regime stepped up its harassment of B92, regular broadcasts continued to be streamed on to the web from service providers outside the Balkans. They were taken up by the BBC World Service and the *Voice of America* and broadcast back to Serbia on short wave.

During the period when B92 was placing updated material on the web it was receiving nearly two million hits and 700 to 800 emails a day from its audiences.[5] Another radio station claiming to be B92, but offering programming markedly less inimical to the Belgrade regime, resumed broadcasting on a powerful transmitter from within Serbia on 2 April shortly after the suppression of Veran Matic's organisation. That succession had been recognised by the staff of B92 long before the event in their slogan, 'Don't trust anyone, not even us!' They continued to argue and demonstrate for it after its suppression and it was formally licensed by the Yugoslav Tele-communications Ministry about a month after the NATO bombing had ceased.

For Balkan and global audiences the web played a crucial role in the reporting of the Kosovo crisis in 1999. It may well have been determining in shaping its narratives as both NATO and the Serbian government came to realise that an open media, even one addressing a still limited audience, meant that many of the old certainties of war reporting and propaganda had to be reconsidered in an era when access to the means of news distribution could not easily be restricted and information both reached its audiences instantly and expanded exponentially. Tom Standage has described how develop-ments in earlier media technologies inevitably impacted upon the conduct of warfare.

> During wartime, the existence of an international telegraph network meant that news that had hitherto been safe to reveal to newspapers suddenly became highly sensitive, since it could be immediately telegraphed directly into the hands of the enemy. For years it had been customary in Britain for news of departing ships to be reported as they headed off to foreign conflicts; after all, the news could travel no faster than the ships themselves. But the telegraph meant that whatever information was made avail-able in one country was soon known overseas.[6]

The telegraph determined the beginning of wartime news manage-ment in the contemporary sense for civilian populations, a process which achieved its apogee in the Falklands and Gulf Wars. As Paul Frissen and others have shown, the fragmenting cultural postmod-ernisation that is accelerated by information networks, far from levelling power, control and inequality, rather tends to concentrate it. 'International networks are intelligently used by transnational corporations. Virtuality does not transform the capitalist system – to some extent it supports it. ICT and warfare are close allies, as the Gulf War has shown. And even the Internet has strong Pentagon origins.'[7] Perhaps the web began to reverse that process during the Kosovo War.

Crucially, for the first time it was possible for populations of warring states to communicate directly with each other through a mass medium. The effect is dramatic and undermines one of the fundamental strategies which enable nations to mobilise for war: the demonisation of opposed populations and ethnic or religious groups. Aldous Huxley's comment about propaganda being '... to make one set of people forget that certain other sets of people are human', is no less true now than it was in 1937. Veran Matic emphasises that the web makes it impossible for NATO to construe Serbia as being 'home only to nationalism, warmongering and sheer brutality'. He goes on to suggest that the silencing of all voices opposed to Milosevic by both the Belgrade regime and NATO would have made 'Yugoslavia a European Iraq and a pariah state for the next ten years'.[8]

The web also defused other strategies of information management. It is now all but pointless for the generals or their spinners to schedule events or conferences for the main news or the morning papers. Their audiences are turning to satellite news and the Internet where they are logging on 24 hours a day for news in real time. As they move towards global audiences the flagship TV and radio news and current affairs shows in America and Europe such as ABC's 'Nightline' and Radio Four's 'Today', are streamed on to the web with lists of content. Their consumers can download those parts of the programme which most interest them at any time of the day or night and view them in the context of a multifarious range of other media.

The sheer speed of the information war on the web also brings with it the capacity to drive out 'bad' information. Don North recounts the fate of the poorly researched Kosovo story filed for the German paper *Tageszeitung* during August 1998. Its writer, on the strength of a single unnamed source, described the 'dozens' of fresh grave mounds, the result of a massacre, on a rubbish dump outside the town of Orahovac. The story was placed on the *Tageszeitung* website, instantly sending Kosovo's 100 diplomatic observers and 300 accredited journalists to the town where the source was identified and found to be completely unreliable. The Serbian explanation, also on the web, and accepted by the diplomatic and media corps as well as the townspeople, was that the graves contained the bodies of some of those 'legitimately' killed in the battle for Orahovac. They had been buried just outside the town because the cemetery was already full. North makes the point that the speed with which *Tageszeitung*'s claims were unravelled on the web prevented the further inflaming of 'already raw emotions'.[9]

From the earliest days of the war it was clear that the implications of the web as information disseminator reached beyond news and its production and consumption to the medium itself. Information and its transmission are commercial products and military necessities as well as media commodities. The United States' trade embargo against Yugoslavia, detailed in Executive Order 13121 by President Clinton on 30 April, led to the American supplier of Yugoslavia's main satellite links threatening to cut them. In a single move the hopes for the Internet of the libertarian left and right as well as those of the electronic democratisers began to look rather fragile. While some of the country's ISPs took their Internet links from a land-based fibre optic line from Holland, the five largest were informed on 30 April by their US supplier that they were about to lose their link. The paradox of the US Department of Trade responding to the air force's success in destroying RTS (Serbian Radio and Television) by removing the country's only source of independent information was brought home to Loral Space & Communication Ltd, the satellite communications company, by an outcry from its Serbian customers. They asked Congress to review the situation and the link was not broken[10] although the embargo remained in place.

The threat was lifted two weeks later although not entirely removed and it continues to pose interesting questions both about the kind of democracy that NATO wished to see installed in Serbia and the future of the web. After two decades of debate over the implications of cultural and media imperialism by America and Western Europe the incident seems to place some doubt against the level of investment that the rest of the world is going to make in yet another medium controlled by the United States. The threat is explicit. Don North describes US military sources as indicating that 'they are prepared to jam Internet connections or even shoot satellites out of the sky if they feel security of military operations may be threatened. Scrambling and manipulating journalists' Internet communications are also options under active consideration to spread disinformation in support of military operations'.[11] The incident was by no means an isolated one. In response to the Iran and Libya Sanctions Act of August 1996 the US National Science Foundation took the unilateral decision to block Iran's only permanent Internet connection. [12]

As journalists were expelled from Serbia and barred from Kosovo itself at the outset of the bombing, the web rapidly became the main source of information about the war for them and, through a range of global news brands and Balkan and Eastern European media sites, for their readers. Websites included those of organisations such as The Kosovo Information Center <www.kosovo.com>, an English language site operated from London by Kosovan exiles on behalf of the ethnic Albanian population, the Serbian Ministry of Information <www.serbia-info.com>, the Serbian Unity Congress <www.sucinfo.com> countering NATO claims, NATO itself <www.nato.int>, the Kosovo Verification Mission <www.osce.org> undertaken by European states as part of the Rambouillet Agreement and the FAS Military Analysis Network <www.fas.org/man/dod-101/ops/kosovo.htm> which offered analyses of the military capabilities of the various factions in Kosovo as well as Serbian and NATO forces, including satellite photos and the latest military deployments.

The Milosevic regime in Serbia had been using the Internet and countering independent voices there and in more traditional media since the beginning of the Balkan War in the early 1990s. By 1996 most traditional oppositional media in Serbia had been suppressed and the regime was examining ways of controlling the web. A draconian Law on Information was passed by the Serbian legislature in October 1998 in which it was specified that web publications committing 'verbal or opinion deceit' would be heavily fined. This was followed in March 1999 by a decree forbidding journalists to communicate any information to foreign media. The decree was difficult to enact since, shortly afterwards, the Californian web company Anonymizer Inc. introduced their Kosovo Privacy Project providing anonymous email and access to web pages and discussion groups for web users throughout the FRY. The system removed all identifying marks from emails and rendered the 'footprint' that web users usually leave on sites that they have visited invisible.

The Allegory of the Good War

John Merrill suggests that the role of journalists, with its professional insignia of objectivity and impartiality, insists that they, and hence the cultural texts that they produce, remain pathologically neutralist and isolated from society. Their reduction of the contingent to 'news' of a world populated only by ciphers such as 'spokesmen', 'sources', 'victims' and 'participants' alienates both them and their readers from the social and cultural implications of the events they are abstracting. This atomisation of society, effected through and advancing what Jung described as the 'psychic isolation' of the individual under massification, is one of the fundamental tenets of Marxist and post-Marxist thinking around the consolidation of the liberal capitalist state.[13]

The main problem with the strategy, according to Merrill, is that it becomes impossible to deliver any narrative about the contingent world, the one which readers and listeners actually inhabit, which makes sense of events other than in fragments and distortions. In the reporting of the Kosovo War the Serbian people were largely characterised by Western journalism around a limited range of stereotypes, thuggish soldiers and police, smug, bourgeois Belgraders or opportunist and backward Kosovan peasants, in a media strategy not far removed from propaganda and little changed since the Boer Wars 100 years previously. Such manifest distortions aside, enemy populations are largely excluded from news footage since, as the photojournalism of the 'turkey shoot' of retreating Iraqi soldiers on the Basra road a decade before had indicated, such stereotypes are fairly fragile and collapse abruptly when depictions of their mutilated and burnt corpses are introduced into the discourse. The pathos inherent in such a death immediately fleshes the most vicious caricature with humanity. Instead, in a strategy which carries less risk of backfiring, the news focuses on a range of equally questionable stereotypes: the victims. In Kosovo those were the children, sometimes wounded, who had become separated from their families, old people driven from their homes and deprived of possessions and formal identity, and young men, signified chiefly by their reported absence.

The web allowed protagonists of the information war to set any sensitivities about the depictions of the real effects of the war aside. While the Western media generally did not use explicit images of terror, partly over problems with provenance, they regularly linked to sites such as the Albanian Koha Detore website which had no such scruples about the graphic recording of the most violent carnage with photography and purported eyewitness accounts.

I am not, of course, attempting to discount the countless personal tragedies which make up any war, but they are able to tell readers little about an underlying situation which is too complex to be condensed into these snapshots and which includes issues which will only expatiate to more considered historical, economic, political and ideological analyses. 'Unable to find a narrative which might organise and make sense of this event, the media resort to telling tales about wounded children.'[14] The response is insidious; where *Time.com* linked to its extended and well-founded analysis piece, 'Winning the Peace: A look at the complex obstacles to implementing the peace', on 20 July 1999, it accompanied the link with an image captioned 'A NATO soldier holds a Kosovar baby at a refugee camp in Albania.'[15] Any explanatory narrative must include depictions of all sides which do not attempt to stereotype them and strive to understand their mobilising beliefs, agendas and ideologies.

From such a standpoint Western representations of NATO's actions begin to look as compromised as Milosevic's. Because it is catering to a highly fragmented audience and its contents comprise a wide spectrum of information the web presently insists on such a plurality of perspectives. Its machinery does not allow the global news brands to maintain the old illusion of news as an entity that is objectively established (by professionals) and somehow natural and self-selecting. News suppliers on the web, both aggregators such as Yahoo! and content providers, largely encourage readers to link to their sources, producing readerships less likely to be blinkered by a 'house' line.

While I might routinely use *newsUnlimited* as my main source of news, the web enables me to also browse both its competitors and, via links from the provider itself, its sources, much more readily and widely than other broadcast forms and in a way that is almost impossible for consumers of print media. One of the roles of journalism in this maelstrom of information is to help readers negotiate the various impasses that arise around bad and contradictory information, even from reputable sources. In July 1999, for instance, *CNN Interactive* reported, on the basis of UNHCR statistics, that 19,000 ethnic Serbs had left Kosovo since the peace agreement on 9 June. *BBC News Online*, aggregating figures from the aid agencies and the Serbian Resistance Movement in Kosovo, estimated the figure to be between 40,000 and 50,000. Given the Albanian backlash that was already being reported the figure was important and informed commentary was needed to interpret the conflicting estimates.

An Allegory for Kosovo

Frederick M. Dolan asserts that the problem is more fundamental and that to the contemporary 'Manichean' mind, unable to penetrate beyond the most simple binary constructions of the world, a narrative project of such depth and complexity is doomed to failure from its inception. Through Paul de Man's work on allegory and symbol he suggests that events such as wars can only be presented, in a consumer culture, through a kind of symbolic theatre or spectacle that forces them into the narrative mould left by earlier events. Such an understanding imposes a heavy functionality upon historiography. With some justification Dolan goes on to propose that any attempt to comprehend the complex factionalising and political machinations that underpin them in their contingent realities will merely lead to confusion and dissipating morale on the part of Western media audiences.[16] He cites the American public's experience of Vietnam as an example of what happens when a war's defining allegory fails to cohere.

Consequently, the Gulf War was articulated by the allied administrations and read by the media through the allegory of the Second World War or as an Iraqi jihad against Israel. Dolan points out that such readings are arraigned against the oppositional one which attempted to understand events in the Gulf through the Vietnam War. The Vietnam War's original mobilising metaphors, such as 'the domino effect', could do little to rouse American public morale as public knowledge of events such as the massacre at My Lai radically undermined and ultimately discredited the founding ideology upon which it was claimed the war was being fought. It became a 'bad' war yet its ideology had been constructed around similar 'big principles' and 'vital interests' to those invoked on behalf of both the Gulf and Kosovo Wars: 'territorial integrity, opposition to aggressive war, and respect for United Nations resolutions.'[17] Dolan suggests that such factors are combined in, and comprehended through, the 'allegorical pre-text' of the Second World War, in which 'economic interests and unassailable principles [are] fortuitously combined to produce a "Good War"'.[18]

Barely two years after what may well have been a wholehearted attempt at a fully fledged genocide in Rwanda, Slobodan Milosevic was caricatured by Jamie Shea, the NATO spokesman, as the 'organiser of the greatest human catastrophe since 1945'. References to the Second World War pervaded much of the Western coverage and commentary on the war, to the extent that Hillary Clinton, pausing for a photo opportunity with refugee children in Macedonia, said that their suffering reminded her of 'Schindler's List'. Where necessary Hollywood was co-opted to make the connection for those whose knowledge of the Second World War was vague or culturally impaired. One of the signifiers which was heavily employed by British and American politicians at the beginning of the war, again referencing the 1940s, was the notion of genocide. The US Secretary of Defence, William Cohen's statement of 7 April 1999 makes it very clear that he saw the war as a crusade, a 'good' war. '[T]his is a fight for justice over genocide, for humanity over inhumanity, for democracy over despotism ... '[19] It is interesting that, at the opening of hostilities, politicians in America and Britain used the word 'genocide' but those closer to the problem, in Italy and Greece, did not.

One of the problems with 'good' wars lies in the very allegories through which they are understood. There must, of necessity, be a moral outcome; endings must be, as George Bush famously promised about the Gulf War, 'not murky'. 'In effect, Bush promised that the war would be fought in such a way as to allow for the telling of coherent realist narratives, with endings implicit in their beginnings and unambiguous resolutions.'[20] The point of the Second World War narrative is that Hitler dies at its culmination and the Reich is reduced to ashes – the forces of good prevail. The implicit ending for the Gulf War narrative was the removal of Saddam Hussein and the installation of a 'democratic' regime in Iraq, neither event which, a decade later, looked likely. In Kosovo it was the removal of Slobodan Milosevic and an autonomous and secure Kosovo, albeit somehow retained within a stable, former Yugoslavia, which had paid its dues and been readmitted to the New World Order.

Dolan is clear that the use of allegory depends upon 'an act of ontological bad faith' in which the pre-texts and the language which triggers them are necessarily suppressed on behalf of the mystification they help to foster. Understandings of the war in Kosovo which proposed Serbia as the new Reich and Milosevic as Hitler were rather at odds with Balkan history and unhelpful in explaining the economic and political foundations of the wars of the Yugoslavian succession of the 1990s.

While the official allegory of Kosovo was the Second World War and the 'progressive' or good war, there were also many oppositional narratives employed in the Western media, including one which pitched American hegemony, or the New World Order (a phrase this time conspicuously absent from the official version), as a kind of cultural, economic and political steamroller on behalf of global consumerism. Both understandings were extensively narrativised on the web, along with many others, yet 'a mere plurality of competing perspectives, however healthy for politics, does not suffice for the purposes of demystification'.[21] Without a good navigator they can merely serve to confuse. It is the outcomes of that 'plurality of competing perspectives', which the web offers so comprehensively and upon which so many libertarian and liberal hopes are pinned, which are here at stake. In themselves they cannot establish a reliable account of events, rather it is in the comparison and evaluation of their conflicting truth claims that demystification might lie and the production of that analysis, ultimately, is the function of journalism. For journalists working in traditional media, hedged by national and cultural boundaries, resort to irony is often the only way of questioning official narratives. On the web, in contrast, they increasingly use its 'plurality of perspectives' and a space where they can fully map out complex issues, to engage comprehensively with those mystifications.

In an information economy, it is not merely journalists who fill the space where public discourse is debated. Many of the interests engaged in the Kosovo conflict used the web as a primary arena of the war, to the extent that, as Vietnam came to be considered as the first TV war and the Gulf the first satellite war, we can usefully understand Kosovo as the first web war. Many correspondents found, for the first time, that they were competing for the attention of their readers with a huge range of what they had hitherto considered as privileged sources and resources. Organisations such as the London-based charity, the Institute for War and Peace Reporting <www.iwpr.net> or Human Rights Watch <www.hrw.org>, used their web pages as journalistic resources which could be accessed directly by the public as well. News consumers responded in their millions. The function of journalism changed from providing parses of those sources to designing comprehensible maps and trajectories through the information as well as underwriting it with assurances of provenance. The sheer volume and range of information on the web also carried radical implications for the way it was read by global audiences and the way the information war was conducted by its protagonists of every hue.

Web reports of the war, from sites as diverse as CNN, NATO, Radio B92 or the Serbian Unity Congress were delivered with an immediacy and, whether we considered them as the most blatant propaganda or not, an authenticity that is simply not available to other media forms. Often the news was delivered directly from the scene of events, through email by participants, in an apparently completely unmediated form. Patently, this proximity with events is very attractive to audiences trying to get an 'honest' feel of the story and the sense of temporal immediacy amplifies it. Immediacy can, however, be expensive in terms of loss of context and accuracy or veracity. Jamie Shea and those journalists who accepted his briefings too unquestioningly might well have paid heed to the experience of Peter Goulding, Assistant Secretary for Public Affairs in the Pentagon during the Vietnam War: 'First reports are always wrong, second reports are usually wrong and don't bet the farm on third reports.'[22]

One of the early losers in the media war was NATO, which, employing strategies including disinformation and evasions which had always worked well in the past, regularly tripped itself on the glut of contradictory information immediately available from other sources and radically undermined its own credibility. The journalism that unthinkingly allowed itself to be spoon-fed by NATO, the MoD and the Pentagon found itself regularly having to make retractions and corrections during the course of the war. Despite the best efforts of Serb and NATO authorities, to quote Merrill Brown, editor-in-chief of *MSNBC*'s online division, 'There's no bottling this thing up by authorities on either side.'[23]

While print journalism becomes a matter of record as it reaches the news stands, and broadcast media often tend to dissipate into the ether, news on the Internet inhabits a tenuous half-life somewhere between the two. As long as a page remains on the main site it should retain the same URL; readers can return to it and links can be made to it from within the provider's site or outside. When the page is removed to the archives it may well be given a new URL, ideally one which embeds the original address within it. The process gives online news something of the integrity of print journalism. Those news providers who used the NATO press conferences to provide the rump of their information on the war were placed in something of a quandary as spokespeople changed their story in response to contradictions which often first appeared on the Internet. To emphasise NATO's prevarications by filing such corrections too frequently would, by implication, have been construed as being unhelpful.

On Friday 14 May, for instance, *MSNBC* filed a headline report, on the basis of information from Serbia, about NATO's accidental cluster bombing of the Kosovo village of Korisa resulting in the death of 87 people <www.msnbc.com/news/230178.asp>. Over the weekend NATO changed their version of the event to claim that the Serbs had used the villagers as human shields. By the following Monday the *MSNBC*'s URL addressed a different story[24] and the Korisa story had completely disappeared. *MSNBC* were using the same URL for all their new Kosovo stories which meant that there was no way for readers to identify errors, corrections and, in this instance apparently, erasures. More importantly, there was a loss of integrity between the page appearing as news and its deposit in the archives. The occultation has disturbing implications for historians wishing to use online news archives as their primary source.

The Virtual Caravelle

The journalist Don North writing to the *General Journalism Discussion* list, describes how, a generation before, he and the other Western journalists in Vietnam were accused of 'sitting around in the Caravelle bar [in Saigon] interviewing each other'.[25] He justifies the practice by suggesting that the bar was the best place to pick up rumour and gossip, the leads that effective journalism relies on. Much more contentious in terms of professional integrity is the manner in which both the Falklands and Gulf Wars were reported under a seamless blanket of total information management by the Allied forces, with audiences being comprehensively denied oppositional views. North's worry is that contemporary journalism, from its new virtual watering hole, will further damage its reputation by merely 'using the same background from the web and filing identical stories'.

It is a timely point. The national TV networks, including the BBC which still has 45 foreign bureaux of its own, increasingly turn to feed-sharing arrangements with CNN (which, with 25 including its office in Baghdad, retains more overseas bureaux than all of its North American competitors combined) and, excluding the *Wall Street Journal*, the 1,600 US dailies employ only 186 foreign correspondents in total.[26] In 1998, in an economic climate where that part of the Western press corps reporting foreign news had been radically reduced in numbers, the web must have appeared as a significant bonus to media management's loath to invest in yet another Balkan war. Many stories did appear in European and North American titles which were obviously 'cut and paste' journalism. Equally, by June 1999 there were over 100 websites dealing with aspects of the Kosovo conflict and many of them were very effectively employed in sophisticated and effective war reporting by many of the major global and national news brands.

Perhaps unsurprisingly the most effective reporting from Kosovo came from news providers such as the UK *Guardian* and the *Los Angeles Times* which continued to invest in coverage from the war zone. Matt Welch concludes his *Online Journalism Review* article, 'Kosovo Highlights Journalism's Failings', with a salutary statistic: 'Editors and publishers who insist that the public just doesn't care about international news should look again. CNN.com's traffic went up 963 per cent after the [Serbian] bombing started.'[27] A decade after the Gulf War, big media had apparently completely forgotten about the crucial opportunity it had left for Ted Turner and CNN. Significantly, by the time that Allied ground troops entered Kosovo, the *New York Times* reported that 2,500 journalists accompanied them.

The online reporting of Kosovo also highlighted problems around both provenance and immediacy. In an arena of competing propagandas from a range of sources, including NATO, it was important that information be checked for accuracy before it was either included in reportage or linked from news sites, and set in context. Information coming from the Visoki Decani Monastery in Kosovo, while it was undoubtedly 'honest', must, necessarily, be read through a different filter from that used to comprehend information from the US State Department or an Albanian website; the website makes it clear that the orthodox monks are Serbs, albeit perhaps, Serbs with a unique perspective on the war. To take mailings from any single source out of context would be to risk producing a severely distorted version of events.

The war, coupled with the accelerating news cycle, provided many opportunities for such distortion. The Serbian paramilitary commander Zeljko Raznatovic, who became infamous during the Bosnian war as Arkan, for instance, seized every chance to intervene in the propaganda war on the web with manifestos, interviews and appearances on IRCs. While the Western press cohort was being rounded up in the Belgrade Hyatt Hotel as the bombing commenced, Arkan even found time to grant an interview to Massimo Calabresi of *Time* magazine as the journalist was having his accreditation revoked by other officials.[28] While he had much to say that was of interest, to have taken it out of the context of racial hatred and terror would have been to abrogate the basic principles of journalism. The CNN page comprising a personal chronology for Arkan, for instance, if taken out of context can easily turn him into a kind of Serbian Rambo. A CNN interview with him described him as 'a well-known businessman'. In the first week of the bombing of Serbia he took part, to much public vituperation, in an online chat on *MSNBC*. The organisation justified its decision to allow Arkan such coverage by describing him as 'a figure of considerable stature in his country. It wasn't much different than putting him on a TV interview show via satellite'.[29] While for *MSNBC* to give Arkan such a platform is understandable, it unquestionably raises issues about the conditions and implications of war reporting on the web.

In the flood of information that is available on the web the formal role of gatekeeper has been largely swept away or defaulted to the reader, but that is not to say that the function of the mediator or filter is no longer necessary. Journalism, if it is to retain its publics' confidence in dealing with complex stories such as Kosovo and renegotiate its roles, has first to admit to the effects of mediation and the sources of its authority. Attempts at mystification by the media now merely produce public cynicism.

The sheer size of the Internet, with its range and immediacy, also means that public opinion, including and beyond web audiences, can be extremely volatile. '... The ebb and flow of opinions on the Internet ... have had the effect of reducing still further the attention span of mass audiences and reducing the role of carefully considered commentary and discussion. And that in turn has contributed to dramatic shifts that leave many audiences with a sense of vertigo.'[30] While I cannot agree with Paul Goble's conclusion about the loss of 'commentary and discussion' – there is now more, not less, space for such discourse – it must be the primary aim of effective journalism on the web to remove that 'sense of vertigo' that he rightly identifies. A war journalism that is no longer willing (or able) to collude with the sleights of hand and obfuscations of military spokespeople will initially compound that sense but, as was clear in Kosovo, those military and official organisations, rather than lose the confidence of their publics at home, eventually have to resort to other tactics, including the truth or approximations of it, and admit to accounts of events which are both partial and partisan.

NATO's bombings of civilian populations in Serbia, Kosovo and Montenegro were at first bluntly denied by their spokesman Jamie Shea. As both television and the web produced evidence that the bombings had occurred, NATO amended their story to blame the Serbian army and paramilitaries. When it was clear that these accusations were also untrue they admitted errors and miscalculations. One of the problems with admission by degree was that it then allowed Serbian propagandists to argue that NATO had adopted a policy of deliberately bombing civilian populations, an accusation that was taken up by anti-war groups in the West. Shea's subsequent statements were noticeably more ready to admit both mistakes and changes in strategy. Truth may well have been the first casualty of war since long before the days of the telegraph, but the web seems to suggest that it can now don khaki with some hope of surviving the first salvo. With the conclusion of the bombing John Pilger wrote a piece in the *New Statesman,* widely disseminated on the web, entitled 'Nothing in my 30 years of reporting wars compares with the present propaganda dressed as journalism.' He may well have been right – many reporters unquestionably stuck rigidly to NATO's line from the first day – but on the other hand this was also the first media war to give Pilger, and others who questioned the West's role, as well as dissident Serb journalists, such a public platform for their views. It also brought a powerful new set of voices into the discourse of war.

News from the Front

More so than natural disaster or personal tragedy, for those who find themselves caught up in it, war is the most traumatic and disrupting experience that human beings have to contend with. The

aphorism about history being written by the victors notwithstanding, wars since classical times have inevitably left behind
eyewitness accounts from a range of perspectives. Kosovo was no
exception, with the difference that its accounts, at least those
coming from citizens with access to a computer and a telephone,
were published during the course of the war, often with other
primary sources, alongside those of the world's journalists. National
and global news providers on the web linked to such accounts,
giving them a global distribution and print and broadcast media
took them up to republish them. J.D. Lasica describes how the email
correspondence between Adona, an ethnic Albanian teenager, and
Finnegan Hamill, a young reporter for Youth Radio in California,
brought the reality of the war to younger audiences who might
otherwise have ignored it. *CNN Interactive* posted the correspondence for audiences around the world.[31] Another account which
was linked on many news sites and published in part in *Arena, Le
Monde,* the *Standard* (Bulgaria) and *Publico* (Portugal), was 'The War
Diary' of a Serbian film-maker working in Belgrade and known only
as A.G. This took the form of diaries and a sequence of videos dating
from 2 March and finishing on 17 June. A.G. makes clear that, for
those who are caught up in it, one of the most unnerving effects of
war is the lack of information.

Wednesday, March 24

We reach Belgrade soon after midnight. Everything is quiet and
nothing happens. When arrived at M.'s home, first thing we do is
turning on the Radio B92, independent radio station. But nobody
knows what's going on. Suddenly, at 3.a.m. local time, Radio B92
was shut down. All TV and radio stations now broadcast the same:
old war movies, patriotic songs, Assembly conclusions ...[32]

The reference to B92 gives an indication of A.G.'s response to the
war, although he by no means accepted the Allied account unquestioningly and found the BBC and CNN websites almost as frustrating
as the Serbian media. As a media worker himself he was very aware
of the clumsy approach to NATO strategies by Serbian military
spokespeople.

Monday, March 29

> M. and me watch TV. A Serbian general proudly talks about successes against NATO. At one moment he says ironically: 'We have only 7 soldiers killed and 17 wounded, after five days of heavy bombing – and they say this NATO is some power ...' What a fool! – would he be happy if there were seven thousand? And he doesn't realise he's just said the greatest compliment to NATO's precision and 'humanity'.[33]

A.G. had access to the Internet and email through his workplace, which was B92-owned, and regularly resorted to it for information although, 'connection is tragically slow, and it works byte by byte'. By 31 March when it was clear that B92's property was at risk from the mobs which had wrecked the US embassy and allied cultural institutions ('I hear that McDonald's is demolished too.') along with those Serbian ones suspected of collaboration, A.G. and his colleagues decided to evacuate the most important equipment from the office – the computers and their modems.

Accounts such as A.G.'s were crucial to journalists attempting to provide realistic accounts of the war, corroborate other sources and provide new information. On 26 March A.G.'s was one of the first accounts to report that the Yugoslav Air Force had removed its MiGs from the runways of Batajnica military airport and sheltered them along the sides of motorways and even in housing estates and the army its soldiers from their barracks to the parks of Belgrade. The following day that information appeared on the world's news.

Many news providers offered such first-hand accounts of the war in a way that has rarely been attempted by mainstream media since the reporting of the Second World War. Such accounts insist that war is not the clinical game that is portrayed by MoD and Pentagon spokespeople, the media spectacle of Baudrillard's analysis that is entirely divorced from its contingent world. The smart weapon that misses its pixellated target by a few metres will produce a tragedy in flesh and blood. Most forms of broadcast news tend to obscure the effects of such events. Personal accounts insist that their readers make those often banal but crucial connections. A.G.'s consuming preoccupation throughout the bombing was the safety of his three-year old son Nikolai who was evacuated on 23 March.

While such accounts, as in the case of A.G's note about the Serbian MiGs, can add substantively to the story, they bring considerable problems with them for the news providers who take them up. They arrive with no provenance and are almost impossible to corroborate while the war is actually raging, yet they offer an immediacy and an authenticity that few other forms of reporting can match. Many Western news providers regularly featured them during the war to place events in a human context. The *Boston Globe*, for instance, opened the account of life in Belgrade by Dragana Zarevac with the headline, 'Awaiting The Bombs'.

Lasica quotes Robert Leavitt, director of Global Beat Syndicate based at New York University, 'It's one thing for a credulous reader to believe whatever pops up on his computer screen. But news organisations have to wrestle with how to remain responsible while capturing the reality and pathos of war.'[34] Leavitt partly resolved the problem by offering a range of viewpoints. Most news providers handle such accounts with circumspection. *MSNBC*, for instance, took the greatest care to distance their editorial position from such local colour by clearly labelling them 'perspectives'. The editor of *Mother Jones*, the American radical journal, headed the email messages by Alex Bogojevic, a US trained physicist living in Belgrade whose mailings vigorously attacked the hawks of both sides, with the caveat, 'These dispatches can now be found on a regular basis on the MoJo Wire, but it is important to note that we have no way of confirming the information Alex sends us.' Such warnings, while entirely requisite, do little to help readers understand the interventions, whatever their intention, and can reduce their impact to that of merely another vicarious gratification.

By enabling private individuals to bypass the media gatekeepers the web has produced an important new genre of reporting. The *Orato* website <www.orato.com> is entirely devoted to such first-hand accounts of international events.

The Information War

The sheer mass and range of information about the war in Kosovo which became available so rapidly meant that it was probably one of the most comprehensively reported wars in history. It consumed bandwidth, TV screens and newspaper columns excessively, in the manner of all wars, but Kosovo was also covered widely and in depth. The web provided both space and access for every aspect of the event to be brought into the discourse and fully explored. Readers, including journalists, were able to place that information in context and use it to inform themselves about the issues that lay beneath the war.

As the bombing progressed and news proliferated from all kinds of sources, NATO seemed to lose control of its information management unnervingly early in the war. It became clear to reporters and news consumers that the bombing war and the information war, while they are fought in parallel, were very different although intricately related events. Since the information war is, *inter alia*, the primary mediator of the bombing war, it is usually in the interests of the warring factions to keep the relationship between the two completely opaque. As became clear in Kosovo, warfare, or its discourse, rapidly collapses into gratuitous bloodshed unless the two remain synchronous; that is when the allegory fails. The spectacle of NATO spokespersons attempting to explain over a period of weeks why their pilots had bombed refugee columns, schools, hospitals and villages ('a system not an individual is to blame') is a clear indicator that the two events had become divorced. When the relationship is intact the information war not only mediates the bombing war, it also vindicates it – in this case as patriotic for Serbia and progressive for NATO – and historicises it either as another assault on the motherland or as the reinforcing of the New World Order. When that seamless, narrative carapace fractures, perhaps through an overload of contradictory information, news consumers become aware of the language that is employed to construct it and the underlying ambitions of the narrators.

The war on the web allowed journalists and news consumers the space to query the sound bites, tallies, accusations and counter-accusations that comprise military press conferences and manifestos. It became clear, as it had in every war that the developed world had been involved in during the second half of the century, that those presenting the war were themselves comprehending it through a new language, one which the military of both sides were already well versed in – the acronyms, neologisms, euphemisms and obscurantisms of information warfare. If there was a difference in the Kosovo

War it was that the Internet brought that war to the closer scrutiny of news readers.

The role of information warrior is adopted not only by the military and politicians but also by corporate capitalism and the large group of freelancers, or terrorists, known as hackers. Its weapons include 'flaming' and 'spamming', or overloading a target's computer with usually inappropriate data, 'firewalls' – the hardware and software that protect information systems from attack from without – deception and counter-deception, 'perception management', viruses, 'hacking' or the accessing of systems or computers without authorisation and the disablement by covert or direct means of the enemy's information systems. While it is beyond the scope of this book to discuss it, the scale and impact of hacking on military information systems should not be underestimated.

> According to the US Defense Information Systems Agency, a Pentagon computer security agency, US Defense Department computers containing non-classified but sensitive data were attacked 250,000 times in 1995, in which hackers succeeded in penetrating the computers in an estimated 160,000 incidents.[35]

Information-based warfare blurs the traditional boundaries through which war is understood and it directly implicates whole populations. The perception of who controls information becomes as important as air or sea superiority was in earlier wars. It is waged over a battlefield that includes the political, economic and, crucially, the social and cultural spheres. Journalism has always been one of its central resources and in the past, especially in wars for which the allegory, both defining and interpreting, has held, it has been willingly co-opted. In Kosovo, as we have seen, that allegory was unsteady from the start. This is unsurprising since the web, able for the first time to present, however unsatisfactorily, the information that 'explained' the war in all its complexity, made the allegory redundant. 'Good' information foregrounds the spurious premises of the allegory. The act of war is as much social as it is political or military and it became more difficult for civilian populations to deny their complicity. That universalisation of the moral burden of war has been a fundamental military principle since the Napoleonic Wars.

... the complex of military activities ... are conducted primarily for their direct, social, economic, political, and psychological impact. The activities, in their purest form, are the interaction of the military with the society-government.[36]

The *US Army Field Manual* is by no means referring solely to enemy societies.

Given that the Internet was originally designed as a military information system it is perhaps appropriate that it should be the device which ultimately demystifies the relationship between war and information. It insisted upon those Serbs who had access to it confronting, whether they rejected the information or not, the plight of the ethnic Albanian refugees in Kosovo and it made them aware of atrocities on both sides. Neither subject was mentioned throughout the war by RTS, which by 24 March 1999 was the only nationwide broadcaster still legal in Serbia. It also made many citizens of the NATO states question what the bombing was really for, and, of course, journalism on the web was ready with answers there as well, ranging from rank apologists for NATO and pro-bombers (including *BBC News Online*) who used the tattered allegory of the good war like a banner, to Noam Chomsky and Ed Herman's assertions on *ZDNet* about the economic agenda of the New World Order or the World Socialist Website's analysis, hinging upon the West's unhampered access to Caspian oil reserves over the succeeding decades. Such larger strategic issues, often, necessarily, articulated from oppositional positions, are rarely tackled by either newspapers or broadcast news. The omission is determined both by form and by affiliation (of course, we might ask why the old media evolved that way) and while the first factor is clearly not a constraint on the web, US Executive Order 13121, even though it was not fully enacted, made it clear to both anti-war and anti-NATO commentators on the web that the latter was.

Journalism, in the larger context of information war, is, of course, subject to the exigencies of war. Websites, both those of news providers, such as the *New York Times*, or sources, such as NATO, will be the subject of attack intended both to disable and to tamper with content. Tom Regan, writing on the *Christian Science Monitor* website, described how hackers attacked US government websites and took the White House website offline for three days in response to the

NATO bombing of the Chinese Embassy in Belgrade.[37] News sites that are merely crippled will be eventually returned online, but news consumers are also vulnerable to information being altered by hackers. When the *New York Times* website was invaded by a group of hackers calling themselves HFG ('Hacking for Girlies') in September 1998 the site remained offline for three days. The hackers left an HFG logo and personal and vituperative attacks on various writers specialising in computer security on the site. When *NYT* producers tried to delete the page it kept reappearing. The *NYT* site, by 1998 amounting to several hundred thousand pages, had to be taken off the web and carefully checked and reinstalled. Clearly there was the danger that the hackers had changed other material, perhaps in the archives, left time bombs in the code that would produce further disruptions in the future or left 'trap-doors' that would enable them to re-enter the site whenever they wanted to. For the US newspaper of record the HFG attack posed considerable problems but in wartime such activity takes on a new and darker mien.

While the Serbs were unable to compete on equal terms with NATO in the local propaganda war, with leaflet drops, airborne TV and radio transmitters disrupting terrestrial programming and, when all else failed, the bombing of RTS headquarters along with the country's civilian telephone and computer networks,[38] they were able to conduct an alarmingly effective Netwar[39] which left NATO looking outdated, out of touch and even vulnerable.

> On the 13th floor of Belgrade's tallest building, a drab pile of brown steel called the Beogradjanka, young volunteers – mainly students whose high schools and universities have been closed by the war – tap away at two dozen battered old computers souped up with new hardware. The electronic boiler-room operation is linked with more than 1000 computer volunteers working at six other centers in Belgrade.[40]

These, mostly English-speaking, volunteers fought the propaganda war on the web for the Belgrade regime. The main task was to keep the government websites, <www.gov.yu> and others, updated, mainly with material translated into English. They also argued about the war in countless chat rooms, networked with anti-NATO groups in other countries and sought out Serbian expatriates, especially in

North America, to become politically active. After they were expelled from Serbia many Western journalists found the Beogradjanka cohort a useful and willing source of information. The 31 March story in the *New York Times* on Belgrade's response to the air strikes, for instance, was primarily based on interviews carried out over the Internet with the students. Their rules were simple – keep talking (always be polite and keep negotiating) and no hacking – although a NATO website in Brussels was taken offline by suspected Serb hackers soon after the alliance began bombing Yugoslavia on 24 March. They did not draw the line at spamming, which successfully slowed down several NATO websites very effectively, or pinging (using computer-generated pulses to derail systems).

There were claims, in addition to the Beogradjanka production line, of irregular teams of hackers who involved themselves in the information war on the side of Serbia. Not least of these was a proto-fascist group calling themselves Black Hand[41] who claimed some successes in bringing down anti-Serbian websites. One of the effects of the visibility of the information war on the web was to encourage interventions from a range of voices, on both sides, who would normally have left the conflict to their politicians and military organ-isations. In the event this element of the Netwar rapidly exhausted itself in a process of attrition. Black Hand destroyed Albanian websites hosted from Switzerland and the site of the Croatian news-paper *Vijesnik*. In return a Croatian group destroyed the site of the National Library of Serbia which led to a Black Hand attack on the Rudjer Boskovic Institute in Zagreb. This conflagration, while perhaps not remarkable in itself – its targets were mainly quite soft – does indicate the potential that such warfare has for attacking the heart of civil life (health, financial and commercial services) with a precision that is not available to the smartest conventional weapon.

The success of the Serbian psychological warfare operation led the British Defence Secretary, George Robertson, to respond, in the battle for hearts and minds, with pages in Serbo-Croat on the UK Ministry of Defence site. The MoD claimed that the site received over 1,000 hits a day from the Federal Republic of Yugoslavia, which seems to represent a fairly high level of Internet access in the FRY during the war. NATO also enlisted the British Prime Minister Tony Blair's press secretary, Alistair Campbell, to overhaul its media strategy. Having set up a Media Operations Centre (largely to bypass the communications specialists of Shape and NATO) he organised a strategy of responding directly to information put out by Tanjug, producing journalism under the bylines of NATO leaders to appear in the European press and, crucially, of co-ordinating the statements of as many NATO organisations and affiliations as possible to keep them on message. His immediate advice was that NATO should stop giving details of its 'friendly' casualties and concentrate specifically on those 'pieces of information which were important to provide to the public'.[42] The strategy harked back to the Bosnian War when Croatian separatists and Bosnian Muslims retained the American public relations firm, Ruder Finn, to fight their media war in North America. Mobilising the allegory of the Second World War, Ruder Finn particularly targeted women and the American Jewish community with its accounts of death and rape camps.[43] Ruder Finn's strategy was highly productive for its Balkan clients and bore results far beyond the groups that were initially targeted. Campbell's approach, while it ultimately saved NATO from a public relations disaster, initially served to leave a void that other news sources on the web rushed to fill.

The rationale for the bombing of RTS, a difficult proposal to sell to Western audiences, was that its broadcasters, by fighting the propaganda war, were implicated in the war crimes that were being committed in Kosovo. NATO spokespeople described it as a 'principal instrument' of the Belgrade war machine, and, accordingly, a legitimate target. Its destruction left Serbian audiences with local stations, such as TV Kosova which is owned by Marija Milosevic, the daughter of the President of the Federal Republic, and an erratic schedule of programmes. Spomenka Lazic, writing on the Alternative Information Network (AIM) Podgorica website based in Montenegro, described a period when the only broadcasts available in Belgrade were in Chinese, 'Belgraders are able to watch sessions of Chinese assembly, Chinese businessmen, they listen to Chinese news, all that in Chinese language.'[44] This was in addition to the hour of RTS news that all broadcasters in Serbia had to transmit after the loss of the state broadcaster's own facilities.

With the jamming and counter-jamming of stations Belgraders could expect, in any one day, random selections from their national broadcasters, NATO, and also SKY News and BBC World in addition to snow. Lazic suggests that most Serbs resorted to 'information dispersed by word of mouth' as the only reliable news. The Pentagon's threat, in an earlier context, to bomb its enemies 'back into the Stone Age' had, for much of the country's infrastructure been vigorously executed and Serbia's limited access to the Internet proved crucial both in terms of information from behind the lines to Western news producers and military observers and to Slobodan Milosevic's internal opposition. While much of what appeared on many websites was propaganda, or heavily distorted news, it was at least possible for informed readers, often by reading information on one site against that on another, to get some idea of what was happening in Kosovo.

I have already recounted the episode of the Orahovac 'massacre' alleged to have occurred some time before the bombing commenced. That was the result of lazy journalism. Other instances of disinformation were rather more calculated. On 9 March NATO announced that the chief adviser to Ibrahim Rugova, the pacifist Kosovan opposition leader, Fehmi Agani, himself a well-respected moderate, and several other well-known Kosovo Albanian intellectuals had been killed by Serb paramilitaries and Rugova himself wounded. The world's press expressed outrage at the killings and published glowing obituaries for the dead men but diplomats with sources in Kosovo were less ready to confirm the murders. The British general, David Wilby, assured the press that NATO had checked their facts and confirmed the killings. The original information came from a 'very reliable source'.

In something of a 'spoiler', the next day RTS televised news of a 'cordial' meeting in Belgrade between Milosevic and a clearly healthy Ibrahim Rugova. For Rugova, as was later reported in *Spiegel*, the meeting was anything but cordial but the following day he was interviewed by Western correspondents at his home in Pristina and insisted that he was in good health and that, so far as he was aware, his colleagues were in the same condition. When Fehmi Agani was subsequently murdered, a few weeks later by Serbian troops, neither was his death reported by NATO nor the earlier report retracted.

Making rumour official in this way, during the first week of bombing, would appear to be less the result of a mistake than of a deliberate decision: to tip the balance in favour of NATO air strikes on Yugoslavia at a time when public opinion was still very sceptical about their effectiveness.[45]

NATO continued with its increasingly rickety strategy of disinformation during the first month of the war while at the same time
repeatedly, and tautologically, accusing the Milosevic regime of
using totalitarian methods to maintain its stranglehold on the
media.

> Night and day, I am under pressure from journalists to justify
> NATO's actions, but I am struck that Slobodan Milosevic is not
> asked to justify anything ... Milosevic is unaware of any
> constraints connected with the media.[46]

That pressure had been noticeably absent at the same stage of the
Gulf and Falklands Wars. This was at the same time that a rather
more specific pressure was being placed on the BBC in London, by
UK government sources, about its war coverage which tended to
'doubt too systematically the validity of the NATO armed operation'.
It was also suggested that its correspondent in Belgrade, John
Simpson, was 'passing on Serbian propaganda indiscriminately in his
coverage of the NATO bombings'.[47] Such desperate measures came
on the heels of the discrediting of NATO as a news source, to the
extent that many global news providers, including the French daily
Libération had removed their correspondents from NATO headquarters in Brussels by the fourth week of the war. This was in the context
of a news management regime that was, by that point of necessity,
much more liberal than the one imposed on Western journalists
during earlier wars. The key to this change of climate was the emergence of an open information economy on the Internet.

By the end of April NATO officials decided to 'thoroughly review'
their communications strategies and Alastair Campbell was sent to
Brussels to replace the mixture of verifiable fact, disinformation and
error with spin. The new regime simply refused to comment on
negative aspects of the war and merely countered subsequent acci-
dents with accounts of increasingly bloody Serb atrocities and flows
of refugees, possibly incremented, they failed to add, by the very
bombs that were being dropped to save them. 14 May, when other
sources reported the bombing of the Kosovan village of Korisa and
the deaths of 87 ethnic Albanians,[48] was accounted a 'good day' by
Shea.

A Wired Country

For news consumers the war in Kosovo brought with it some seemingly irreconcilable contradictions. It was fought by NATO with a 'zero-casualty' strategy which, while it was expensive for the chancelleries of the Allied states, shifted the entire burden of mortal risk to the target populations not only of Yugoslavia but of Kosovo as well. The founding assumption of such a strategy, derived from an unspoken allegory this time of Vietnam, was that Western taxpayers would stomach astronomic costs and the loss of unnumbered Balkan lives, even those who NATO was purportedly bombing to save, but not a single Allied death. NATO entered the war with the belief that the strategy could be sold to global audiences by employing the news management systems that had worked so well in the Gulf War. Four months saw the loss of much of the infrastructure of Serbia and a looming environmental disaster as well as the patent destruction of Kosovo as a practicable society. In addition, many of the ideological fractures which had marked the Cold War seemed for a terrible moment to have been fully restored. That something had gone terribly wrong was clearly apparent to those who took their news from the Internet.

For television news viewers, in contrast, the one-sidedness of the conflict turned it into an arcade game of atrocity-fuelled slash and kill completely insulated by its packaging from its contingent reality and obscuring the contradictions of its outcome. Even when it confronts its audiences with the 'realities' of death, despair and suffering, television refuses to dwell on them, immediately erasing their bleak images with sport or advertisements for breakfast cereal and the good life, all in over-saturated primary colours. In Kosovo the medium was largely served by a generation of journalists who had been systematically excluded from the more malign effects of war ensuring that print and broadcast media began the war in the same militarised condition that had prevailed for them during the Gulf War. 'Intelligence sources' or 'NATO spokesmen' was attribution enough to corroborate the most excessive story.

Television coverage, and the audiences that it draws, tended to influence how the war was conducted at a political level with, for example, the insistence on no NATO casualties. That coverage largely comprised a series of only loosely connected anecdotes –

human interest vignettes which denied any indication of the complexity of the underlying issues. The refusal to face the effects of the bombing of Serbia, and ultimately the economic and political causes of the war, was in the interests of both the NATO governments and Milosevic. The stress on the emotional and the personal, lost children in the refugee camps for instance, served to remove the world's attention from other children simultaneously subject to the Serb pogrom inside Kosovo and the bombing by NATO.

In a war served by news reports of five minutes and less the founding ideology becomes crucial. The war is understood through its allegories and, indeed, the very attempt to distinguish between propaganda and objective reporting becomes redundant. The context for the war is largely mythical for both sides, and hence is better served by propaganda than by objectivity. Tony Blair assured the world that NATO was 'fighting not for territory but for values' and the 'new internationalism'. He distanced himself even from Margaret Thatcher and the Falklands War (an inappropriate allegory tainted both by the risk it incurred for Britain and the sinking of the Belgrano) by declaring that he was one of a 'new generation' of leaders who 'hail from the progressive side of politics'. For the television war such sound bites were enough to guarantee the NATO victory on every front.

For those who followed the more complicated war on the web Blair's declarations rang hollow and the evasions of Jamie Shea sounded increasingly unlikely in the face of a mass of information from the battlefield itself. Kerrin Roberts of *CNN* sees the decisive difference between the Balkans and the Gulf or Argentina as technological. '... Yugoslavia is a wired country ... It wasn't that our coverage was different. But the reaction is different. In this conflict, people are able to communicate directly in chat rooms with people in the conflict zone ... Here, it is a global community.'[49] Where such direct communication is possible, even across the lines of battle, the fog of myth soon condenses.

Carol Guensburg quantifies that community: 31 million related pages viewed for CNN on 24 March, the first day of the NATO air strikes, more than 154 million views by the end of the week and Yugoslavian usage of *CNN* up by 963 per cent in that same week. 'The country, which usually ranks 30th among foreign countries in visits to the CNN site, rose to sixth place.'[50] Roberts' comments are interesting in that he seems to be suggesting not only that the web allows events such as the Kosovo War to be mediated in new ways, but that the mediation is being met by a new kind of subjectivity, one that is determined by its global as well as its national or ethnic affiliations. His statistics suggest that the disjunction between the Belgrade web user and her compatriot policing Pristina before the ceasefire was rather wider than that between her and other *CNN* consumers in Los Angeles or London.

While news of the Kosovo War on the web followed the reporting in other media – indeed, with its constantly widening bandwidth it became the final repository for much of that reporting – it also allowed the space for journalists, scholars, schoolchildren, politicians, soldiers and those caught up in it to explore and represent aspects of it which in previous wars, if they appeared anywhere, were left to the history books. That spectrum of information meant that it was difficult for web users to contain their understanding of it within the bounds of the 'official' allegory. Even if they did not follow all of the available links the complexity of the situation was clear from any news provider's Kosovo pages on the web in a way that television and newspapers, of necessity, obscure.

Veran Matic suggests that the web enables journalism to reassess its practices and its values.[51] The principles that B92 and *OpenNet,* the ISP that it gave rise to as the radio station was being forced off the air, aspire to are particularly suited to the Internet. These include the interlinking of reports, with individual events being considered in context. He insists that all reporting, every story, be written from, and directed towards, its context. The strategy allows journalism to focus on processes and issues rather than unconnected elements which can be easily appropriated by ideological and economic agendas. For the same reason, people should be depicted as individuals rather than as members of ethnic, religious or social groups. Finally he suggests that '… you should ask yourself whether self-censorship or repression of reports by other authors helps reduce violence …'

Matic's view of the web, unsurprisingly given his experience of the vulnerabilities of traditional media under a totalitarian polity, is perhaps over-optimistic. While it must be recalled that he had the support of several global media brands including state-funded organisations such as the *Voice of America,* he remains far from uncritical of them. On B92's transition to the web he concludes:

The distribution of programming was virtually unstoppable. The Internet provides a variety of solutions to overcome obstruction and interference. In order to stop program distribution, the regime would have to cut all the telephone lines connecting this country to the rest of the world. But satellite phones, in combination with the Internet, could overcome even this restriction.[52]

5
'Too Fresh to be True': Acceleration, Ethics and the Spectacle

> The publication on the World Wide Web of Kenneth Starr's blow-by-blow account of Bill and Monica in flagrante marked an inflection point of sorts. It was, some thought, the moment the Net came of age rather as the coronation in 1953 marked the moment when people in this country decided television was not a fad but a necessity ... The comical spectacle of television reporters solemnly reading to camera the contents of Web pages which viewers had already digested will take a long time to fade.[1]

The 1998 publication of judge Kenneth Starr's federal grand jury report on the web, following a vote in the US House of Representatives, marked one of the high points of a news story that had obsessed readers around the world since the beginning of President Clinton's second term of office. The publication marked a global media event. It was read in English by 55 million readers, rapidly translated into other languages and led directly to the introduction of an AltaVista site that machine-translated the report into six languages.[2] This dissemination of a political document, largely bypassing the press, seemed to presage a new set of relationships between politics and the public. The web itself had already featured conspicuously in the story when Clinton's relationship with Monica Lewinsky was revealed on the *Drudge Report* website then carried by AOL.

Drudge's website, notoriously anti-Democrat and anti-Clinton, by no means limits itself to political news and rumour. Perhaps unsurprisingly, since it is based in Hollywood, it also features the gossip of the media industries. It was Drudge who first broke the news about the creation of *MSNBC* by NBC and Microsoft and about the comedian Jerry Seinfeld insisting upon $1 million for each episode of his sitcom. The *Drudge Report* comprises an aggregation of links to global and North American news providers along with tabloid 'reports' often breaking stories from sources more constrained by traditional editorial practice. Drudge's network of sources regularly throws up contradictory and opposing readings and commentary upon current stories or even material which attacks the *Report* itself. Drudge refuses to discriminate and moves on to his next 'exclusive'. On 1 January 1999 Drudge 'broke' the 'global exclusive' revealing President Clinton's alleged black teenage son. In fact, allegations of the sort had been circulating in the tabloid press since 1992 and their mendacity regularly exposed. On this occasion Drudge's by now global currency led to the allegations being taken up by the *Times* and *BBC News Online*. The story then spread to the *Washington Times* under the headline 'Media Abuzz with Rumors that Clinton Fathered Boy'.[3] It took more than a week for the global media frenzy to abate with *Time.com*'s report that a DNA test had revealed no relationship between the President and the boy.

A similar escalation had occurred twelve months earlier with the Monica Lewinsky story. *Newsweek* reporter Michael Isikoff, through his source Linda Tripp, had heard tapes of the Tripp/Lewinsky telephone conversations which were to prove so incriminating for Clinton. *Newsweek* spiked Isikoff's story on the subject in early 1998 because of editorial uncertainty about the provenance of the tapes and also at the request of Kenneth Starr, who was investigating scandals in the Clinton White House. *Newsweek*'s postponement of the publication of Isikoff's investigation decided an associate of Linda Tripp to force the issue by giving the story to Drudge. He broke the essentials on the *Drudge Report* forcing *Newsweek* in turn to publish a fuller account on its own website. Right or wrong Drudge's scoop took more than thirteen million readers to the *Drudge Report* website in the month after 10 August.[4] The story would have eventually broken without Drudge, but his intervention clearly accelerated the news cycle. A year earlier Drudge had pulled off a similar coup by forcing the publication of allegations of sexual misconduct against the President by the White House volunteer Kathleen Willey, who had refused to substantiate them for *Newsweek*.

Drudge's role as media *agent provocateur* against both the Democratic administration and the mainstream press can be seen as his seizing the agenda from a media still encumbered by traditional journalistic values. In removing the role of gatekeeper, and hence agenda-setter, from the traditional media, the web does not necessarily place it directly into the hands of its consumers. It becomes available to be contested by a variety of agents including those consumers. Drudge ensured that the Clinton scandals received a coverage that they would not necessarily have received in either the traditional media or on the web. In the limited news-hole of the traditional media, that coverage deprived other stories and issues of exposure they might otherwise have received. The debate around Monicagate almost completely erased, for instance, President Khatami of Iran's visit to the United States and developments in the Northern Irish peace process in the global press. The effect is hardly new. Richard Nixon attempted to deflect the impact of the reporting of Watergate with the observation, 'After two weeks and two million words of televised testimony ... we have reached a point at which a continued, backward-looking obsession with Watergate is causing the nation to neglect matters of far greater importance to all of the American people.'[5] The criticism ignores the reality of a discourse which depends not on entities or events in its contingent world but on the products of newswork. As long as the world's media were consumed by Watergate the scandal was, by definition, the news.

While the web's wider bandwidth allows journalism the space, although not necessarily the attention and the readership, to change this, it also provides Drudge and others with a constituency that print tabloids, such as the *Globe*, the *National Enquirer* in the US and the *Sun* in Britain, never had. J.D. Lasica sees the process as a kind of feeding chain in which credible media organisations stand on the shoulders of increasingly shaky sources, including those mavericks like Drudge who are effectively short-circuiting the news cycle.

> Stories of doubtful provenance, ignored by the traditional press, find a home in the fringe media or supermarket tabloids; the reports make the rounds on the Internet, where they transmogrify and take on a new life; soon they bubble up to the surface on talk radio, cable talk shows and late-night monologues; finally they

appear in more traditional conservative publications. The story achieves a level of acceptance at every stage.[6]

The web has become part of a new media economy in which it not only acts as a link in the chain but also accelerates the whole process and detonates those stories in a global arena. The fact that news providers report a story, even where it is offered as unconfirmed, in itself gives it the credibility to merit repetition. The emphasis placed on such reports, which often consist of half-truths or suppositions, also has the effect of blurring the line between news and those media spectacles constructed, sometimes spuriously, from conflict, celebrity and catastrophe. These are churned up with stories such as elections, train crashes, roller-coaster stock markets and legal trials which are all given similar spin. Perhaps the distinction is merely between tabloid news and traditional, so-called value-driven journalism. Lasica suggests it is more and finds Larry Flynt's 1998 list of Republican party adulterers whom the publisher, in a kind of *quid pro quo* for Starr, intended to flush into the limelight, redolent of 'nothing so much as McCarthyism'.[7]

The world's news consumers' fascination with the events putatively exposed by Drudge and later, more formally (and also on the web) by the Starr Report, should not be confused with the crucial issues around the attempted impeachment of the President of the United States. The spectacle of sex and abuse of power drew attention away from the political process. Bob Woodward, one of the *Washington Post* reporters who worked on the Watergate scandal, sees the two events as very different; the Watergate affair saw the media reporting and attempting to comprehend historical events in the contingent world, Monica-, or Zippergate as it came to be known, was largely fabricated by the media and its cohorts including political lobbyists.

> The big difference between the Monica Lewinsky scandal and Watergate is that in Watergate, Carl [Carl Bernstein] and I went out and talked to people whom the prosecutors were ignoring or didn't know about. Here the reporting is all about lawyers telling reporters what to believe and write.[8]

The difference in the reporting of the two scandals went far beyond the journalistic process. Woodward and Bernstein claimed a commitment to the principle of enabling their primary constituency, the citizens of America, to participate fully at all levels of democratic life. Drudge presents himself in that tradition of American investigative journalism, as a muckraker and whistle-blower on the hypocrisies and abuses of the powerful. The thumbnail image on his website depicts a cultural anachronism complete with rumpled jacket, pork-pie hat crammed onto the back of his head, top button of his shirt loose and tie askew. He can be seen in the tradition of the jobbing printer of the eighteenth century, a throwback to the radical press in which the citizen-journalist had immediate access to, and indeed often owned, the means of production.

Drudge can simultaneously be viewed as doing little more than meeting the demands of a hyper-inflated consumer market. In an economy built on the primary commodity of information as entertainment there is little investigation and fewer checks in what often amounts to merely a web gossip column and what Rosenstiel and Kovach describe as a 'journalism of assertion'.[9] The assertions are still bound by law and convention and are hence constantly undercut and rendered provisional. Their apparent legitimacy, all the more plausible because of the candour with which the claims are qualified, can make them lethal. The following extract of only 24 words contains three such qualifiers. It is far from untypical. 'In an unverified report the Ministry of Agriculture and Fisheries claimed that animal rights activists may have cut the brake-cables of Ministry officials' vehicles.'[10] This presentation of uncorroborated and conditional information achieved a kind of paroxysm during the Kosovo War, especially on the web, although the trend was already well established in traditional media before 1994. Its content both derives from and feeds the media rumour-mill, often as deliberate disinformation. Such material comprises the mass of email leads which Drudge claims to receive every day, some of which he posts on to the site. Through the sheer proliferation of such material Drudge is well aware that readers are forced to evaluate it carefully. More significant perhaps is his mode of operation. Before the web it is doubtful whether such a phenomenon, a journalism exclusively of assertion, could have existed and as he himself has said:

We have entered an era vibrating with the din of small voices. Every citizen can be a reporter, can take on the powers that be ... time was only newsrooms had access to the full pictures of the day's events, but now any citizen does. We get to see the kind of cuts that are made for all kinds of reasons; endless layers of editors with endless agendas changing bits and pieces, so by the time the newspaper hits your welcome mat, it had no meaning. Now, with a modem, anyone can follow the world and report on the world – no middle man, no big brother. [11]

Drudge's willingness to publish unverified material (often uncovered, rejected or awaiting verification by others) brought critical attention to the willingness of some of the web's editors to take advantage of the medium's capacity for instant publication. The fact that the web allows journalists to publish breaking stories almost instantly leads to managements insisting on rapid-fire publication and a 24-hour news cycle.

News, whether it be print, broadcast or webcast, no longer allows the luxury of confirmation by at least two sources – the principle that Woodward and Bernstein insisted upon as they broke the Watergate story 25 years before Linda Tripp's claims about Monica Lewinsky. In many American states, and in other countries, the willingness to publish a retraction can have a strongly mitigating effect on cases of libel and Drudge defended his libels and bad judgements by claiming that he could and does publish retractions as swiftly as assertions when necessary. In the case of many of his Clinton revelations, as we have seen, that particular stable door was swept off its hinges as they were immediately followed by an uncontrolled journalistic feeding frenzy. It is very difficult for the retraction to ever catch up with the untruth that spawned it. One of the equations that online journalism needs to solve is a way of balancing instantaneous release of news with equally immediate critical feedback. The problem with instant news is that when it is wrong it tends to be buried, sedimenting into and reinforcing its context, rather than corrected.

The reciprocal of the argument, of course, is made by those who, for whatever reason – perhaps the sensibilities of polititians and advertisers – would have the facts constrained within 'acceptable' parameters. In describing Hillary Clinton's response to Drudge's revelations about Monica Lewinsky in 1998 Jonathan Wallace says that the First Lady's worry was not about untruths but about 'balance'. Asked about the regulation of the web she replied, 'Anytime an individual or an institution or an invention leaps so far out ahead of that balance ... and throws a system – political, economic, technological – out of balance, you've got a problem, because then it can lead to the oppression of people's rights, it can lead to the manipulation of information, it can lead to all kinds of bad outcomes which we have seen historically. So we're going to have to deal with that.'[12] The argument is the one that is regularly employed to cow the tabloid press when it presses too close upon the heels of power.

However, Drudge's willingness to have information, true or false, on his website within five minutes of its discovery rapidly turned him into a celebrity journalist, to the extent that by mid-1999 he hosted a television talk show for Rupert Murdoch's distinctly conservative Fox News Channel and a radio show syndicated by ABC across the major cities of the United States. 'I've been called a muckraker, but also the most powerful journalist in America. That is because I am just seconds from publishing, without having to ask anyone, and with no money.'[13] His style proved not to be entirely to Fox's taste and by November his contract had been terminated. Fox executives declared his approach to be 'completely unprofessional'. For his part Drudge had always said, 'They can always throw me back to the Internet if they have to.'[14] While his blurring of news and entertainment cultures cannot be entirely blamed on the Internet since it merely develops existing trends, it is perhaps interesting that in this instance a self-styled 'information anarchist' armed only with a computer and modem should be deemed suitable for such well-rewarded media jobs.

One of the effects of Drudge and others like him, symptomatic of a general speeding up of the cycle of production for news, seems to be a reduction by media generally in the time and effort devoted to checking stories. Perhaps the most notorious example of such abrogation of responsibility are the reports, derived solely from mischievous information placed on the web (via Usenet), that TWA flight 800, which crashed off Long Island in 1996, was brought down by a missile. As consumers increasingly turn to the web for breaking news so they, and the news providers, become more vulnerable to such outright hoaxes and to the fudges and elisions of Drudge-like journalism. More positively, as we have seen, the web is able to provide readers with the background and depth to place stories such as the one that rapidly came to be known as Zippergate into their political and cultural contexts. It can link them straight to the White House statements on the subject as well as the tapes and transcripts, the Starr report, commentary, parallels with historical scandals, reviews and biographies and provide time lines which set the story into its context of the Clinton administration and the larger political economy of the United States.

David McClintick suggests that the two effects are merely different faces of the same paradigm shift for journalism, that perhaps the Drudge Report 'foreshadows the role of the Internet as a new and different journalistic medium and as a catalyst of broader trends towards democratisation and devolution of the power of big institutions, especially in the media worlds of New York and Washington'.[15] Drudge's rapid incorporation by that same big media notwithstanding, McClintick goes on to propose him as a 'modern Tom Paine' who, while he is willing to take their dollars, clearly does not share the corporate consensus of the global media cartel.

Matt Drudge derides journalism as a 'fraud' and claims that his readers 'believe what I'm saying. It's entertaining'.[16] The problem with news as entertainment, of course, is that the shift compromises both its legitimacy and authority. The stabilisation and commodification of news ensures the large audiences of popular media forms. Unfortunately, large audiences do not automatically bring high credibility, and consumers, while they are clearly willing to enjoy the vicarious gratifications of the detail of the Clinton/Lewinsky affair, can simultaneously discount them as news.

News as media spectacle is driven by the commercial imperative for news providers to retain and expand their audiences and to produce the same profit ratios as other branches of the entertainment industry. News providers are now part of the same conglomerates which produce entertainment and compete for the same investment capital. The ideology that naturalises news as one of the central commodities of the information age insists that it too becomes subject to the drive for profit and is operated by its owners as one of a series of profit centres. The determination of news as entertainment foregrounds a range of cultural factors, not least shortening audience attention spans or what Todd Gitlin has described as 'communication compression'.[17] The era of the sound bite has radically changed the relationship between readers and the actors of the news.

The trend can be seen as part of the transformation of the media in general in which news is reconfigured as a secondary and separate part of the general political economy of the developed world. From a role which supplemented the primary sectors – manufacturing and trade, education, the military, etc. – including those institutions which Althusser described as the 'ideological state apparatuses', with a kind of annotation or commentary, news and the media have shifted to the centre of capitalist production and consumption. The incorporation of news into entertainment, a process in which Littleton and Kosovo are given the same treatment as Zippergate and celebrity weddings, sees as its outcomes new cultural or media products such as 'real-life action' television and some of the more polemical forms of talk radio.

Similar quasi-journalistic forms are emerging, often around gossip, on the web, sometimes merely formalising a discourse already active on the Usenet. The primary function of such products is to draw viewers to advertising sites. The news, instead of assisting its consumers to understand the conditions of their existence – in Marxist terms, the alienation that is the subjective product of industrial capitalism – becomes one of the commodities that allows them to imagine that they can escape it. 'Communication compression', far from a dumbing down, can instead be understood as a strategy enabling news to convey apparently contradictory messages, the 'polysemic and flexible' signals that John Fiske sees as fundamental to viable popular media. Such messages often include the incorporation of information from decidedly uncertain sources as news. The results of informal polls, based on unverified and self-selecting constituencies masquerade as or accompany news. A poll suggesting that 62 per cent of readers thought that Paddington Station was unsafe to reopen appeared on the main news page of *newsUnlimited.co.uk* on 1 October 1999, a week or so after the Paddington rail crash, accompanying links to fresh reporting of the tragedy. It was one of a series of polls appearing on the front page of *newsUnlimited* which, while it did not allow readers to repeat votes, appeared to do little other than signal and corroborate the editor's decision to lead with a particular story. In 1999 many online news sites carried similar polls.

The Spectacularisation of News

The reproduction of knowledge, including news, as entertainment is one of the defining activities of the contemporary 'culture industry'. Its status in the information economy was articulated by Guy Debord as early as 1967 as 'the star commodity of the society of the spectacle'.[18] Kosovo, Zippergate, as well as the most banal of domestic situations are reconfigured as 'spectacle commodities'. The ideological function of the news spectacle, as it has been argued by Habermas, is the formation of public opinion.

> Opinion management with its 'promotion' and 'exploitation' goes beyond advertising; it invades the process of 'public opinion' by systematically creating news events or exploiting events that attract attention.[19]

It must come as no surprise that the commodity of the news spectacle is predominantly consumer-driven. News on the web as in the traditional media is now led by scandal, celebrity watching, weather reports, sports scores, the market, health and lifestyle, and consumer information including listings. News that is not amenable to spectacularisation – the more complex issues that demand economic or political analyses – are summarised and may well eventually disappear from broadcast systems. As the web becomes the dominant channel for issue-driven news it will transform it dramatically.

Steven Johnson has pointed out that, as long as consumers use a range of browsers, the output of their news providers, however scrupulously designed, will be presented to a range of aesthetic considerations or design parameters. Browsers can be adapted to individual preferences and Netscape can handle HTML very differently from Internet Explorer. Consumers also face the prospect of products 'that actually filter through information based on *semantic* variables. ... Today's browsers alter the look-and-feel of the data they convey; tomorrow's will alter the meaning of that data, by emphasising certain stories over others, or by punching up sections that are particularly relevant to the reader'.[20]

Traditional broadcast journalisms have, by their nature and however ineffectively, covered a spectrum of news. Pull-technologies, however, employed by many news channels on the web, allow consumers to bypass completely those stories about which they know nothing and wish to know less. The *Fishwrap* and *Daily Me* models allow them to filter them completely out and the web, in such a context, becomes a network of elite sources of information and niche news products including, on the one hand, political and celebrity gossip vehicles such as the *Drudge Report*, and on the other, purveyors of specialist high-value information such as the *Financial Times* and the *Wall Street Journal*. Of course, as long as the web continues to attract mass audiences advertisers will ensure that those channels exist alongside mass audience titles as well.

Such publications, for instance tabloid websites such as *USA Today* and the UK *Mirror,* will construct the bulk of their content, including news and information, as entertainment. Stories are presented in narrative forms which gratify their audiences with recognisable conventions and the catharsis of closure, often with a moral that serves the interests of the current dominant ideology. News as infotainment rarely strays far from human interest stories, vicarious excitements and just deserts. Human interest includes dramas such as Timothy Leary's decision to 'die' on the web on 31 May 1996,[21] and births. On 16 June 1998 the first birth was recorded live on the healthcare site *AHN.com*. Many, much more banal human activities seem to make equally riveting web entertainment. Web stars such as JenniCam <www.jennicam.org>, whose lives on the web include sleeping, eating, watching television, defecating and having sex, can draw more than 100,000 hits a day making them as good a prospect for advertising as many regional news shows or more traditional entertainment. The web has enabled the spectacularisation of the private and the everyday in the way that television appropriated more public events in the past.

Daniel Dayan and Elihu Katz have described how public events such as the Olympics, deaths and weddings and defining political moments such as Watergate or Anwar el Sadat's visit to Israel ('Contests, Conquests and Coronations') have been adapted by television to serve specific ideological functions. For such events to carry the social and cultural resonance that they do, their representation demands the active involvement of audiences. We can see the web inviting its audience's 'ritual participation', often to much more banal events, in similar ways. As on television the aesthetic of the web is created by 'offering free [on both television and the web more usually for a fee in the days of 'pay per view'] and equal access, creating a liminal space, rehearsing the ritual order, and positioning the viewer so that he can both identify as observer and respond as participant'.[22]

That status 'as observer' is not, of course, as disengaged or unimplicated as the phrase might suggest. In the case of a media event such as Zippergate the protagonists, both the prosecution team led by Kenneth Starr and the White House, were actively seeking ways of influencing public opinion. The 445 pages of the Starr Report, placed on the web in raw and unmediated form through a number of content providers by the Office of the Independent Counsel, were clearly intended to provide the basis of the extended political debate which rapidly followed. The subsequent discourse, while it did not exactly follow the direct path to impeachment anticipated by Clinton's Republican opponents, comprised a significant media spectacle lasting many months and drew global audiences to all news media but particularly to the web. It included extensive analysis, responses and rebuttals from a range of political positions, background information as well as interactive and other discussion forums. The story drew upon links from the US House of Representatives and the White House as well as many North American news providers. Documents such as the Senate Court of Impeachment Trial Memorandum[23] placed on the web under terms of the United States Freedom of Information Act, drew hundreds of thousands of readers.

What the posting of the Starr report on the web clearly did not do was to direct the information exclusively to an 'elite' group of gatekeepers and commentators. The web gave those readers who wished to focus on the more salacious aspects of the report, the sex, scandal and private lives of its subjects, full rein to do so. The American press, even those elements more inclined towards the Democrats, were sucked into a vortex of prurience. Public opposition to the decision of the Grand Jury to publish the unmediated report led to comments in the American media about the wisdom of bypassing the filters, ideological and ethical, of journalistic 'scrutiny'.

That response, largely self-serving though it is, does reveal some understanding of the vulnerability of traditional journalism faced with the web. In the short term Kenneth Starr and the Republican party strategists used the Internet to sidestep the liberal press but the media is designed around a larger game. Zippergate was another spectacle geared to keeping audiences hooked and, through edited versions of the report in print editions, to bringing as many as possible on to news websites where they could link to the whole report. The web publication of the Starr report brought a surge in the readerships and audiences of traditional news media and was instrumental in bringing many new readers to the web. By using the web to influence public opinion directly the report also foregrounded the problem of disintermediation and the evasion of the political process. Kenneth Starr and his team effectively neutralised journalism by simply bypassing it.

The audiences of scandals such as Zippergate comprise the customers of the advertisers who capitalise the news industry. Such a story attracts large global audiences which, especially if it is drip fed by maverick providers such as Matt Drudge, subordinating journalism to political expediency while at the same time imbuing it with a frisson of the illicit, can be sustained over long periods. Excess brings readers to websites in the same way that it has always sold newspapers. In this case Drudge, and Starr himself, helped the whole process to evade the media 'gatekeepers' and, in what is clearly to be a standard model for the future, the story took on a life of its own. Unhampered by the checks and inflections of professional commentators, and largely bypassing the political process, it was consumed wholesale by audiences, spin doctors and lobbyists. Ultimately it eluded even those who had released it and proved impossible to direct towards its intended political goals.

This is not to suggest that unmediated information becomes somehow autonomous or without bias. While such spectacles do not necessarily serve the hegemonising functions of Dayan and Katz's carefully mediated 'Contests, Conquests and Coronations' they unquestionably and directly address the demands of the media corporations for audience share and as such they are both apolitical and destabilising. An 'unfiltered' spectacle such as parts of Zippergate, including the Starr Report, cannot be understood, for instance, through Chomsky's 'propaganda model' of media. The 'manufacture' of social consent to government is necessarily predicated upon a heavily controlled and screened media. Those controls may well be imposed by systemic factors such as the economies of scale imposed by a mass form rather than any corporate or state agent, which partly explains why they are able to fail so readily when the system is renewed by an emergent technology.

Bias itself is seen, at least for consumers in the West, to be part and parcel of 'the news'. Readers understand that news is inflected by its source, that it is mediated. It is that inflection which explains why it has been elevated from its *actualité* and gives it meaning. A news spectacle like Zippergate carried a range of different meanings for Republicans and Democrats, and for Americans and the citizens of other countries. The Starr report, deprived of its political spin – its bias – remains merely raw and confusing information. When the values subsequently applied to it are those of entertainment rather than news, its political meaning becomes subject to significant category distortion.

Baudrillard suggests that such a distortion is systemic, that scandals such as Watergate and Zippergate function in the same way as Disneyland, that is as 'imaginary effects' concealing the lack of 'reality' or moral principle both within the park and without.[24] 'Whoever regenerates ... public morality (by indignation, denunciation, etc.) spontaneously furthers the order of capital ...' The claim is that by repudiating the immoral and the licentious, capital, itself completely without principle, provides itself with a moral facade or 'superstructure'. Its agents, whether they be Matt Drudge or Woodward and Bernstein, place that superstructure in the hands of capital in the form of scandal or rather news of scandal. That news, in its unmediated form, seems, however, to neutralise the moral order (an ideological form) leaving an indifferent readership and the scandal of a rapine capitalism unconcealed. The media's consumers then accuse it of dumbing down, of selling out to advertising. Capital's claim to a social contract, founded on a moral probity which exposes scandal and conducted through the global media corporations, is itself exposed. One of the scandal's of Zippergate was cruelly exposed in the failure of the American public to become interested in the abortive impeachment attempt upon President Clinton.

There was interest, however, expressed elsewhere. One effect of the web is the globalisation of news, however local, which is not necessarily to imply, as we shall see in Chapter 8, a 'global' news but rather a local inflection on the global. Zippergate was a world story with implications for readers everywhere. The *Star.arabia.com* website, an English language site from Jordan whose main constituency is expatriate Jordanians, saw the story mainly as a 'Jewish plot against the President of the United States, aimed at distracting the US from implementing their proposals for the stalled peace process'. The same feature ponders whether 'Clinton will resort to another foreign policy adventure ... to deflect attention from home',[25] perhaps prefiguring the Kosovo intervention.

Zippergate thus comprised a genuine global spectacle commodity. On one hand, it produced a set of images and texts through which journalists from opposing political factions in the United States, no less than in states and cultures around the world, were able to redefine their social realities. On the other, it was also produced, distributed and consumed around the world as an entertainment product, a spectacle of infotainment.

Myfirsttime.com: the Banalisation of News

The web can by no means be blamed for turning the news into spectacle. Dayan and Katz see the trend as endemic to the media as a whole and a function of massification. The Olympics, the Watergate hearings and the wedding of Charles and Diana were all media events. After Leni Reifenstahl's *Olympia* it seems almost irrelevant to use veracity as a criterion for evaluating such representations. They become aesthetic, moral and cultural events rather than, or in addition to, news. The recategorisation also construes other, more banal, events such as lottery draws and human interest stories such as Timothy Leary's death as part of the category. The banality of news has been accelerated on the web.

The trend encourages disinformation and fraud. In July 1998 media around the world reported that a teenage couple in America were planning to lose their virginity live on the web. A few moments' thought should have alerted editors to the spurious nature of the claim. However, just as with Matt Drudge's Clinton rumours, the story spread like some pernicious weed and took millions of visitors to *www.myfirsttime.com* to meet Diane and Mark. The rigorous checking of the *St. Louis Post Dispatch* revealed that the site was owned by a former video pornography retailer whose web broadcasting was to be conducted by a company more usually associated with selling sex videos. Perhaps unsurprisingly viewers would be charged $5 to access the webcast. The quite legitimate decision to charge for such questionable entertainment coupled with its dubious provenance led to the world's news organisations dropping it rather sharply but do not alter the question of why they were so willing to be gulled by it in the first place. The website subsequently offered a plethora of alleged 'first time' accounts, some, interestingly, in fabricated pidgin languages geared solely, it seemed, to search engine software, and advertisements for sex products and sex websites.

Such ersatz news stories as *myfirsttime* and the exaggeration of celebrity as news value, for instance in the over-coverage given in 1999 to the marriage between Posh Spice and the footballer David Beckham draw attention away from issue-based news. Even though there is space enough on the web for both kinds of news such fabricated spectacles, geared to attracting mass audiences and the advertising that accompanies them, are allowed to lead and, of course, in the limited newshole (that area of the newspaper page that is left for the news once the advertisments and headers have been set) of print and broadcast news, they can deprive more complex stories of any coverage at all. The issue stands at the centre of the development of journalistic ethics. The economic model which determines printed newspapers insists that their contents, news and advertising, are delivered to a fixed proportion. For most newspapers the ratio is about 40 per cent news and editorial to 60 per cent advertising. The print newshole is a severely limited resource and late twentieth-century media management styles and the rise in the importance of selling copy meant that it shrank fast. Journalistic ethics policed the decline as best it could. The development of the web as a primary carrier of news, with its potentially unlimited newshole, has forced a review of those standards.

Journalism Ethics on the Web and the Crisis of Legitimacy

Before the wholesale flight of news providers to the web, editors and journalists were already reconsidering the core values of their craft. 'From "balance" to "balance/fairness/wholeness" and from "accuracy" to "accuracy/authenticity".'[26] Joann Byrd, writing in the

American Editor, sought ways of widening the grasp of journalism's guiding principles. The ability that hyperlinks give to readers to 'drill down' into sources and the issues that lie at the heart of a news story should certainly help to provide balance and wholeness. They will also create new ethical problems for editors by taking readers to partisan information, in some cases hatred and obsession, advertising and other news media. Are they responsible for the information they have linked to? Having transported their readers to this information how do journalists then get them back to set it in context with their own 'balanced' conclusions and should they offer some evaluation of the credibility of those sources and competitors? How far should interactive forms be employed to enable readers to intervene in narratives? What about those groups who do not have access to the web?

Byrd also raises the problem of accuracy and the authenticity which demands context and nuance conducted 'in a medium which moves at the speed of light'. A potentially unlimited newshole enables a comprehensive coverage of issues and communities for the first time. Archives, guides and listings will remain available to readers, adding to the depth of reporting on current issues. While such information may well point up journalistic errors of judgement and inaccuracies in the past, their erasure or correction points to much more serious problems around authenticity and integrity. The *Drudge Report* seems to illustrate a dramatic shift in standards around this issue.

Journalism ethics are the moral benchmarks through which journalists gauge their practice. They map a set of standards which govern the economy of principles within which journalism would operate and are most frequently brought into play in the relationship between editorial and advertising; the wobbly line where 'church' meets 'state'. Once news coverage is determined, even in part, by advertising, the standards are breached and the issue becomes one of press credibility. The partition between church and state, while it may, in practice, be vulnerable to the occasional erosion as advertising income insists that coverage of particular topics is reined in or emphasised, usually assures readerships of the integrity of their daily news.

However, the emergence of news providers on the web, many with no background in traditional news media, has led to the wholesale discarding of the values which have developed through and which pertain to traditional media, including that crucial separation. Some of these providers are the more successful independent start-ups but more usually they are global media conglomerates such as Disney or Microsoft and their news and portal sites, *Go* and *MSNBC*. In an economy which survives on narrower margins than the entertainment industries in general, many online managements, driven by their business departments, regard the separation of editorial and advertising as anachronistic and 'linear'. The arguments suggest that consumers who 'get the web' are savvy enough to be able to tell the difference between editorial and advertising, and even if they can't, does it really matter in the new speed-of-light economy? Such thinking permeates the web and impacts directly on the relationship between websites and their readers.

The use of cookies – tracking users as they wander around the network and creating the profiles that will subsequently be employed to present them with the adverts that they are likely to be interested in – is generally regarded as fair exchange for content which mostly arrives free. The question of invasion of privacy hardly arises, much less legislation such as the European Economic Commission's consumer privacy guidelines of 1998 or the UK Data Protection Act of a decade earlier. Similarly, the print conventions on adjacency, which prevent advertisements being positioned in such a way as to suggest that they are endorsed by editorial copy, tend to be discarded in the design principles that dictate the appearance of the *Daily Me* and ignored by web providers.

This mechanical approach to composition can lead to wildly inappropriate placement of adverts: the airline advertisment next to news of the latest air disaster. The abandoning of the rules on adjacency coupled with cookie technology means that the advertising on web pages can be powerfully tailored around several criteria simultaneously; the display advert for the latest release by my favourite band on the review pages of my regular music ezine. At the same time your browser will configure the same page with an advert for your favourite band's latest music. When the ad is clicked on and the music, in whatever form, is purchased, the zine, or in other cases the *New York Times* or *Salon.com,* earns up to 15 per cent commission on the sale. The transaction radically changes the relationship between advertisers and the media, especially if the editorial or sales office of the vehicle carrying the advertisement is tempted by the prospect of increasing that commission by pushing the music with favourable reviews.

Neither does the web adhere to the conventional standards of traditional media in its recognition of ownership; it is often difficult to distinguish advertising or retail websites from entertainment or even news sites. The problem is compounded with the 'affiliate' agreements, mentioned above, between news providers and their advertisers which allows the news provider to receive a percentage of each sale made by the e-merchant through a reference from the news site. While it can be argued that this arrangement merely restructures earlier agreements between advertisers and the media it is hard to see how the new relationship cannot but further erode the 'glass wall' between the media company's sales and editorial offices. In a parallel failure of integrity the relevancy of many search engine results is a commodity that can be bought and sold; a large payment can see the name of my book-retailing company appearing at the top of every reply offered by the search engine.

Such direct interventions by advertising into what consumers might expect to be editorial – or at least independent – domains in some sectors of online news are a clear departure from the ethical standards claimed by traditional media. The effects include the re-introduction of a pro-corporate bias into news on the web that had largely disappeared from the media in Britain and North America early in the twentieth century. That flamboyant, intensely partisan reporting was then called 'yellow journalism'.

Since scandal and spectacle have become the dominant genres of news across most media including the web, the values of journalism must be reassessed to take account of them. It is hardly sufficient to write them off as failing to meet standards which may be anachronistic and obsolete. Scandal and muckraking sell newspapers, it is true, but, as is evidenced in the press allegations against politicians such as Richard Nixon and Jeffrey Archer, they also expose corruption and crime. Nor can the steady decline in the consumption of print news be laid entirely at the door of Rupert Murdoch. Large sections of society in the West see news, at least in its traditional forms, as simply irrelevant. The institutional dialectic which structures news, including such issues as the relationships between sources, reporters and media owners, as well as accuracy and fairness, while it is clearly related to that attrition, tends also to be placed in perspective against it.

The whole discourse of press ethics, the conventions about exactly what may be said and which voices are privileged to be heard and which are not, usually becomes visible only when, as with Matt Drudge's interventions, it is perceived to have been transgressed. Furthermore, 'In order for an issue to achieve the status of being ethically problematic, there must exist an appropriate forum for the generation of such a discussion.'[27] For newspapers and the broadcast media the defence of news values has largely been conducted around opposition to the market orientation of owners and business offices. The historical discourse of objectivity, for instance, can be construed as having been entirely driven by the impoverishment, distortion and ultimately appropriation of the public sphere by political and commercial factions. Once those factions had ensured that they owned the expert voices who alone were privileged to speak and had silenced genuinely open debate with the muzzle of objectivity, there were few points remaining where any journalism, however radical, which met the terms of the new professionalism, could successfully apply leverage. Since objectivity's primary claim is for a correspondence with reality all other versions are necessarily discredited. Hard news was implicitly objective. The situation does not, however, transfer wholesale to the web, and the proponents of 'hard news', clearly an ideological construction, have lost ground in the transition. Gaye Tuchman extends the understanding of journalistic objectivity to include a 'strategic ritual'[28] or set of procedures which journalists employ to validate their work. Clearly this protective mode of objectivity achieves little more than a narrowing of journalism's focus.

In addition to objectivity, Jeremy Iggers qualifies the fundamental principles at issue in the debate as conflict of interest, accuracy, fairness and sensation. We might add a predilection for closure to that list. The conflicts of interest that news journalism is subject to are largely the effects of ownership in the hands of a global media cartel vigorously defending its interests in other fields, including advertising media sales to its primary customer, global manufacturing. Among the effects of the increasingly partisan nature of big media are its almost complete failure to report corporate crime, partly reflected in its diffidence around pro-consumer and pro-labour issues. The spurious scandals of media which are politically biased to the left or to the right, to Labour or Conserative, Democrat or Republican, are merely a screen to mask the disgrace of a media that is almost universally pro-corporate and anti-labour.

The rise of objectivity in the news, which Iggers and others have located as the key to the professionalisation of journalism (most commentators seem to agree that it emerged in the half century between 1870 and 1920 and I have already indicated the nature of the lock), is perhaps the value which has been most thrown into question by the ways in which the Internet is forcing a rethink of journalistic practice. Deprofessionalisation, exemplified, it is claimed, by practitioners such as Matt Drudge, and deskilling, exemplified by Steve Case's insistence on the blurring of the difference between journalism and 'information packaging', places pressure on accuracy as well. Drudge has made it clear on many occasions that he sees accuracy as being neither possible nor necessary in an information economy that makes immediacy a prime value. The inaccurate can be expunged as fast as it is included.

As for fairness, it is often used as little more than a euphemism for objectivity; however, it can also represent 'a more thoughtful articulation of disinterested reporting that covers all the bases rather than simply "balancing" two sides'.[29] Sensationalism, which panders to the morbid curiosity of readers, tends to be constructed around scandal and, arguably more legitimately, spectacle. It is usually comprehended through standards of taste which, since they are cultural, makes it difficult for the arbiters of journalistic standards. Since so many events are, in any case, presented, even designed,[30] as news spectacles, the whole concern of sensationalism becomes one of genre and style as much as ethics. News as spectacle and the systemic changes determined by the technologies of the web seem to compound the crisis of legitimacy which traditional journalism finds itself in.

Iggers sees the function of journalistic values, particularly objectivity, as in translating 'property rights into social power. The norm of professionalism provided a restraint, never completely effective, on who could be a producer of news and the norm of objectivity further constrained what journalists could report and who could serve as a legitimate source of news'.[31] The *Drudge Report*, on the face of it, completely overturns that principle and might productively be employed to comprehend the model. The restraint, in retrospect, seems to have been more technological and economic than professional.

The key determinant, tightly controlled by owners until the emergence of the web, was a range of ever more expensive news production technologies which both constantly reduced the levels of skill required by newsworkers across the whole process – from news collection to dissemination and distribution – and raised the stake that those wishing to enter the industry had to invest. Iggers proposes that other factors also contribute to 'the foundations of autonomy and accountability [of newsworkers] ... being systematically dismantled'. He includes:

> ... the reorganization of the newsroom into teams, following the corporate model
> ... a shift to a 'market-driven' approach, in which market research replaces the expertise of the reporter as the basis for judgements of newsworthiness and the objective of satisfying the customer replaces the goal of informing the public
> ... a shift from 'news' to 'information', and
> ... a shift in emphasis from the narrative to the visual.[32]

The net impact of these changes mitigates against a journalism built upon a set of specific professional skills and for the packaging of information. News packagers are necessarily highly skilled in the use of a limited range of software but hardly encompass the knowledge and experience which enable the judgements about taste, value and appropriateness which comprehend newsworthiness.

The soundness of such judgements is what separates journalism from scandal, gossip and raw information. Journalists exercise news judgement, based on a shared set of values and conventions, when they decide what to cover and how. Subsequent decisions about the appropriateness of sources, judgements about what should be omitted, what is interesting and when and where to run the story are all based on that professional responsibility. Increasing competition online and the loss of the 'news cycle' have deeply eroded the criteria upon which that judgement rests.

One of the effects of a journalism so constrained is that it is unable to defend its autonomy and becomes a tool of media business, set to snare the big advertising budgets. A further effect – one that has been so far unsuccessfully reappropriated by proprietors such as Rupert Murdoch – who so successfully drove the market-centred approach in Britain – was the appearance of a new journalism in publications like the *Drudge Report* in the USA and *Scallywag* in Britain, and their many imitators (some markedly more successful than their epigones).

Drudge is able to publish from his two-room flat in Hollywood by employing a technology that demands very few overheads. His 'team', mostly comprising other news providers such as *Slashdot*, mobilised by no more than a link to their website, are virtual in the extreme.

> His nerve center is a fluid cacophony – a cheap Sanyo television monitor tuned to CNBC, another to CNN, another to C-SPAN ... a Sony radio purring phone talk, an RCA satellite dish bringing in European news, show tunes, and extra TV channels, a police scanner looking for local action, and, most importantly, two computer screens linked to chat-rooms, e-mail, news wire services, and the Internet.[33]

Without wishing to elevate Drudge as the contemporary counterpart of the printer publishers of the great age of radical journalism, William Cobbett or Tom Paine, his newsroom also serves as his printing press or transmitter. The *Drudge Report* makes no concessions to its readers in terms of visual appeal or newsworthiness. Its sheer lack of style or discrimination is breathtaking to the readerly eye that has been educated in the contemporary news' aesthetic. *Newsweek*'s satisfaction at Matt Drudge's sacking by Fox News, especially after his forcing their publication of the Monica Lewinsky story, must have been tempered by his immediately leading with a link to their own (slightly triumphal) report of the event in November 1999. Any report of the death of journalism in the emergence of Drudge was premature, however the craft, with its skills and its determining principles, was certainly changing.

The Return of the Real

While Drudge's journalism may well be unappealing to many, including as it does distortions, inaccuracies and a more or less complete dependency on the work of others, at the same time it firmly reharnesses news to politics and to the affairs of the community. This might seem to be one of the fundamental objectives of journalism, yet it has been routinely ignored by corporate media in its ever more precise matching of readers and audiences to advertisers and patterns of consumption. Drudge's is a journalism, however imperfect, that enables citizens to participate once more in the democratic process. The same argument can perhaps be made for the traditional press in the continued presence of such publications as *Private Eye* in Britain; however, the traffic over the *Drudge Report* averages at about 6 million a week. During a period when it is breaking a story traffic is equivalent to or exceeds the mainstream news sites such as *New York Times*. *Private Eye*'s circulation, on the other hand, depends on an ageing readership and steadily declines.

Citing the philosopher Fred d'Agostino, Iggers argues that the logic of any claim for journalistic objectivity gives it an Archimedean perspective, outside the system that it would intervene in. It is a 'God's eye view', or, quite literally, the 'view from nowhere'.[34] Hence it is a perspective that forecloses on the possibility of dialectic, conversation or interactivity. This contradicts the major potential of the web and may well be why objectivity is increasingly eschewed for other values such as freshness or immediacy by online journalism, values which encourage response rather than refuse it. The trade-off comes with severe implications for the accuracy of news which, in turn, further discredit the general claim for objectivity. The 'view from nowhere' collapses anyway when it is revealed as journalism's resort to the repeated and tired views of a limited range of recognised experts. Journalists 'cannot report [their own inferences] as facts. If someone else draws the inferences – and usually this someone else is an official empowered to do so – then the journalist can treat the inference as hard facts'.[35] For reporters and editors under pressure from deadlines it becomes routine, a kind of shorthand for the news. The tabloids have long indicated that the market demands something else. As 'the Internet becomes a gigantic repository for so much copied, mutilated and spin-distorted information and misinformation, it becomes ever harder for readers to know what is true, what is rumour, and who can be trusted',[36] and we have clearly moved to a new paradigm for news, demanding new readership skills which render the routine redundant.

Rumour further undermines the God's eye view since its source and its intention is unashamedly secular and social. Whether it carries any truth or not, it forcibly reintroduces the social into the discourse of news. It brings new values to news suggesting 'the existence of physical volume in the event. [Rumours] counterbalance its pedagogic cool, its ironed-out flatness'.[37] That 'physical volume' reconnects it to the lived world and perhaps begins to explain the gimcrack attractions of online news against the falling constituencies of the traditional press. The web discards the exactitude and precision of the technology that hosts it for much fuzzier, and perhaps more socially productive, albeit risk-laden, standards of information.

As Daniel Dayan and Elihu Katz have shown, news in the decades before the emergence of online media was increasingly concerned with the 'pseudo-event'. The term includes those spectacles ranging from sports festivals (World Cups and Olympics) to political summits and royal weddings which are staged for the primary purpose of being reported. Clearly such weddings and meetings must still occur in a world with different media priorities, but they would take very different, and more subdued, forms. Such events have become axiomatic for news, redefining our understanding of it within a comparatively short historical period. In so doing they have displaced other kinds of information that journalists might cover, including other sets of political relations, environmental issues and the edgy dialectic between consumers and manufacturing corporations. Dayan and Katz view such media events as essentially anti-democratic in that they encourage the process of disintermediation – they enable political leaders to speak directly to their constituencies over the heads of parties and parliaments.

> However liberating this style of communitas may seem to be, disintermediation may be an ominous step toward enactment of the mass-society scenario, insofar as it may involve the weakening of representative and grass-roots institutions.[38]

The process not only eliminates those intermediate layers of representation but it also reduces the role of journalism itself as reporters face the choice of either becoming partisan storytellers (was the President guilty or not?) or interpretive experts, in this instance on the strategies and processes that would or would not lead to a successful impeachment. In both cases analyses of political substance are scrupulously avoided for what Daniel Hallin describes as 'horse-race journalism'. The decision of Kenneth Starr to publish his report on the Clinton Whitehouse directly on to the web short-circuited both the political process and the news cycle. It can be seen to be at once advancing a quite radical democratising trend but at the same time, through such an immediate access to the American public, undermining the very social and political structures that have evolved to support democracy. The publication of the report may well have marked a defining moment for the web but it also signalled a much darker potentiality. The intervention not only informed the public about the scandal, it also rewrote that public's understanding of the administration and attempted to insist that a particular set of moral values be recognised by the community.

While such a demand signifies a moral function, it is one which, when it comes from their politicians – and Starr was seen as being a political appointee – is not always welcomed by the public. It was perhaps not surprising that much of the American public ignored Starr's alarms. By alerting the public to Bill Clinton's inappropriate behaviour Matt Drudge, on the other hand, had fulfilled a central function of news media. It is 'one of the most influential means of circulating the moral norms of the society, for circulating the conversation in which disagreements about those norms are debated and resolved, and for circulating the new vocabulary that signals changes in those values'.[39] Whatever *Newsweek*'s motives were in failing to publish the Monica Lewinsky story once they had corroboration, and however salacious the details of the story might have been, they were clearly failing to fulfil such a moral function.

The crisis of legitimacy for news journalism, both in traditional media and on the web, arises when the press no longer addresses its readers as citizens. Much of the press commentary around the Starr report was couched at a level that manifestly failed to address the political issues, seeking instead to satisfy vicariously a range of consumer desires. Politics as pornography articulates its citizens as customers (in fact the customers of the media's advertisers). 'To the degree that it ceases to place its duty to the community first and to address its audience as members of a community, the newspaper is abandoning both journalism and its larger moral role.'[40]

The role, a vehicle for citizenship, includes the provision of a record of the life of the community and in that representation the press produces the primary construct through which the community recognises itself. The manifest community, idealised in a set of moral values, exists first in the news. It will later be mediated through other forms and genres. Local media's primary role can be seen as defining the local and creating identity or a sense of belonging. However, as Bagdikian has pointed out, too often local media, even in metropolitan areas, is controlled by a monopoly whose main interest is in controlling advertising. The identity of the community is subsumed into the single activity of consumption and the conditions of the reader's personal experience are erased in a continuum of products providing links to the imaginary universe where media events, royal weddings, wars and cup finals occur. Bagdikian is referring to the media in North America but the same patterns of ownership have recurred in Europe, Asia and Australia.

The web permitted an interruption in the spiralling costs of media production and allowed the possibility of local and, in the case of Matt Drudge, unaffiliated, ownership. Cheap production and dissemination do not demand massive inputs of advertising revenue; however, when local advertising looked as though it was going to follow readers to a revived online local news many of the corporate owners of local media, Northcliffe in the UK and E.W. Scripps in the USA for instance, began to devise and promote new models of news or reverted to older models which recorded the life of the community rather than merely hosting advertising. News in the era of the web has an unnerving capacity to become despectacularised. Drudge's intervention in the Monica Lewinsky scandal defused it for all the subsequent commentary, even in the *New York Times*. It was difficult for readers to differentiate between moral high ground and gossip. The resolutely shoddy appearance of the *Drudge Report* refused to allow the Clinton impeachment hearings the same glossy status of the reporting of the Watergate hearings. As journalism becomes local and issue-driven again it allows readers to identify in and with the social. The effect may well be provincialising, even parochial, but that is hardly surprising given the rise in the account of gossip, as the 'real' is abstracted from cosmopolitan media events, from somewhere else, and returned home.

What I am claiming, on the insubstantial evidence of the *Drudge Report* and a few other websites such as *Not CNN*, used by journalists to oppose or contradict the global news establishment, and a rapidly growing number of local news sites, is the emergence of a journalism on the web which limits the ability of the media cartel and its agents to completely define and dominate social reality. This journalism insists on the revival of a public sphere, not, however, the institution that Habermas described: the determining instrument for the rise of the bourgeoisie, which gave rise to the liberalism that ultimately destroyed or heavily constrained the very communities which emerged with it. This public sphere does not, as the one formulated by Habermas did, insist on coherence, rationality and an educated elite, but instead it thrives on gossip, erratic intervention and breadth as well as depth of knowledge. It attains public consent by colouring, as much as by shaping, public discourse, often by introducing a cynicism that corrodes the power of institutions and the individuals who represent them. In their place this journalism foregrounds and reinforces much more informal social structures; it eschews the official voices of objectivity for families, clubs, groups of friends, ethnic and religious associations, neighbourhoods and *ad hoc* social groupings of one sort and another. It reframes social reality away from the commodity and in terms of those informal associational structures. We can look beyond formally constituted journalism to the millions of websites and newsgroups which now constitute so much of the Internet, which includes very small but very active groups mobilising around interests as various as Barbie, Sacramento and Esperanto, Doom and osteo-arthritis.

Conclusion

Journalism as infotainment is produced to the demands of the marketplace rather than to those of its audiences. News becomes a media commodity just like any other, in some cases as easily consumed as confectionery and providing the same instant gratification. In such a context the reporting of the local can be problematic; it rarely has the gloss and hence the universal appeal of the manufactured media event. The local is often difficult to abstract according to the logic of the commodity. It stubbornly clings to its associations and its context. The attraction, for a regime of infotainment, of events and actors specifically designed for media, is obvious. As we have seen, the demands by the technologies of contemporary broadcast and print media for massive investments of capital, drawn from the public in the form of share capital and in a context of global capitalism, insist on such regimes.

The emergence of new, or revived, journalistic forms on the web seems to offer some hope for a kind of participatory democracy in an depoliticised era. By returning a voice to the public, journalism gives it the possibility of rethinking itself and untangling itself from the commodity. In 1927, on the cusp of the age of high massification, John Dewey saw that only some new form of communication could create the 'great community'. Forms such as rumour and gossip, consigned to the gutter although not exactly ignored by traditional journalism, allow individuals to intervene in the social process rather than being forced into the role of spectator. In information structures which can accommodate provisional truth claims those informal modes of communication are useful. It is for journalism to 'continuously try to explore and to disclose the frames of reference and the conscious and hidden assumptions from within which they ... operate'.[41]

Absolute truths delivered from the single, and implicitly uncontestable, perspective of objectivity make a nonsense of any notion of the plural society. Iggers proposes a new set of values that would encourage an active citizenship rather than refuse it. These include 'accessibility, respect for persons, fairness, interpretation, and skepticism ...'.[42] Such a system of values renders the media event a historical curiosity. The World Trade Organisation talks in Seattle in November 1999, for instance, were clearly intended to offer one kind of media spectacular to global news, but instead a whole range of oppositional groups hijacked their representation with an alternative spectacle. The approach forced the reworking of a set of debates that will define all of our futures. Iggers suggests that an accessible media, willing to promote dialogue, would actually do away with the need for such global summits. Such events are deliberately constructed to produce narratives of confrontation, triumph and defeat and to deter any intervention but the official. A dialogue from the grassroots would seek, on the other hand, compromise, reconciliation and access. Journalism can become a vehicle for the debate itself rather than news of the spectacle of confrontation. Journalism on the web has the present potential of becoming an interventionist form of civic or public interaction operating from within or alongside its constituencies. As the primary determinant of social reality it will continue to draw advertising but it need not continue, itself, to be determined by that advertising as merely another entertainment, or infotainment, form.

6
'Undertakings of Great Advantage'

I think we'll look back at this as the golden age of the Web, not because everything was exceptionally good but because it was free. There will probably be a tremendous war of attrition in the next two or three years, because we've built too much premium content that we can't support.[1]

Newsweek's Michael Rogers' pessimism is, I suspect, at least partly misplaced. He also fails to mention the speed with which the infrastructure and primary content of the 'golden age' was assembled and the extravagant optimism and huckstery upon which so much of the venture was premised. Edward Chancellor's study of the South Sea bubble describes earlier speculative schemes, designed to absorb the flood of money chasing the South Sea flotation in the eighteenth century, which became increasingly tenuous. They included a proposal, not dissimilar to some of those being floated in the late 1990s for projects on the web, for 'carrying on an undertaking of great advantage but no one to know what it is'.[2] In 1999 alone more than £1 billion[3] was invested in British Internet start-up companies including media ventures, and commentators were drawn to make comparisons between the crash of the 1720s and the financial black hole of Internet stocks. The valuations of companies such as Yahoo!, Amazon (the online book retailer), Freeserve and *Lastminute.com* seemed to bear little relation to either the volume of business that they were transacting or any reasonable evaluation of their prospects.

This frantic activity coincided with the endgame of a thirty-year cycle of acquisitions and mergers among continental and global media corporations and the emergence of an oligopoly controlling the global media, communications and information sector. By the late 1990s much of the world's media industry, at every level, had fallen to a handful of companies. This is perhaps hardly surprising in an era which saw information as both the fundamental resource and the primary commodity of both the primary and retail sectors of the advanced global capitalist economy. The Internet served as an appropriate arena to stage the final act of the metamorphosis from an industrial- to an information-based economy. It would also comprise the central infrastructure of that economy. By removing our focus from the technology and examining the new business models that are emerging on the Internet and the dealing and politicking which fought over it as it found its place in the market we can learn much about the new media.

The US Department of Commerce study 'The Emerging Digital Economy'[4] provides an interesting comparison to gauge the initial growth of the Internet. Its figures suggest that, in North America, radio gained 50 million users after 38 years, television took 13 years to reach the same sized audience and the Internet four. There were 40 million users of the Netscape Navigator browser within two years of its launch; more than any other computer application.[5] The astonishing rate of growth of the first truly global medium was pursued, over-enthusiastically some said, by equally astronomic investments. Chip Brown suggests that in 1998 development of online news cost US providers $203.7 million.[6] The total, as we shall see, does not account for much of the basic research and development that went to establish the Internet. While the precise total spend is difficult to establish it is clear that the global news providers – the brand names – spent heavily often to the detriment of the development of their traditional media holdings. The same applies to many national, regional and even local providers. While the UK's Department of Trade and Industry (Future Unit) report, 'Converging Technologies: Consequences for the New Knowledge-Driven Economy', suggested that the main opportunities for the traditional press, *The Times*, the *Daily Mail* and *The Economist*, etc. lay in 'leveraging "trusted" brands into new markets' ... acting as 'islands of trust in a sea of change', many in the industry were not so sure.[7] In the USA there was evidence that some readerships (including the so-called 'generation X') associate the traditional news brands with an approach that is inappropriate, both in terms of content and presentation, to contemporary life. These emerging readerships turned to web start-up brands such as *Salon* and *ZDNet,* and rebranded media such as *HotWired, newsUnlimited, Nando Times, SzonNet* (the rebranded *Sueddeutsche Zeitung*) and *The Mercury Center* (the website of the *San Jose Mercury News*) for their news and information. Marc Auckland of the BT Global KM Group expresses the not entirely ironic commercial argument for web start-ups over the re-engineering of established brands for new media in the equation:

$$NT+OO = COO$$
New technology plus old organisation = costly old organisation[8]

What is more certain is that online news, however it is branded, like other information products has a finite constituency. It is that which will ultimately determine the sector. Furthermore, as this chapter suggests, the diversity of brands and organisational styles on the web obscure a remorseless tendency towards a proprietorial cartel.

Much of this investment, built on the sudden and apparently irrational decision to begin giving news and other content away free, was made with no clear idea of how it would ever be recouped. Yet perhaps the rush to the web was not so irrational. Brown makes the point that newspaper owners had been trying to escape the bulky physicality, the 'crushed trees', of their otherwise very profitable product and the problems with distributing them, since the oil crises which had forced the West's primary industries to re-evaluate their business practices in the 1970s. In 1998 *Time Inc.* spent over $1 billion dollars on paper and postage.[9] Perhaps unsurprisingly, in their enthusiasm to get away from such an expensive, bulky, anachronistic and inconvenient delivery system many media companies overlooked just what all that wood pulp physically carried into homes and workplaces was: often more than 50 per cent advertising. It was often an advertising which was either locally based or which carried coupons and for which, before the Internet, newspapers were the most effective medium. They were also unwilling to calculate the real costs of online news. For many traditional news suppliers it was difficult even to assess profitability since production costs – including journalists' wages and infrastructure charges such as wire-feeds charged to the print or broadcast newsroom – were never properly passed on to the online desk.

A superficial view of the web does not alter the fundamental economics of news production since it merely offers a new channel of distribution for existing categories of information; in the case of shovelware it barely even changes content. Even its capability for interactive communication, often seen as subversive to traditional media, has been harnessed to extend the power of advertising. However, as we have seen, that change seems to disturb the whole structure, even the rationale, of 'the news' to its very roots. Where the web becomes a truly mass medium and the main source of news for its constituencies, by altering the functional relationships between consumers and producers, and hence between producers and advertisers, those changes carry a knock-on effect for societies, cultures and their economies.

A useful historical analogy offered by libertarian netizens for news on the web is the period before mass advertising – when it was still possible for radical voices and small, independent presses, usually subscriber-driven and with agendas wider than the all-consuming pursuit of profit – to make themselves heard through the clatter of advertising sales. Later, in the period of massification a project like Labour's ill-fated *Daily Herald* in the UK – its massive circulation (more than 4.5 million in its last year and nearly double that of the *Manchester Guardian, The Times* and the *Financial Times* combined) only matched by the paucity of its advertising income – was unable to survive. Advertising, perhaps contrary to popular expectation, is not attracted to high readerships, mass audiences or popular forms. It wants to extract specific groups from those entities, namely the buyers. Perhaps the *Daily Herald* might have succeeded on the web, which does not carry the prohibitive production costs of print journalism and where there remains, at present, the space for different business models. After its effective failure over decades (arguably a century and a half and certainly since the 1960s) in both Europe and America the web has seen the re-emergence of an ideologically determined press. Perhaps the alternative press of North America (less so in Europe) never went away, but, at least for a while, the web made it more accessible to general readerships. Of course, in a climate in which free content becomes normative and drives out paid-for material the web could just as easily strangle those providers barred

from advertisers' money through ideological, ethnic or other affiliations regarded by big business as unpopular or unhelpful.

Brown describes the spirit of the post-1970s for mainstream media
producers as a 'spendthrift techno-romanticism ... when many
papers were seduced into ill-advised ventures in audio and videotex
services. There were deals with cable TV companies, and by the mid-
1980s many newspapers were hoping to cash in delivering their
product by fax. That none of these gambits really caught the public's
imagination didn't stop newspapers from piling into cyberspace'.[10]
Perhaps the Gadarene rush can be explained by a closer look at the
economics of the industry.

The News Online

One of the key junctures in the development of the printed press, as
it is understood through the Whig interpretation of its history, was
the move from capitalisation by political and class factions,
including the state, to 'financial independence', recognised by
Marxist historians as a euphemism for dependency on advertising
revenue. It is more like an addiction; Bagdikian assesses it as a '5-to-
1 dependence on advertisers ... Newspapers, magazines and
broadcasters in 1981 collected $33 billion a year from advertisers and
only $7 billion from their audiences ... [It] has insulated these media
from the wishes of their audiences'.[11] A seamless continuation of
that relationship exists, or was assumed to exist by sources of capital,
between news on the Internet and advertising, involving similar
opportunities and tensions between consumers, providers and advertisers and based on the same understanding – that the media
provider's primary product is the delivery of an agreed quantity and
quality of readers. Content, news or entertainment, is not merely
incidental to that end. It is the bait. The Internet brought the added
advantages, where there is no need for advertisers to limit themselves to a 30 second off-peak slot, of unlimited space and time as
well as the ability to quantify usage very specifically in markets in
which every consumer can be individually targeted and catered to
with a personalised media mix.

Rosalind Resnick, writing in mid-1994[12] describes what was then
a brave, perhaps even foolhardy departure, for news publishing on
the Internet. Hitherto, news providers – she mentions the California-

based corporation Knight-Ridder, one of North America's largest
newspaper owners, but in 1994 there were others – had gone online
in association with ISPs, in Knight-Ridder's case AOL. News was
offered to the ISPs subscribers as an extra charged service with the ISP
taking a large proportion of the income. In the first nine months of
service Knight-Ridder attracted 5,300 customers. Resnick compared
Knight-Ridder's progress with the *Palo Alto Weekly*, which had taken
the then novel approach of publishing an edition directly onto the
Internet. The non-subscription service, admittedly in what was
probably in 1994 the most wired neighbourhood on the planet,
received 4,500 hits in its first two weeks of operation.[13] Other titles,
notably the *Raleigh News & Observer* in North Carolina, *Online
Wisconsin*, an electronic news journal started at the University of
Wisconsin and *Kommunal Rapport* in Norway were also experimenting with free access over the then new World Wide Web.

While the technology was clearly a very effective way of distributing news, and consumers flocked to the sites, what those pioneers
needed was a way of setting their projects into a workable economy.
Bill Johnson, publisher of the *Palo Alto Weekly* believed that his
profits would come from classified adverts and display advertising
from real-estate brokers. 'One of the neat things about the Internet
is that a small paper that serves a very focused area can, with
minimal effort, offer the community a way to engage in collective
dialogue.'[14] His reasoning proved to be only partly right. In the
event specialist suppliers and national, even global providers, found
it just as easy to offer the service. On the web they could be simultaneously as local as the *Palo Alto Weekly* or as global as Yahoo!

The *Raleigh News & Observer* undertook a more ambitious
approach and spent half a million dollars on a comprehensive,
largely free online service called *Nando Land*. It included email,
games, local and educational reference material with the electronic
edition of the newspaper available to every public school and other
community organisations in North Carolina. In 1994 *Nando* also
offered unlimited access to Reuters and AP news services and was one
of the first news providers with online archives. Less successfully, the
paper also attempted to launch an expanded subscription edition.

In blinkered adherence to the formula of 'multiple revenue
streams' (subscription, advertising and transactions) news publishers
continued to attempt to sell titles by subscription over the web for

the next half decade. However, in an economy where consumers were rapidly gaining the expectation that most of the content, including their daily news, would be free, the strategy produced only dwindling traffic. Subscription was a business model which, outside of very specialised sectors such as share-tipping and commercial and financial information, including, successfully, both the *Financial Times* and the *Wall Street Journal*, was never sustainable for online publication. Even for the *Wall Street Journal* – by 1999 one of the few news providers on the web making a profit from online news – the venture hardly produced the expected bonanza. Of the 600,000 registered users who used the initially free interactive edition only 50,000 took up the offer for an annual subscription that was significantly cheaper than the print edition ($59 in 1999 and $29 for print subscribers). The Danish financial newspaper *Boersen* only offers (free) subscription to its online edition to subscribers to the print edition, many of whom take it up. The approach naturally attracts premium rates to advertising on the site. Another niche market that has been able to employ the subscription model with great success is political analysis. The *National Journal*'s online edition, *NJ Cloakroom*, charges $1,047 per annum to subscribers and attracts 600,000 page impressions per month (1999).

The initial failure to attract paying subscribers by Microsoft's online magazine *Slate* – in October 1998 the free section of the site attracted 400,000 readers against the 20,000 who subscribed – gave a clear indication to the online news industry that, for the majority of sectors, the subscription model had failed. What was needed was a range of mechanisms including subscription, which clearly succeeded in some niche markets, but which also allowed consumers to purchase specific content at affordable prices, perhaps a fraction of a penny for a single newspaper article, as well as advertising, e-commerce, sponsorships and affiliations and a culture which understood assets such as news and photography archives as value-bearing commodities.

The general repurposing of news and news images as archive appeared within two years of the first online news providers. Titles found that these (comparatively shallow) archives often drew as much traffic as the main site and, in some cases, they began to invest in the long process of placing historical archives – some of which pre-dated the web by a more than a century – online.

Since readily accessible news archives, the first drafts of history, draw readerships so effectively then clearly advertising space in this new medium might, at moments of peak traffic, carry premium rates. Much of the commentary on Judge Hervé Stéphan's September 1999 ruling on the causes of Princess Diana's death, for instance, carried links to the extensive reporting of the event itself in 1997. The web has also transformed photographs and other images into retail consumer items with companies such as Bill Gates' Corbis licensing images for non-commercial uses such as home pages or school projects at $3 per image while retaining the full market rate for commercial applications.

Until workable 'digital cash' systems appeared, allowing consumers to give their credit information to transactions clearing houses which would aggregate payments to suppliers and charges to consumers, the idea of 'micropayments' was not able to progress. Furthermore, when it did arrive, the whole notion of micropayments would have a radical impact on the way in which news providers and consumers understood content. A newspaper such as *The Times* might contain, on average, well over a hundred items not including advertisements. Subsidised by that advertising we routinely pay substantially under £1 for the whole package. Even at a micropayment of two pence per item the cost of the newspaper would more than double for readers but, of course, they will not want the whole paper. Even for free content online consumers are more discriminating than readers of print news and access only those parts of the online edition that most interest them, perhaps 10 per cent or so of the whole. For consumers to click the button enabling payment options they have to be sure that the item is of value to them. Free access to headlines, section indices, lists of content and leading paragraphs or abstracts might allow the effective negotiation of those reader decisions.

The *Wall Street Journal Interactive Edition* has also experimented with a daily 'pass' paid for through microtransaction. In 1999 this cost $1.95 to the print edition's 75 cents. As with other microtransaction models, any market in which the electronic edition costs more than twice as much as the print one seems to make a nonsense of the much touted 'benefits' of online news for consumers.

A more effective way of encouraging readers to extend their use of sites charging for individual features and articles might be to link or chain stories more coherently than print journalism does. They could be offered links to associated items as well as a range of presentations of the same story going into progressively more detail. Steve Outing makes the point that such a system also allows newspapers to sell information, often of high value, which is in excess of the capability or utility of print editions. The complete reports of local planning meetings or parliamentary debates, for instance, since they are unusually printed in full, are of consuming interest only to small sectors of readerships. Online news could easily make them available and at premium prices.[15]

Even with the advent of digital cash though, the problem for newspapers on the web was far from solved. In 1994 Bill Johnson was absolutely correct in his wish to protect his advertising, especially his classifieds. For many newspapers up to 50 per cent of advertising revenue comes from classified advertising. For those which have managed to make particular sectors of it their own, such as the UK Guardian's dominance of recruitment advertising for a whole range of industries in Britain, it is their lifeblood and must be protected above everything, even content. 'Panic ... has been the driving force. Simply put, newspapers are spending money to keep from losing their classified ad base.'[16]

The problem for newspapers is that classifieds sections are really only databases. It makes much more sense for a teacher who is looking for a new job to seek an appropriate recruitment site rather than her local or national newspaper. She can type in her subject and level and the database will tell her all the jobs currently available for secondary school maths teachers in her own region, the UK or Europe, and with a few more clicks the rest of the world as well. The same applies for second-hand cars, garden planning, antiquarian books, ponies, and day care for infants. The service is free and allows consumers to make the kind of comprehensive searches that would have been unthinkable with newsprint. Newspapers are losing a significant portion of their classifieds revenue. By 1999 large North American news providers were already buying back their classifieds business from web start-up companies. The classifieds provider AdOne Classified Network was purchased by a consortium including MediaNews Group, Hearst Corporation and E.W. Scripps.[17] Of course, the spectre of e-commerce places many traditional service and retail suppliers, from auction houses to booksellers and pharmacists, in the same position.

The DTI (Future Unit) 1998 report agrees that the press will be threatened by 'loss of advertising revenue, particularly for business to business advertising. This will be particularly acute for local and regional media'.[18] It goes on to stress the importance of the online press developing new models for their advertisers.

One of the initial problems with the web economy was that it was initially both unquantifiable and unqualifiable. Advertisers do not spend the large amounts of money that they do on faith; they require audited circulation or audience figures, detailed demographic information and, once they have tested the market, information on how particular constituencies are responding to their communications. Until the international audit organisations such as the Audit Bureau of Circulation, BPA International and Nielsen's in North America were able to agree standards, even a language (the difference between 'hits' and page impressions) for measuring web traffic, most advertisers were suspicious of the new medium for all its claims. Did audits include users employing browsers or software capable of removing advertisements? What about the many hits from robot programmes either testing links or collecting information?

That suspicion, coupled with the dawning realisation that advertisers were no longer competing for a finite resource as they had in print and traditional broadcast media, led to advertising rates online actually falling as the audiences grew exponentially in the 1990s. Banner ads, usually at the top of the screen, and often taking readers to the advertiser's own site, were charged at between £15 and £25 per thousand page impressions (CPM) in 1995 and by 1999 that had fallen to £2 or so, although they still comprised more than half of all advertising on the web.[19] The problem with them was that by 1998 rather less than 1 per cent of traffic clicked on them. Web users had rapidly become blind to them although their sheer ubiquity continued to allow them to perform well in brand awareness campaigns.

So poor was the performance of online advertising on media sites that many companies had ceased using it by 1999 and were using advertising in traditional media to draw customers to their websites. Other forms of online adverts now supplemented banners including pop-ups and extramercials which appear in their own windows on top of other content, and interstitials, which appear as browsers move from page to page, have been tried but they continue to employ the paradigms of old media advertising, print and TV. More inventive are ad-bots which monitor conversations in chat rooms and other interactive environments. They are programmed to intervene in private conversations when they come upon trigger words and phrases suggesting a potential recipient for their particular commercial message.

Some of the characteristics of the Internet – hyperlinks, the fact that it is a network, interactivity and the notion of telepresence – radically differentiate it from the traditional media upon which conventional models of advertising and marketing are based. It is, of course, quite possible that the 'natural' form of online advertising has simply not appeared yet and that the medium still stands where photography did in its first decade, trying to replicate its subjects as paintings.

Some of the determinants for these new forms can be extrapolated from the differences between online media and their precursors. Firstly, as I have already indicated, traditional media sell space to their advertisers on the basis of its scarcity. When readerships or audiences rise, media companies do not produce more pages or longer programmes to meet the rising demand for opportunities to reach that audience, instead they raise their prices. In contrast, on the web not only are there a potentially unlimited number of channels, but even the most successful of them can simply serve up more pages to meet the demands of their advertisers.

In this media landscape of plenty, online advertisers are able to target their markets much more specifically. The content of websites automatically filters their constituencies with a precision that heralds advertising's Promised Land. Information about individual consumers is gathered from their computers by files known as 'cookies' which are attached to every page, sometimes every file. In addition to the series of files that will comprise the web page, the server and client computers exchange other 'background' information using the innocuously named cookies. Most web users are unaware of this dialogue since their browsers are set to ignore the traffic, although cookies can easily be either made visible or even disabled.

With the main text file (sometimes one arrives with every single file and, as we have seen, a web page can comprise ten or fifteen separate files) a cookie will arrive to generate a small text file on the user's computer. The file will allow the information server to exchange and record information as the transaction progresses, sometimes for as long as the user is logged on and can even alert the server about future log-ons. It allows the server (the news provider or advertiser) to learn about the user. It might track every move through the site (or subsequent sites or visits) and compare that information to earlier visits. Potentially, it could even track the user to other sites. While cookies can be intrusive or pointless in most cases their activity is benign. For the user they can help the site to expedite the next visit and for advertisers, of course, they are the most powerful consumer feedback device so far developed.

Cookies, by now ubiquitous on news sites, allow managers to know exactly who is browsing their sites, how many times they visit it, which parts of the site, including ads, they are interested in, what other sites they visit and how long they spend there. Most browsers tend to spend much longer on news sites than they do on portals or aggregators but, of course, they tend to visit the latter more often. That detail of profiling allows advertisers to tailor websites individually to each visitor they receive, with visitors being offered a particular portfolio of ads based on past personal preferences. Broadcast ads might appeal to less than 1 per cent of their audiences, print ads perhaps marginally more, both media effectively wasting most of the advertiser's investment. Online advertising can maximise that investment in a way that makes the advertisers' wildest dreams come true. The reciprocal of that precision is that advertisers know exactly how successful their adverts are. The difference between browsers who visit a site and those who click on their banner gives a very precise gauge of performance, impossible in traditional media and invaluable to advertisers. As the cycle of consumption moves online advertisers know who clicks and who stays to buy. Informed by cookies their advertisements address individual viewers by name and arrive with insights into their most intimate desires.

The Free Content Revolution

For many consumers the key change dictated by news going online appeared to be that, quite suddenly and apparently by universal consent of the media industry, news, which had hitherto cost the average news reader upwards of £300 each year, became free. Perhaps they should not have been surprised by the development since information in cyberspace is effectively limitless and therefore cannot sustain the value of scarcer resources. One of the outcomes of this superabundance of information was that readers and audience became intimidated by the sheer scale of it. They came to believe that it could not be handled without the specialised filtering skills and technologies available only to the largest, and hence most credible, media corporations. The very idea of the 'information economy' seemed something of a paradox. Whatever the currency of the new economy was based upon it did not seem to be information.

Some managements saw free content as a temporary device to attract readers to the new medium but, once instituted, it proved very difficult to reverse. Proposals to begin charging for news sites generally saw precipitous drops in traffic resulting in advertisers seeking reduced rates and, anyway, media owners who charge for content are locking out consumers whom their advertisers will happily pay someone else for. In a bid to increase traffic some titles boost already free content with additional rewards systems for consumers. Regular users of sites are able to accumulate points which can be redeemed against retail goods and charged online services. Similarly, in 1999 there were ISPs offering shares to those who would sign up for their already free services. For news sites, of course, free content can also perform as a 'taster' encouraging subscription to a print edition that offers extra or more up-to-date content.

In some cases free content does seem to impact negatively on circulation for print titles. Henk Rijks cites the Dutch daily newspaper, *Het Parool*, which had traditionally and profitably published a weekly omnibus edition, mostly for overseas subscription, comprising special reports and abstracts. The target audiences were largely Dutch expatriates and embassy staff. When in 1996 the company instituted a daily web edition many of the subscribers to the omnibus edition failed to renew. Perhaps unsurprisingly the log files of the website showed that more that 50 per cent of visitors were from outside Holland.[20]

Whilst specialised databases such as *NEXIS* can still cost up to $200 an hour to access, most information on the web is free to all intents and purposes. The move to free content loses something of its radical appearance when placed in context. The medium is only free to those who have already been able to purchase a computer and modem (or set-top device) with an ISP or cable subscription. Accordingly, the Internet acts as an excellent filter to remove the poor from an important public arena. The provision of free news is a small price for advertisers to pay for the ability to segment society so readily into the haves, who, by virtue of the fact that they are browsing the web have already proved that they can afford to purchase the glossier products of late capitalism which feature in the web's adverts, and the have-nots, who can only consume vicariously and so are much more easily catered for by television.

The concentration of global media ownership combines with that crude economic determinism to encourage a bifurcation of both editorial and advertising content into popular (broadcast) audiences and other higher socio-economic (webcast, including video and audio streaming) constituencies. While popular entertainment and news is fragmented into a myriad of increasingly expensive pay-per-view channels the web continues to offer its wares gratis.

> Today's Internet has a flat-rate billing. Or maybe it's no billing. Its designers never figured on charging for service, so packets sent across town or across the ocean are all charged the same – nothing … users aren't paying for the infrastructure – it's heavily subsidized.[21]

As the following sections suggest, that subsidy is drawn from the larger political economy. In the age of consumption there are no free lunches. Consumers pay a high price, in a range of currencies including the aggravated fragmentation of their society into information haves and have-nots, for what appears to be free.

Church and State

With the perceived collapse of the value of online advertising on news sites (as I have indicated, largely arising from a misconception) their managers, driven by owners' pressure to profit, sought other ways of parting advertisers from their money. While banners remain the predominant, albeit heavily discounted, model of web advertising, news providers also sold sponsorship, advertorials, interstitials, traditional displays (which are merely print adverts scanned for the web), the hosting of local e-malls and email newsletters. In an economy where dependency on advertising was total, the advertising was actually dwindling or returning to traditional media and in their rush to secure not profitability but continued existence, the wall between editorial and news (traditionally comprehended by newspeople as the church) and sold advertising content (the state) began to crumble. Where advertising was the sole source of income for news sites it was perhaps not unreasonable that they should wish to weight the relationship in favour of commercial sustainability.

Where there is any doubt about the source of material, as in the case of so-called advertorials, it should, in the light of traditional journalistic ethics, be clearly marked; yet in 1998/99 the web saw a wave of 'stealth' sites containing marketing material, often technical and consumer reports of electronic equipment, masquerading as news and editorial. Even where the problem was not so pronounced news sites were looking increasingly like billboards.

The problem is compounded by the fact that in traditional media, with its recognised conventions and forms, readers readily differentiate between editorial and advertising content, to the extent that they even know where particular advertisments are likely to appear in papers and what space is likely to be news. On the web, as producers continue to experiment with form, new graphical forms and emerging multimedia technologies, such discrimination is more difficult. Adverts can pop up anywhere on the screen, even, as we have seen, between screens. Links can deliver readers to sources and other news materials, or, with no warning that the church walls have been breached, to advertisers. *Caveat emptor* must be the rule, labels such as 'Infosite' and heavy and repeated suggestions within the text notwithstanding. Frequently, the reader must scroll right to the base to find the name of the advertiser who has sponsored and perhaps even produced the page. Where such promotional material has been designed to imitate its host medium it becomes very easy for readers to stray from one domain to the other without realising that they have crossed a boundary. The boundary is further blurred by the tendency of some news providers to sell advertising on a performance basis. Where a proportion of advertisers' sales accrue to the news provider they have arguably forsaken their core business and their ethics for the retail trade.

It took the press in Europe and North America nearly half a century to persuade readers, in some – Bagdikian and others would say most – cases spuriously, that they were not influenced by advertising money. The blurring of church and state on the web took less than half a decade to endanger that hard-earned credibility. The problem is partly a function of the bubble-like economy of the web itself. The Internet Advertising Bureau and PricewaterhouseCoopers' report of 1998 suggested that US online advertising that year was growing at a giddy rate and would top $2 billion. Clearly, the gold rush had begun since 53 per cent of that income came from the already discredited banner advert. The impact of such figures on the venture capitalists who had funded web start-ups, including news providers, led many of them to insist, says Lewis Perdue, on a 'return on investment for every page. If that page doesn't generate enough income, you don't continue writing'. He worries that 'if performance-based advertising becomes the norm, the web will become a gigantic infomercial',[22] which is exactly what much of the licensed press was before the advent of the journalistic ethics system designed to forge a trust between the press and its readers and an integrity that would retain them.

While old-media news brands, the *Guardian* or the BBC, tended to apply the same ethics system that they employ in the print or broadcast media to the web, many of the start-ups such as the portals and aggregators which were built around the successful search engines and the media conglomerates' 'super-sites' of the web's first decade had no such tradition. Many search engines do not even see themselves as being in the business of news and blithely charge to place advertisers' services and products at the top of the lists of recommendations with which they respond to web users' requests. Such practices, which exclude those alternative voices already marginalised by traditional media, clearly ride roughshod over any notion of disclosure. But even when disclosure is made – as is usual in the case of sponsorships (which make no claims upon the content with which they are associated) and advertorials (which do) – unless it is made clearly and the delineation between editorial and advertising clearly marked, audiences will raise questions about influence and integrity. On the other hand it is those very practices which create new opportunities on the open market of the web. At the beginning of 1999 I found myself increasingly irritated by certain assumptions from the search engines I had depended on for some years, including those employed in the researching of this book. Seeking search results that were determined by my criteria rather than by the advertising industry I experimented with new ones and rapidly moved my allegiances to *Google* and *AlltheWeb* which I have used ever since.

The news media's understanding of itself as church and state is predicated on a belief that, even when it is owned by corporations whose products it advertises, it can retain an autonomy, a defendable integrity. While things were not so clear-cut when the analogy first arose at least it served as a healthy aspiration. It is an understanding less easily defended in the cluttered and over-packed media of the twenty-first century. Organisations such as the American Society of Magazine Editors, aware of the erosion of trust, institute standards aimed at separating church and state. Their code includes:

1. The home page of a publication's website (or other electronic venue) shall identify the publication by displaying its name and logo prominently in order to make clear who controls the content of the site.
2. On all online pages, there shall be a clear distinction made – through words, design, placement, or any other effective method – between editorial and advertising content.

It does not take long to find breaches of these and all their other principles of conduct on the web at present.

The Media Oligopoly

In 1983 the American journalist and academic Ben Bagdikian published *The Media Monopoly* in which he expressed the concern that, as a result of the repeated rounds of media deregulation sponsored by America's corporatist conservatives and legislated by administrations increasingly cowed by the political power of those who controlled the flows of information to their constituencies, media ownership would fall into fewer and fewer hands. He traced 46 corporations which controlled the mass media in the USA in 1981. By 1992 that group had shrunk to 23 and in the most recent edition of *The Media Monopoly* (1997) Bagdikian cites Christopher Shaw, a Wall Street media arbitrageur, as suggesting that by the early years of the twenty-first century all North American media would be in the hands of six corporations.[23] The situation is echoed in Europe. Bagdikian also makes explicit the fact that those same companies hold the reins of a whole range of media sectors. The logic of such vertical integration was tested to destruction in Italy during the prime ministership of Silvio Berlusconi when advertisers who wished to buy time or space on a FinnInvest vehicle often had to use a Berlusconi advertising company and make their purchase through a Berlusconi media-broking house.

Bagdikian suggests that, while it does not prevent the media from responding to superficial cultural changes this concentration of ownership has a stultifying effect on society. Conflicts of interest between church and state have existed since the *Corantos* but, with the consolidation of ownership in an information economy they become critical, posing serious threats to the public interest. Big media's interventions are designed to protect the interests of its owners and its advertisers from both competition and adverse legislation.

> The news media are not monolithic. They are not frozen in a permanent set of standards. But they suffer from built-in biases that protect corporate power and consequently weaken the public's ability to understand forces that create the American scene ... This institutional bias does more than merely protect the corporate system. It robs the public of a chance to understand the real world.[24]

The news media oligopoly is, of course, global in reach and while, since Bagdikian was writing, it has had to contend with the upstarts of the web, AOL, Excite, Yahoo! and Microsoft itself, it has accommodated them easily, not disturbing the trend towards corporate gigantism in the slightest. It either devours them in a seemingly endless stream of takeovers, replicates them, as Disney has done, on the models of portal sites such as Yahoo!, with *Go*, or entered into partnership with them, as NBC has done with Microsoft, the *New York Times* with *Compuserve* and *News Corp* with Yahoo! The main incentives for this consolidation are profitability – and as we have seen the web holds the grail of the total market, capable of extracting maximum profits – influence and the eradication of true (and necessarily expensive) competition. While media moguls and stock markets justify the consolidation of the industry with words such as 'synergy' it can also be understood through the notion of 'vertical integration', a system which encourages the ownership of the means of production, promotion and distribution under one roof.

Such an understanding is rather contradicted by the Future Unit view that online distribution drives 'industry structures away from conventional vertical integration to more complex structures based on the ability to contract out many elements at reduced cost'.[25] While such a move might well have implications for the creation of media content the report offers no clear reason why it should impact on ownership. Clearly, a range of problems arises in terms of fair competition and quality when a media provider owns both the content and the means of distribution, as is the case with cable television operators in many countries. As the web increasingly becomes available over cable, accessing the last, and largest, portion of the mass market that is so far untouched and turning the web into a truly popular form, ownership of distribution becomes a problematic issue. In most countries ownership of bandwidth, or channels such as telephony, is vested either in the state itself or in communications companies carefully hedged about with regulation. The 'common carrier' offers, or should offer, full and equal access to individuals and organisations wishing to sell content. It was the existence of the convention of the common carrier which enabled the growth of the Internet beyond its military roots.

The combination of control of information and political and economic influence on a global scale seems to leave little choice available to all those who are affected by the actions of the oligopoly and their associates, particularly consumers but also competition, employees and the general public. An example of the way in which media companies weight the news agenda can be seen in NBC's lack of interest in reporting the nuclear industry after the 1980s, when it was purchased by nuclear plant contractor General Electric[26] and *MSNBC*'s apparent obsession with healthcare in the late 1990s as its owners circled that lucrative market.

While the web did seem to arrive at the right moment to stall at least the stranglehold of the global media oligopoly it is easy to over-estimate its democratising effect. I have described how for those who used it and its supporting networks it was possible to 'read' a very different Kosovo War than the one reported on the traditional media. That is true, but even on the web, there are many consumers who do not stray from the portal sites that claim to give them all the news and information they need. A reader taking his or her account of the war from *BBC News Online, newsUnlimited* or *MSNBC* (and chose not to click to their external links) would not be very differently informed from viewers of TV news or readers of the *Telegraph* or *The Times*.

Increasingly that consumer inertia is contractually formalised and only parts of the web are available as providers such as ISPs and cable TV companies filter its content to their subscribers. It is too easy, and quite legal in most countries, for a local newspaper whose online content is distributed to a large part of its readership over cable to have part of its content, perhaps its classified ads, filtered out. The cable operator might reasonably see that advertising as a useful addition to its own portfolio. It is just as possible for the cable operator, unregulated as a common carrier, to refuse to carry the paper at all. The strategy of limiting or filtering content is claimed to make the Internet more user-friendly for many users, but it also deprives them of the medium's eclectic heterogeneity, including much of its less corporate material, and incorporates the web firmly into the dominant economy of big business.

The Privatisation of the Internet

Popular notions of the ontology of the Internet are based on a fundamental misconception ...

> ... that the Internet is merely 'virtual', when in fact there is a physical aspect of the Internet which is often ignored. The foundation of the Internet is very much physical, a core system of switched data lines that comprise the 'backbone' of the Net. This tangible property is increasingly in the hands of large media monopolies, a fact that threatens the very democratic life of the system.[27]

I have alluded to threats to the hardware of the system in time of war but it is clear that that highly vulnerable entity, the common carrier, crucial to the web's very existence, is also at risk of depredation in the normal course of business. At the time of writing there is little governmental willingness and only fragments of legislation in the USA and Europe which could be used against a concerted attempt by the oligopoly to appropriate that backbone completely. As that process is completed the web's use and development will be entirely determined by the logic and the demands of capitalism.

Heather Menzies has described how communications technologies tend to accelerate the 'transfer of assets [including the technologies themselves] from the public sector to the private and the consolidation of power into the hands of larger corporate units'.[28] The privatisation of the nodes and networks, which were originally paid for by the US government with massive investments from other public sources such as American and European academic research funding, was instrumental in changing the culture of the web from public information arena to cyber-mall. As many commentators have emphasised, 'The Internet was a brilliant technical achievement that never would have happened in the free enterprise marketplace.'[29] Its privatisation began in earnest with AOL's purchase in 1994 of 12,000 miles of leased fiber-optic circuits and other assets from MCI, one of the corporations charged by the Bush administration with overseeing the transfer of the Internet from public to private hands.[30] By 1995 all US data lines were in the ownership of the private sector. Among the implications of this shift was the fact that, as early as 1996, it was impossible for all but the very well-heeled to break into the American (by far the largest) Internet provider market. This was presented as part of the normal maturation of an emerging industry. 'What appeared to be an ideal form of democratic participation and communication has now become a very sophisticated method of reaching a geographically dispersed, high income consumer market.'[31]

Where news is the content of any communication which itself carries and implicitly mediates advertisers' messages, it cannot be seen to contradict them too openly. Where it attempts to do so a censoring mechanism, geared to policing and correcting the content and distribution of information, is rapidly activated to bring content back 'on message'. The meta-message of news providers across all media including the web articulates the benign influence of the global corporations and the integrity of their projects, friends and products. The IGC/Peacenet annual 'Project Censored'[32] programme identifies the stories that fail to make the headlines. In 1998 they included stories such as the genetic sterilising of the seed produced by GM crops with the so-called 'Terminator' gene, chemical companies which trade simultaneously in cancer treatments and known carcinogens, the development and actions of corporate paramilitary forces to protect First World investments in the Third World and the failure to implement planning restrictions on housing developments built on flood plains and areas below sea level in Europe and North America in an era of global warming and rising sea levels.

In an economy of interlocking boards of management and cross-holdings of large blocks of shares between media companies and other industrial sectors such stories are unlikely to be aired by brand-name news providers. There is the example of the documentary on lung cancer and tobacco interests which was shelved by an American network, whose board of directors included representation of the tobacco industry. The propensity of Internet users to bypass such controls and disseminate information unhelpful to the oligopoly, while it will probably not be entirely lost, will be curtailed by restricting interactive forms and coralling more and more users into heavily filtered areas of the web. AOL, for instance, responded to the US Telecommunications Reform Bill (with its Internet censorship amendment) by radically curtailing its customers' use of the Usenet. 'Corporate media conglomerates are working very hard to ensure that the National Information Infrastructure is built as a system of consumerism and commodification, not a system of grassroots, two-way communications.'[33] Such trends seem to discount any pluralist analysis of the impacts of web ownership.

Graham Murdoch's view of such an approach suggests that as media corporations reach a critical mass their control moves from the owners to a management elite.[34] The problematic, in which day-to-day management separates from ownership is described by economists as the 'agency problem'. The global dispersal of stock ownership means that it is very difficult for owners to retain even a strategic view of agency or actions, allowing for the production on television of such shows as *South Park* and *The Mark Thomas Comedy Product* or the journalism of John Pilger and Jim Hightower, which, while they are commercially successful, soapbox the scandals of capitalism and effectively critique its values. There is, of course, no reason to believe that the management should perceive the interests of the company differently from the owners, or protect them any less vigorously. 'Moles' such as Mark Thomas or Michael Moore, operating from inside the media corporations can equally be seen as evidence of an overweaning confidence and a desire to take profit from the very limits of their constituency rather than any vulnerability. As importantly, Murdoch suggests that 'control is not a quantity [the largest shareholding] but a social relation',[35] the ability of shareholders to work in concert across a range of companies to dictate a whole industrial sector.

Again, some strands of cultural studies and media analysis propose a model which stresses the autonomy of the consumer. Drawing on a range of feedback devices it places the determining agency of what is programmed and how in the hands of media consumers. Corporate decision-making is determined solely on the strength of a classical understanding of the market economy. Both models seem inadequate in the face of the oligopoly and an economy based on advertising, not least since audiences only see content that has been 'pre-filtered' by a media hierarchy that knows what its advertisers expect. The 1999 scandal of genetically modified crops was constructed around the wilder claims of environmentalists. Neither the economic argument – that the owners of the new products were using them to turn global agriculture into a closed market – nor the consumerist arguments around choice were examined in most news coverage. Outright censorship is unnecessary in traditional media where hegemonic control works as well and where producers, at the editorial and newsroom level, have learnt to police themselves.

On the web, regular panics around issues such as pornography, universal failure of copyright and political extremisms are rapidly producing a similar hegemony and can be understood as part of the machinery that is driving it into private hands. Hegemonic control of online media is increasingly reinforced by the state. The DTI Future Unit report looks towards the state to 'pioneer regulation for the new digital knowledge-driven economy, to provide the vital positive framework of institutional support for business'.[36] The market and Big Media are likely to be further advantaged as Internet 2 is developed in association with business and we see the emergence of what Eric Meyer has called the 'new, new media' which will once more lock independent and small producers out of the means of media distribution. The cable television industry in North America, with its eyes fixed on interactive systems capable of delivering video, audio and text, is developing very high-speed, high bandwidth systems that will run in parallel with the Net. Such systems, by no means common carriers, will exclude most of the web's content, including those independents originally attracted by the low costs of publishing online.

> With telecommunications becoming a 'product' controlled by private enterprise on a global scale, there is little doubt that a huge segment of the world's population will be denied the benefits of high-speed telecommunications. The technology will go where the money is to be made. Bill Gates and his fellow 'visionaries' are not altruistic humanitarians. They are capitalists with a vision of ever greater profits, and unfortunately this appears to be the vision that will guide the information highway.[37]

Nicholas Baran's assessment is probably too bleak but it is certain that any vision of the Internet as a force for democracy and the real-isation of the 'global village' needs to be radically reassessed with the privatisation of the web.

Electronic Capitalism

> Beneath the rhetoric of the 'information' society, and the cowboy frontierism ('frictionless capitalism' and such) of Internet enthu-siasts, the ideology of monopoly capitalism is being consolidated (and hegemonized) in forms that are all the more total and total-izing for being invisible and ubiquitous.[38]

In 1996 the US Secretary of Labor, Robert Reich, employed the phrase 'electronic capitalism' in a *New York Times* piece to describe an economy in which capital is unconstrained and completely mobile – it can be moved anywhere around the globe instantly.[39] At the same time workforces, increasingly comprising two-wage-earner families, are increasingly tied to particular locations by property, social links and obsolescent skills. For its workers electronic capi-talism is very different from the mass production economies of the recent past. Reich makes it clear that 'electronic capitalism ... enables the most successful to secede from the rest of society' that the moral link of capital to the community has been severed.

> The word 'community' right now is very appealing ... connotes very appealing images. But in reality, very few people live in socioeconomically diverse townships. In fact, we are, as a nation, segregated by income to a much larger extent than ever before. Zip Code marketing has become the rage because marketers know that where we live has a lot to do with what we can afford to buy. And remember that the local tax is still the major revenue source for schools, libraries, infrastructure, and many social services. It's not surprising, therefore, that we're seeing a wider and wider divergence between the public services available to those living in very wealthy suburbs and exurbs and people who are in working-class and poor towns.[40]

The process that Reich describes is accelerated by electronic capitalism, in which the information sectors, including media and news providers, are not constrained by national borders. The financial news sector, and to a lesser extent what was traditionally considered as the broadsheet press, is geared to a global readership, but hardly a contemporary mass readership. More importantly, it is a readership that can be readily understood as a community, one for which a shared media provide common social and institutional understandings weaving identity for their subjects as nation states and regions have done in the past. Such an understanding of media foregrounds the work of journalism especially in its roles of gatekeeping and agenda-setting.

Reich's conclusions impact heavily on those industries at the breaking edge of the information economy – the media providers. The rapidity with which electronic capitalism grinds though its business cycles constantly puts the brands at risk. Just as in other markets, news media face an economy of lowered costs and global audiences in which opportunities can be identified, exploited and dissolved in weeks or months rather than decades. Thus the large-scale media spectacles such as the Olympics will see opportunist news sites spring up to capitalise upon them and move on. Similarly we have already noted the traffic that is drawn to the online media local to natural disasters and events such as the Littleton killings. Increasingly local brands are technologically ready to capitalise on events in their patch. For those who are not so prepared there is always someone who is. In the words of the report of the Chatham House Forum, 'Unsettled Times' (1996), 'Markets become even more prone to amplifying success and failure.'[41] It is not only workforces who are penalised but also those media providers who fall behind the defining markets and technologies.

It is not only capital that is unfettered in late capitalism. All the factors driving the economy are accelerated, which raises the possibility that the life cycles of the technologies that enable them might be foreshortened accordingly. While print was the dominant media form for five or six hundred years and the telegraph continued to be profitable for a century or so perhaps television will not make its century and the web will take Microsoft with it after only a few decades.

Conclusion

This analysis offers a model of the news industry that is completely embedded in and determined by a market system that is profit-orientated and funded by advertising. While it offers a less constrained understanding of the media than Chomsky and Herman's 'propaganda model'[42] it does suggest that many of the possibilities offered by the technology, and indeed tested by the online news media, may be inexorably foreclosed upon. The determinants of news, across the range of media and technologies, remain largely ideological and geared to serving elite, corporate ends.

The early years of the web saw an open online news media because the oligopoly only realised the full implications of the new technology around the mid-decade. It was not until 1994 that Bill Gates recognised the 'sea change' that was about to sweep global media and trail computing with it. Traditional media executives were several years behind him. The interregnum provided the opportunity for more autonomous media forms such as news lists and bulletin boards to establish themselves on the Internet and migrate to the new web, with an ethos that was distinctly non-corporate. When News Corp, the BBC, *MSNBC et al.* arrived they were able to usefully appropriate some of that existing infrastucture, and even use it to rethink existing practice (around free content, for instance). Other elements, the notion of cheap or even free and universal access, for example, may ultimately prove rather more problematic for them.

> Some argue that the Internet and the new communication tech-
> nologies are breaking the corporate stranglehold on journalism
> and opening an unprecedented era of interactive democratic
> media. There is no evidence to support this view as regards jour-
> nalism and mass communication. In fact, one could argue that
> the new technologies are exacerbating the problem. They permit
> media firms to shrink staff while achieving greater outputs and
> they make possible global distribution systems, thus reducing the
> number of media entities.[43]

And rethink those entities. The traditional newspaper is an information carrier derived from print technology and cohering around a
particular revenue model which brings together several disparate
businesses: news dissemination, weather reports, display ads, stock-
market reports, classified ads, listings, entertainment, etc. With the
obsolescence of its defining print and broadcast technologies there is
not necessarily anything remaining to hold the package together. Its
rationale disappears and specialist publishers will rapidly appropriate
the various parts of the business to repackage them as discrete
products and deliver them more effectively and, as we have seen,
more cheaply.

7
'That Balance' and the New World Information Order

Anytime an individual or an institution or an invention leaps so far head of that balance (contemplated by the Founders) and throws a system, whatever it might be – political, economic, technological – out of balance, you've got a problem, because then it can lead to the manipulation of information, it can lead to all kinds of bad outcomes which we have seen historically. So we're going to have to deal with that.[1]

Hillary Clinton's reservations about the web on Matt Drudge's revelations about her husband and Monica Lewinsky were shared by many. A similar call came from Chris Smith, then Labour's heritage spokesman in the UK: 'Current laws were framed in the age of print. We need a new framework of rules for the age of electronic communication.'[2] Public opinion on issues such as privacy and free speech tends to swing violently depending on how it is inflected and is, in any case, riven with contradiction. Most Westerners, for instance, after Voltaire, jump to a visceral defence of free speech, until that freedom triggers some cultural limit such as paedophilia, euthanasia or abortion. It is by no means only totalitarian or fundamentalist states which continue to regard the Internet with the deepest suspicion. Access for the subjects of many states, even to email, is deeply hedged about with legislation and surveillance and for many censorship remains a 'twin-headed, fire-breathing dragon that burns high-speed data connections just as readily as banned books tossed into a bonfire', as Jeffrey Perlman evokes it. 'One head is focused on regulating access. Another draws a bead on content.'[3] For the political and religious dissidents of many countries, any resort to the web as a means of carrying on debate within their own country or taking the struggle abroad, has to be undertaken through third parties.

In some countries access to the web is so scarce and so expensive that even that resort is barely worth the risk. In Iraq and North Korea the infrastructure that would enable access to the web is, for most of the population, effectively illegal. In Burma access is against the law and violation can be a capital offence. Even in the USA many news sites are blocked by public access providers such as libraries and colleges panicked by the terms of the Communications Decency Act (CDA) which was enacted as part of the Telecommunications Act 1996. The so-called Exon amendment of the CDA (sponsored by Senator Jim Exon of Nebraska) sought to make the use of any computer network which displays 'indecent' material criminal unless the provider imposes an 'effective' restriction upon that material for consumers under the age of 18. While the act was found unconstitutional by the US Supreme Court in 1997 the following years saw a series of similar acts proposed both at state (where many such, largely unenforceable, acts passed into law) and national level. The acts are viewed as a model by governments around the world. They are generally worded in such a way that information about AIDS and indeed most gender issues tend to fall foul of them. Most responsible news organisations are, accordingly, liable under them as well.

The 1998 New Mexico catch-all bill banning 'any information' that could harm children is a case in point. The Child Online Protection Act, October 1998, attempting to block material 'harmful to minors', replacing the term 'indecent' in the 1996 act, had enforcement blocked four months after it was passed by a District Court judge in Philadelphia.[4] Of course, pornography is not the only target of this flood of legislation. It also seeks to outlaw hate speech and, as addressed by Hillary Clinton, libel. Equally obviously, much of the targeted material is already subject to legislation which protects victims whether it occurs on the web or elsewhere. In the UK in addition to the Obscene Publications Act 1959 which bans any publication with a tendency to 'deprave or corrupt', the Post Office Act 1953 renders it a crime to post anything 'indecent or obscene'. The same test, thanks to the Telecomms Act, applies to traffic on other public carriers such as phone lines, including all ISP traffic. In the USA the Post Office Act of 1865, after a similar panic to the abuse of the mail, criminalised sending 'obscenity' through the mail. Most other signatory states of the Universal Postal Union have similar laws, many of which already embrace telecommunications of all sorts and hence are applicable to the web. The panic about pornography on the Internet is clearly not about gaps in legislation.

Publications such as the pro-life 'Nuremburg Files' website, while they certainly exist in print and pre-dated the web, were never disseminated beyond very limited constituencies. On the web the list of names, addresses, images and other personal information about those who work in America's abortion clinics was eventually shut down as incitement to murder. The names of doctors killed by anti-abortion activists were routinely crossed out on the site and those who had been wounded greyed.[5] In a 1997 report the Simon Wiesenthal Center indicated that there had been a 300 per cent increase in websites (to over 600) run by white supremacists and anti-Semites since 1996. By March 1999 the number had risen to 1,400. In Britain there were about 20 white supremacist sites owned by groups such as Combat 18 and Blood and Honour which offered hard-core fascist material. The Center called for legislation to control the Internet but, again, they might have more profitably sought to control publication of hate sites with existing legislation which in many countries is quite adequate to the task. The UK Internet Watch Foundation's chairman, Roger Darlington, points out that in Britain at least, such material is often criminally racist and is specifically outlawed under the 1986 Public Order Act which 'makes it an offence to publish material designed or likely to stir up racial hatred'.[6] Perhaps the panic is as much about a misinformed fear of new technology or an entrenched traditional media defending its markets as it is about extreme content. On the other hand Brian Loader has pointed out that the claims of the libertarian netizens, in refusing to recognise the context in which the Internet was developed, are equally unfounded.

A ... weakness of the cyber-libertarian formulation of cyberspace is the notion that it comprises a virtual reality which is somehow alternative and unrelated to the 'real' world. Yet such an understanding is surely to ignore the fact that the very technologies enabling 'virtuality' have been developed for military, educational, public and increasingly commercial use.[7]

The point is well made and can be extended. In restructuring the ways in which we store and use information, including journalistic forms, the Internet cuts across and forces slippages in the hierarchies and divisions of the social. Society's complex of public, private and intermediate or mixed domains, including markets and the apparatuses of ideology, are thrown into new relationships. The principles embedded in regulation and governance which define those relationships may have to be rethought.

Gatekeepers in the Machine

In North America, and increasingly elsewhere, many libraries and colleges now offer access to the Internet that is restricted by filtering software. Products such as SurfWatch, Cyber Patrol, Net Nanny and CyberSitter make no claims about the law. Their primary markets are parents and public institutions serving children and young people such as schools and libraries panicked by stories of the excesses of the Internet. By targeting particular key words or proportions of the screen mapped to a restricted range of flesh tones, they inevitably block innocent sites as well, including news and education sites. The Utah Education Network's filtering software, for instance, prevented students from accessing both the bible and the US Constitution.[8] Most filtering systems also use regular scanning by employees as well as software scanners and are moderated by Oversight Committees of interested groups such as teachers, clergy, the Anti-Defamation League and the Gay and Lesbian Alliance Against Defamation. However, with more than 800 million pages of content to monitor (February 1999)[9] that hardly seems a viable method of evaluating the web. One of the sites blocked by Cyber Patrol is Deja News, the Internet's major archive of messages posted to Usenet's discussion groups. There are more than 50,000 such groups; some 168 of them are concerned with sexual matters and a few others promote hate politics. Others, however, are focused around archeology, parenting, gardening, health, the exiled politics of police states; in fact every subject that humans are interested in. While graphics and photographs are unavailable since Deja News only archives text it is still the depository of a considerable amount of material of encyclopaedic range.

We have more than 300 gigabytes of data, representing 250 million messages dating back to March 1995. Over 4 million people access our site, viewing over 90 million page views each month.[10]

Cyber Patrol blocks all of this. Other large archives of general content, more than a million pages at *members.tripod.com*, are also regularly blocked by filtering software in its efforts to prevent access to material that might be limited to one or two pages. For public libraries to use such a blunt instrument to block access to information resources of such magnitude might seem perverse but it is no more so than those churchmen who wanted to curb the perceived excesses of printing during the late medieval period or those who wanted to abandon the general postal service in Victorian Britain because it was being used to disseminate pornographic material. That problem was resolved, as we have seen, with a series of Post Office Acts in many countries, which targeted abusers of the postal system rather than the technologies that enabled it. When the moral panic around pornography and the web has died most countries which do not already have it will enact similar legislation to deal with the present problem. In the UK a relatively minor amendment to the Obscene Publications Acts of 1959 and 1964 in 1994 brought the Act up to date with electronic storage and transmission of information.

Censorware, for now, is little more than a spurious sop to a media induced panic. The software cannot possibly meet its claims without blocking large amounts of quite innocent material, including most news sites. Some filtering software offers a more sinister facility in the audit trail function, allowing installers to check the sites and newsgroups that users have attempted to access. While most browsers offer similar trails, albeit of more limited duration, as a matter of course, they are not necessarily apparent to casual users. The potential for tension and isolation in both the workplace and the home that such information offers seems to mitigate against its employment. PlanetWeb, the web browser packed with the Sega Saturn game console offers the option of actively blocking information on alternative lifestyles which may well signal a more general development in the design of browsers as the web becomes a genuine mass medium.

While the inherent flaws in censorware will not prevent them from finding customers regulatory legislation is a more difficult proposition. The huge amounts of small bits of information that comprise a network at any moment make it impossible for ISPs or sysops (system operators) to police messages in the way that a print publisher or broadcaster does. If the legal role of publisher devolves to individual users does that entirely remove any responsibilities about content from ISPs? For the purposes of defamation or obscenity the traditional conception of publishers' liability needs to be completely rethought.

Filtering software promises a more insidious attraction. Like the *Daily Me* and other pull-media, it can offer news consumers worlds in which information about terrorism, disasters and hatreds is simply screened out. All news can now be good news, or sports news, or entertainment news. It could be argued that such partial constructions of the world are hardly exceptional. Prior to the mass media the informed individual belonged to a small elite which excluded large elements of the population, often including women and the poor. The world views of the information-unenfranchised, however, while they were collapsed to the village or even the household, were not usually distorted by such a systematic erasure of whole topics. The fragmentation of mass-media forms, already advanced by the mid-twentieth century, enabled consumers to become more specific about their media consumption; newspapers were designed to allow them to discard easily the sections that they were not interested in, radio addressed quite specific interests, but it was still difficult to avoid the news completely. Cable television and the deregulation of radio encouraged a further diminution of that public space but it was with the arrival of the web, which allowed consumers to select all their media to be delivered in one package, that they had the power to switch off everything that they did not want to know about.

In his book *Data Smog* David Shenk sees the trend as entirely contradicting any notion of global consciousness and the web as leading instead to a parochialism which while it is as efficient as a library cataloguing system, since it cannot offer the serendipity that such systems offer their users as they wander the stacks, is radically divisive. Shenk's 'nichification' leads to increasingly narrower domains, walled and gated global villages populated entirely by Marxists or Republicans, pagans or stamp collectors. Perhaps these polities are more like medieval city states than villages. As personalised news services and filtering software such as Cyber Patrol become more effective, as they must, the world view of web users risks becoming ever smaller. As the flow of information increases to become overload, consumers are forced to filter and the information they most readily filter is that which produces dissonance or which threatens their construction of the world. Increasingly, we will seek to reinforce our opinions and prejudices about the world and blot out everything with which we might disagree.

Portals and service providers are also able to gain an editorial hold on consumers by offering unique, often sanitised views of the world. Companies such as Yahoo!, Freeserve and AOL, by providing an interface for information from other providers, also control access to that information. The larger ISPs package their own news as well as pages of information on cities and communities, weather, retail and entertainment – the information that people plan their lives around. Providers such as *Ukplus.co.uk* make this intermediate status their main selling proposition and guarantee users a medium that gives 'all the fun of the Internet without too many unpleasant surprises along the way'. While it is reasonable enough to wish to protect oneself and family from hate and pornography, the protection becomes insulation when unpleasant news is also filtered.

Through cookies and other feedback, portal providers know their customers intimately. They control the first layer of links into the outside world and, increasingly, many consumers never click beyond that first layer. For those consumers the ISPs, or their editors, have taken over the role of gatekeeper once occupied by the news editors of our print and broadcast media. They are able to shape their customers' worlds by foregrounding certain sites, censoring others and adding a portfolio of pop-up information and advertisements very specifically tailored to individual consumers' tastes. Totalitarian states have always aspired to similar control.

Censorship

Since September 1996 China's main commercial network, providing access for more than 80 per cent of users through state-run ISPs, has blocked access to websites offering information in a number of categories. These include dissident sites hosted abroad, especially those focused on the Tibet and Xinjiang independence movements and news sites from Taiwan (considered by Beijing to be a rebel province), many Western English-language sites including the *Wall Street Journal, CNN Interactive* and *BBC News Online* including, more specifically, anti-Beijing China-watching publications, and some sexually explicit sites such as *Playboy* and *Penthouse*. The official explanation for the clampdown, reported by Kathy Chen in the *Wall Street Journal,* was the rise in 'spiritual pollution' carried by the web but it was implemented in the context of a general tightening of controls on information entering the country.[11]

China's sensitivity with regard to networked communications is perhaps to be expected. In 1989, when the government confronted and killed students in Tiananmen Square one of the main conduits of information about events in Beijing to the outside world, along with fax and telephone, was the Usenet. It carried reports, appeals for help and announcements about meetings and visits by activists to other countries. The government responded to this activity by cutting telephone links and monitoring bulletin boards and computer conferences on the Usenet. Western news providers such as *BBC News Online* and CNN were also blocked. China felt threatened by the web on several fronts. On the one hand, Madeleine Albright, the US Secretary of State, has stated her opinion on many occasions that the Internet will 'open up' China to new ideas and on the other, oppositional groups such as the Falun Gong sect and the Democracy Movement have used it since 1989 to help mobilise against the government.

In January 2000, the government imposed further controls on its 9 or 10 million web users, then mostly located in or around Beijing. The Communist Party newspaper initiated the clampdown with the statement that 'all organisations and individuals are forbidden from releasing, discussing or transferring state secret information on bulletin boards, chat rooms or in internet newsgroups'.[12] Western commentators were quick to point out that since no one in China knew exactly what exactly was entailed by 'state secret information' the clampdown was fairly swingeing. In 1999 Lin Hai, an Internet entrepreneur, was charged with 'inciting the overthrow of state power' and sentenced to two years in jail for selling an email address list to a web zine based in the USA.[13] At the same time websites in China were prohibited from either disseminating news or hiring journalists to generate content. Websites were also required to employ 'secrecy checkers' to monitor content on behalf of the government. China is far from being alone in such attempts to control the flow of information within its borders. Almost exactly one year before the promulgation of the 'state secret information' controls in China the Bulgarian government adopted a law aimed at licensing all the country's ISPs. The granting of a licence was conditional upon 'a full description of turnover, clients, etc. and a tax consisting of a percentage of the turnover'.[14]

The Internet, however, is uncontainable by design. As in the case of the independent Serbian websites during the Kosovo War in 1999, as fast as sites are closed down their content is mirrored to new sites. To quote John Gilmore, it 'deals with censorship as though it were a malfunction. It routes round it'.[15] Even in the case of China the state network is by no means the only one available to informed users. Furthermore, once it is placed online, information tends to replicate (it is copied from site to site, archived and mirrored for a range of reasons) and to proliferate by attracting annotations, refutations and synopses. While Beijing might be able to block access to the *Wall Street Journal* for its citizens it will hardly be able to track all of those sites which, legally or not, have copied material from the *WSJ*. My source for Kathy Chen's article was the Electronic Frontier Foundation censorship archive but it exists in at least a dozen other locations as well. Once online it is impossible either to track those replications and proliferations or to remove the article.

While some regimes refuse to countenance access to the web it is impossible for them to prevent content from being written to it. The Internet was designed to resist attempts to interrupt the flow of information. Where breaks occur in networks the information simply finds a new pathway. Thus Arab journalists based in many Middle East states, which all use the same language, file their stories on the Arabic Media Internet Network (AMIN) website[16] to overcome problems 'of censorship of local [home] news, but papers can cover news of other Arab countries. Our aim is to break the censorship of local news by getting Jordanian news, for example, from Syria or Palestine'. Journalists from the region can file uncorrupt versions of stories to the site which can be compared with their printed versions, making the physical censorship of newspapers worse than useless since readers can clearly see exactly what it is that their government wishes to obscure.[17] The more general effect is that in many Arab countries the web has made government censorship of imported books, magazines and newspapers completely ineffective. By March 1999 the AMIN website was receiving around 46,000 hits each day, mostly from within the region. Material that has been banned is either placed on the web or bulk emailed into the countries which have suppressed it. The effect is to create a much greater stir than the original material, allowed into the public domain, would have made. Websites that consider themselves vulnerable to repression by governments or other agents can mirror their content to servers in safe countries as the Yugoslav radio station B92 did during the Kosovo War.

In earlier conflicts radio stations were amongst the first targets of repressive regimes and revolutionaries, and firebombed newspaper offices tended to remain quiet. There was an early recognition by repressive states that, if the web is a mass medium, it is very different from television, print and radio. It is neither partisan, nor can its bandwidth be packed with friendly information. It has forced governments and corporations to employ more subtle means of censorship; they are now as likely to employ disinformation as forcible co-option or closure.

There is a thriving cottage industry producing very credible and completely misleading websites and email press releases to a variety of ends. The tendency is alarming in the light of PublicAgenda Online's 1999 survey revealing that slightly more people have 'some' or 'a lot' more confidence in the web than they do in television.[18] More people have confidence in newspapers rather than in television, yet both forms of traditional news media, due to the nature of their production apparatus, have considerably more integrity than the web. Brian Whittaker describes the bogus websites that are employed by states such as Tunisia and Syria as follows:

> Internet users in Tunisia who look up <http://www.amnesty.org>, for example, are likely to be directed to a site resembling that of Amnesty International, the agency that campaigns for human rights. But instead of seeing data documenting the country's poor record in the field, they will be offered descriptions of the Tunisian government's wonderful achievements in human rights.[19]

Countries such as Tunisia attempt to control the Internet even further by legislating for a monopolistic, state-controlled Internet Service Provider, which often charges its service at rates which exclude all but the elite and the very rich. The evidence of the use of fax machines and photocopiers, both heavily restricted technologies, in the Iron Curtain countries in the decade prior to the fall of the Curtain, suggests that the only way of stopping the web from reaching such populations is by completely decommissioning telephone and other communications networks.

The threat, veiled, as we have seen, in a concern about indecent and extreme material, extends to the Western democracies, many of whom have rushed bills similar to the CDA into law. France, Germany and Sweden had all enacted such legislation by the end of 1996. The UK proposed a Europe-wide law. The Broadcasting Services Amendment (Online Services) Bill restricts the Australian public from either providing or gaining access to 'material deemed unsuitable for minors as determined by the Australian film and video classification standards'.[20] In other polities the political agenda, while it is still shielded by the moral panic, is more clearly stated. The Singapore Broadcasting Authority (SBA) polices similar legislation, aimed at 'protecting the national interest and shielding children from objectionable material', in which the definition of the word 'objectionable' is extended to include all content 'which tends to bring the government into hatred or contempt, or which excites disaffection against the government'[21] or, further, which 'runs counter to Asian values'. The SBA's Class Licence Scheme (1996) is intended to regulate the Internet and promote 'healthy development'. The scheme specifically recommends that local ISPs employ access control devices such as Net Nanny, SurfWatch and Cyber Patrol. All ISPs and content providers placing information on the web for 'business, political or religious purposes' are required to register with the SBA and the law specifically demands the licensing of 'On-line newspapers targeting sales in Singapore through the Internet'.[22] The same law targets audiotext, videotext, teletext, broadcast data services and other online services. In the event Singapore licensed only three ISPs and insisted that they screened all material accessible by clients.

While it is easy to accuse states such as Singapore, and for that matter parts of the USA, of coercion in their efforts to regulate the

Internet, the possibility must be considered that many of their citizens have voluntarily surrendered 'privacy and autonomy in return for quality of life. That is, governmentability in cyberspace suggests that power relationships based upon public compliance and subject identity will continue to play an important part in human interaction'.[23] Stated in such bald terms the proposal seems at odds with our understandings of liberal democracy and yet, on the issue of encryption of networked information, Dorothy Denning continues to argue in favour of the governments which vigorously seek technologies and powers 'that would assure no individual absolute privacy or untraceable anonymity in all transactions. I argue that this feature of the technology is what will allow individuals to choose a civil society over an anarchistic one'.[24] Such interventions and the widespread use of censorware, however clumsy, by both private individuals and the state seems to signal a decided nervousness about unfiltered, and unfettered, information. The implications for a journalism attempting to fulfil its traditional roles are serious.

One option that is no longer available to governments is the unilateral and comprehensive termination of Internet connections when things seem to be getting out of control. There have been instances of such a resort, for example in Hong Kong (23 February 1995) when Hong Kong Internet Gateway Services, as a result of interventions by the Police Commercial Crime Bureau and the Hong Kong Office of the Telecommunications Authority, cut all the circuits to local ISPs and their many thousands of customers. While news and information are effectively short-circuited in such an event, commercial activity is also lost and, already by 1995, Hong Kong was a significant supplier of regional corporate accounts. Goh Mui, writing in the *Eastern Express* newspaper, suggests that this particular instance resulted from a confrontation between the local ISPs and the gateway services rather than any political motivation but the effect on freedom of information is the same. 'This episode has set back the business use of the Internet in HK by 2 years. Why on earth should anyone trust the Internet as an efficient business tool any more when the plug can be pulled without warning.'[25] The lesson is clear for governments: once e-commerce has established itself on the web, regulation has to be handled with some circumspection. The Singaporean ideal of balancing the conflicting aims of exploiting the Internet to the full while continuing to insulate citizens from undesirable influences is not so easily realised.

Privacy and Surveillance

> ... privacy in the contexts of our social relations protects us from social overreaching – limits the control of others over our lives.[26]

There are many factors, not least, for most of us, the economic one, which prevent us from such overreaching. Some statutory guarantee of privacy, in many cultures and polities, is the slim support of personal autonomy. Privacy itself is a historical and cultural anomaly, the product of a particular mode of consumption. It cannot be said to have existed anywhere before the nineteenth century and in our time those inhabitants of the planet privileged enough to have it fight fiercely to keep it; yet already we see it beginning to atrophy. David Schoeman describes it as relating 'exclusively to personal information and ... [describing] the extent to which others have access to this information. There is an even narrower conception, one that limits the range of privacy to personal information that is "undocumented"'.[27] His caveat has significant implications both for journalism – it lies at the heart of many of the debates on journalistic ethics – and for the subject of the information society, a society which regulates itself, indeed exists, through a global project of documentation. For the subject or any other body to be undocumented is to place both recognition and identity itself at risk.

In large parts of the developed world, significant elements of its populations' lives now leave clear information trails. The subjects of the contemporary corporate state can conceal less and less of themselves. The shift of much information work – in which I would include teaching, law, journalism and media of all descriptions – on to the web has rendered that process almost complete. All of our important financial transactions have been traceable for some time, as well as the histories of our health and education. In addition to creating profiles of our behaviour, such traces are also used to monitor and discipline us. Computers allow work itself to be tracked with a mechanical precision and data workers, from call-centre operatives to some journalists, can all expect to have their every key stroke monitored. The Internet allows our thought processes to be monitored as we chase ideas and intuitions with search engines and through directories. The arrival of Internet 2 and enhanced bandwidth will mean that most of the media that we consume is also logged. With every service that is supplied to consumers and every response they make, electronic networks also produce new data which itself can be used to make new connections.

The information economy might well be global, and thus beyond the grasp of the state, but that does not mean that both the state and other agents will not use the potential for surveillance that the Internet offers to constrain its subjects radically. The real possibility of agencies accumulating large amounts of electronic detail about individuals from a huge spectrum of sources places existing laws on privacy under some pressure. As Paul Frissen has it, 'Scale becomes an obsolete factor to organisation and to governance. Instead of economies of scale, economies of scope become crucial.'[28] A potentially infinite amount of information about the subject, including the barest minutiae of his or her life, can be recorded, and, for the first time in history, effectively processed.

Can the right to republish material that is nominally already in the public domain but which makes new sense when it is assembled differently go unquestioned? Any database which brings together my religious and political beliefs, details of my daily information consumption, my shopping habits and my sexual interests could leave me vulnerable on a variety of fronts. While such information about readers might not have traditionally been the concern of studies such as this where consumption of media, including news, can be tracked so directly, the issue of privacy becomes crucial. The possibility that surveillance can track my every act of reading is unnerving even in a liberal democracy. The bomb-making primers read on the web by the boys who attacked their classmates at Columbine seem to condemn them outright.

The favoured metaphor for the study of surveillance has, in the past, been Jeremy Bentham's Panopticon, particularly in Foucault's version which construes it as an instrument of moral reform and subjectification. We could apply a simplistic model of it to information technologies, locating the server as the eye at the centre of the Panopticon, which might well include an analysis of crude key-stroke monitoring software. In a wider context Net Nanny offers corporate employers ways 'to ensure that employee productivity ... is maintained within the workplace', to quote its promotional literature.

Such analyses might not prove so adequate in dealing with the individual's encounters with local and global networks. Many software agents, including cookies, track the web surfer's progress through layers and across vectors of information. The record of those moves and the shards of information they have captured, a modest enough toll, is enough to pay for the reader's access to the day's news or news archives. Such agents are not secret; browsers can be set to recognise and announce – even reject – them, but the matrix of information that they render must, inevitably, remain opaque to their subject. The subject is caught in a surveillance network comprising the telltale track, from website to website, that she leaves and the countless cookies that report her progress. An AT&T survey in 1999 found that less than half of Internet users were worried about the privacy issues raised by cookies and more than 10 per cent did not even know what they were,[29] yet by 1998 Tim Berners-Lee admitted that he was 'very concerned about the privacy aspects of the web'.[30]

Several web-based organisations including the Electronic Freedom Frontier have been monitoring freedom of speech and the individual's right to privacy for some years. Aspects of the debate have momentous implications for online journalism. PublicAgenda Online, an organisation composed mostly of journalists committed to bringing the defining issues around the web into the public domain, proposes a debate that can be argued from at least three positions.[31]

1. The libertarian position, safeguarding the individual's rights to privacy, especially against the state, and unequivocally guaranteeing the right to freedom of speech.
2. The liberal position which suggests that it is up to consumers to protect themselves; that they, not regulators, should be empowered to decide what they don't want to see online.
3. That the state (or other agents) should apply and enforce mainstream social standards on the Internet and that citizens should accept limits to what remains confidential on the Internet.

Setting aside the general arguments about freedom and society it seems clear that the third argument, potentially giving governments and corporations the ability to censor large parts of the Internet, would be deeply problematic for most responsible journalisms. Speech is already rigorously controlled by the laws of libel and, depending on national boundaries, other legal instruments. Its further policing, more than the conduct of reporters, would clearly have direct implications for the social beyond the limited domain of the media, including the economy. The solution would necessarily give the state direct access to all information on the Internet and, as with the CDA, leave the law open to constant erosion as the definition of subjective conditions such as 'obscene', 'pornographic', 'degrading' and 'fascist', all subject to semantic slippage from a whole spectrum of cultural agents and mores, are endlessly debated. The reporting of the Monica Lewinsky scandal would have been reported under rather more restrictive conditions than the Christine Keeler story was in the puritan Britain of the mid-twentieth century.

At present the issue of surveillance is most acute in large companies, more than a quarter of which in America routinely read employees' email. While most of those companies seem to disclose their privacy policies to employees the monitoring of such traffic has implications for whistle-blowing and the exposure of corporate crime as well as to the larger issue of how citizens keep themselves informed.

Censorship or Constraint

The tendency by governments to restrict and curtail activity on the web can be viewed in another light. The censorships targeted at web publishers and free speech, if successful, could be of immense commercial benefit to the global media establishment. At present, when a Drudge or a *SlashDot* can attract a larger readership than the *Washington Post, The Times* or Disney's *Go*, there must be a great incentive on the part of big media and its friends in government to handicap the web's upstarts in any way they can. The technology itself might well eventually weed out such mavericks and newcomers as Internet 2, with the massively expanded bandwidth required to transmit full-featured streamed media, demands an equivalently expanded entrance fee. That development will leave the traditional press, already badly mauled by the new web providers in the loss of their classified and display advertising, and without broadcast technologies, doubly vulnerable. The arrival of RealAudio in 1995 left the world's traditional radio industry, weighed down by nearly a century of investment, limited bandwidth and, in many countries, onerous regulation, and just beginning to come to terms with the digital age, equally handicapped. The age of the personal radio station had arrived abruptly and, it seemed, universally.

Many of the stories published and broadcast in the traditional media which seek to panic their audiences about the Internet are clearly just that: panics. 'Journalism has failed in a major and shameful way to live up to its obligation to inform citizens about that which we need to know in order to remain a democracy. All this porno on the Internet, all these stupid scare stories about hackers and pedophiles and no explanation of the winners and losers in the telecommunications deregulation.'[32] The winners, in Howard Rheingold's argument, are plainly the global media cartel who, as they see it, will eventually have Internet 2 fall to them as well as most of the web. The archetypal bogus scare story, derived from a study in a law journal, appeared as a cover story on *Time* magazine in 1995. 'Cyberporn' by Marty Rimm claimed that more than 80 per cent of Usenet discussion groups posted pornographic images.[33] The purported university study about this massive preponderance of pornography on the web was rapidly discredited by a campaign organised from *The Well* online service. The statistics that claimed to underpin the study and which comprised the main evidence presented by Senator James Exon in his proposal for the Communications Decency Act in the USA proved to be entirely bogus. It was merely one in a series of scares that continue to suggest that the Internet needs to be regulated and restricted, that only professional media organisations are to be trusted with their hands on the 'publish' button.

Scares and the 'popular demands' for regulation that they inspire are only one of the ruses used to marginalise independent web news content providers. The mainstream listing directories tend to only list those who form part of the cartel. The *Drudge Report*, for all its conservative and Republican leanings, is rarely listed. The high bandwidth networks designed to provide video on demand will not be configured as a common carrier in the way the Internet was. It will never feature Drudge and the many like him from a political spectrum wider than any dreamt of by the mass media of an earlier age.

Copyright and Intellectual Property

The formal protection of intellectual property on an international basis began with a series of accords agreed in Paris in 1883. In countries subject to those accords copyright protection is automatically granted when any work 'is fixed in a tangible medium of expression' and under most jurisdictions computer memory, obviously including that of web servers, is considered a 'tangible' enough medium to cover its contents with the rights of copyright. Ownership of copyright prevents others, unless they have been granted specific permission, from copying, displaying or distributing copyrighted work and it also defends the work from unauthorised performance, from modification and from having parts of it included in the production of new (derivative) works. Clearly the existing accords leave some grey areas with regard to the web. While in most jurisdictions it remains legal to link to, and hence display, a file on a remote computer, to download it and save it on that computer's hard drive is against the law. Yet that is exactly what browsers do when they cache, however ephemerally, web pages that have been linked to. The abrupt and hyperbolic development of the web left international law in some disarray on this issue with some states attempting to criminalise unauthorised linking to web pages.

By the last decade of the twentieth century the World Intellectual Property Organization (WIPO) was still aggressively lobbying for updated copyright laws to take account further of electronic media. Many saw the new proposals as much more restrictive than their predecessors. Copyright laws are intended to provide protection for global media companies against media piracy, which, in the past was often based in the developing world. Many of those states, with their business classes and intellectuals, have come to regard copyright and the treaties that protect it as a tool of First World elites. They see its primary aim as the closing of markets to cartel outsiders and WIPO's proposals for the future as further disadvantaging them.

Current law allows for different levels of copyright protection in different countries. This often entails payment of royalties on a scale in which, depending where they are, users can obtain legal copies for different prices. Global networks make something of a mockery of such a system.

Global networks make it easy to order copyright works from other countries where they are cheaper, even though current UK law allows rights owners to restrict commercial imports of copyright works from outside the EEA. On-line delivery will make this even easier, and also raises concerns about control of material placed illegally on the internet, where those placing the material on-line may be outside the rightholder's jurisdiction. Increasingly, copyright material may need to be licensed on a global basis, and new international treaties making it easier to apply and enforce copyright protection, wherever material originates, should therefore be brought into force as quickly as possible.[34]

The enforcement of copyright at flat, global rates, while it might be more convenient and would eliminate such frauds, would certainly penalise poorer users and include another barrier to media production in their countries. The existing intellectual rights of providers such as *Go* and *MSNBC* would be protected along with large portions of future global markets.

The current round of WIPO legislation looks further than piracy and also aims to curtail what is known as 'fair use', that is to allow research, education, news reporting, parody and commentary about copyrighted materials, in existing acts. The proposals would prevent writers, journalists, academics, scientists, librarians and students from citing information that they can now use freely. It would make a text such as this, which is based on hundreds of sources from every continent, unsustainably expensive. Some multimedia texts, drawing on many sources including proprietary materials, are already wildly expensive to produce and beyond the resources of all but the largest media corporations. Copyright, orginally designed both to protect and promote knowledge and discourse, would become the key instrument preventing its dissemination in many of the new media forms. The furtherance of knowledge demands constantly proliferating links and connections. The Internet seems to provide a healthy environment for this expansion.

Most of the important sources for this book, for example, either exist online or can be readily traced in one of the web archives. Where knowledge is deprived of those connections, where it is too closely protected, it will decay. When copy protection ceases to be maintained through consent, when, for instance, it is enforced by technology, perhaps encryption, it will force the emergence of new information paradigms based on paucity rather than abundance. The pirates will be able to crack most forms of encryption but media consumers will limit their horizons to what they can afford, and in many cases that will be what they already know. The Internet is now the predominant tool for journalism and such restrictions would affect the dissemination of news more than any other activity.

The web has brought other copyright-related problems to news providers. In 1996 several large North American media companies brought an action against *Total News,* an aspiring news portal site. *Total News* used frames to capture content from national providers such as the *Washington Post* and *USA Today.* While the files remained on the sites of the companies that owned them, to the reader using the *Total News* site, because of the way the content was framed, it looked as though the documents were part of *Total News.* In fact while some of the data on the screen, including, most contentiously, advertisements, was being downloaded from *Total News,* the news itself was coming from other media sites. *Total News* vigorously refuted the claim for copyright infringement. The whole area of online news is fraught with many unresolved legal landmines. In a case brought by the *Shetland Times* against a local competitor it took nearly two years to achieve an interim interdict on the fundamental principle that news sites in Britain could hyperlink to material hosted elsewhere.[35]

The Scottish case raised the eyebrows of journalists everywhere. While other news providers were desperately seeking ways of encouraging news readers to their websites, and one proven way of attracting such traffic is to have good links to your page, here was a news site attempting to use the law to prevent such links. It was already perfectly apparent that it was impossible to sell news effectively and simultaneously restrict access. By 1999 most news providers, the *New York Times* excepted, had even removed the demand for passwords. The shift is exemplified in the general move from admonishments which warned users that copyright of site information should not be breached in any way to the provision of buttons which provided printer-friendly versions of files or which encouraged users to email features to themselves or friends.

The World Information Order

Both the problems and the possibilities that surround the Internet arise from its globality. Even during its first decade – when much of the hardware was physically located in North America and when both hardware and software were predominantly the products of American corporations – it could not be usefully construed as an American entity. There was no attribute, like the language of rock or the narrative structures of Hollywood, that particularly insisted upon its Americanness. It required no adaptation to be used by Japanese schoolchildren or Zapatista guerrillas. Most efforts to regulate its content, however, refused to recognise this nature and were local and, doomed to failure, provisional. While groups such as the G7 Ministerial Conference on the Information Society conducted a series of conferences to discuss issues such as national regulation, access, copyright and encryption, cultural pollution and free speech, the issue of global regulation, while it was hedged around and remained largely unspoken, was clearly the major agenda item.

The legislative precedents for bodies such as the European Council, in its 1994 report on 'Europe and the Global Information Society', were radio and satellite television, which, if they were not global were at least continental in scope, and which, as traditional mass media, tended to be controlled by elite groups who already had close links with government. Accordingly, in both cases a series of treaties and understandings had been quite readily agreed, often co-opting or steam-rollering even the pariah states of the late century such as Libya and Iran. Since the Internet was clearly a universal as well as global medium in a way that the traditional mass media had never been, the G7 information group had to tread more carefully. However, some of the forces lobbying most strongly for regulation were their friends in the traditional media, the very elites who took advantage of the deregulation of the media in the second half of the twentieth century and who, two decades later, wished to protect the massive investments made subsequently. That hiccup for the global media cartel's plans for monopoly may well be only temporary. The higher bandwidths of Internet 2 and beyond will come with much higher entry charges and the prizes in media markets will once more go to those with the deepest pockets.

The reverse side of this difficulty is that the principles of freedom of speech, constitutionally guaranteed in many countries, are not protected on the Internet in the same way. In both Germany and Australia, for example, they exist for newspapers but not for the Internet. Perhaps those elisions in national law should be capitalised upon and some form of self-regulation or charter as suggested by Mitch Kapor and John Perry Barlow, the founders of the Electronic Frontier Foundation, outside of national law, be considered by the users of the medium. Declan McCullagh agrees that the regulation of the Internet should not be a matter for sovereign governments at all and that a 'new way of looking at cyberspace' must rapidly emerge to pre-empt a world information order that is imposed by some national alliance or even, leveraging its technological advantage, by the United States itself.

> Some precedents exist. Maritime law, for example, says that no single nation has jurisdiction over the oceans. Medieval Europe recognized a separate law for merchants that had its own judicial system. Antarctica is not governed by any single country's laws. The Catholic Church is a multinational institution that largely governs itself.[36]

Far from being multinational Barlow sees the web as an autonomous 'seamless global-economic zone'[37] which makes the nation state redundant. While it is difficult, at the time of writing, to imagine the world's nation states conceding such a position and yielding such power to what must ultimately be little more than a user group, perhaps it is the only solution if the Internet is to become the consummate common carrier. Historically, journalism has often possessed liberties denied to the private individual. It has also been aware of the provisional nature of those liberties and protected them fiercely. Journalism has been one of the social institutions, worldwide, to grasp most actively the opportunities inherent in the trans-national Internet and it is also most vigorously involved in defending and codifying those freedoms. Unfortunately there are many news workers who, perhaps in best faith, are nervous about such freedoms attaining a universal currency. Norman Solomon cites Katharine Graham, the once campaigning owner of the *Washington Post*, talking to CIA officials in 1988:

We live in a dirty and dangerous world ... There are some things the general public does not need to know and shouldn't. I believe democracy flourishes when the government can take legitimate steps to keep its secrets and when the press can decide whether to print what it knows.[38]

Graham's contradictory statement, at first sight quite breathtaking coming from the executive who enabled the Watergate investigation, is clearly articulated by one who regards herself as an insider. It is a mindset that helped to compromise the press in the eyes of many of its readers in the period after Vietnam and Watergate. By the time the *Post* and most of the other news providers of the West came to report the Gulf War it was generally understood that the capability of the news media was, as Philip Hammond and Ed Herman have characterised it, 'degraded'.[39] Any claims for critical objectivity and independence were paper-thin.

Such a degradation of the press effectively matches the work of the most draconian regulation. The collateral loss of credibility merely exacerbates the degradation until the press fails to serve any useful social function other than the 'orders for the day' of totalitarian regimes. As Bagdikian has pointed out, for the West this becomes a clarion to fresh feats of consumption and little else.

As we have seen, the web mitigates against such collusions of the press and power as well as any justification of it. Martin Bangemann, a member of the European Commission in the 1990s, was the author of the series of papers on the regulation of the Internet. He regarded local solutions to this regulation by the world's nations as pointless. Problems with and evasions of such local legislation would be simply effected by crossing national borders at a key stroke. The real effect of such legislation would be to handicap electronic commerce in those countries which enacted it, with the concomitant loss of jobs. A better solution might have been the harmonisation of national laws; however, 'given the complexities of the question and given in particular the number of countries with different laws and cultures, the prospect of having clear rules in the form, for instance, of an international treaty, at least in some reasonable time, is rather low'.[40]

In partial agreement with Internet libertarians such as Barlow and Kapor, Bangemann favoured a compromise based on an international charter built around a range of principles and basic rules policed by the users of the networks themselves. Bangemann's charter provided a framework 'covering such issues as the legal recognition of digital signatures, encryption, privacy, protection against illegal and harmful content, customs and data protection'.[41] He saw the main instruments for achieving the charter as 'mutual recognition and self-regulation'. Formal regulation by the state(s) would be the final resort.

At the root of Bangemann's new world information order is the recognition of the need for fundamental shifts in the economy and society, a 'paradigm change in policy' that would trigger the opportunities preferred by the information society. Bangemann recognised that while the world stood on the cusp of epochal change the world network would conflict with laws, habits and culture in many, if not all, of the countries it served. Accordingly, he proposed three principles, which remain enshrined in many of the EU's proposals about the Internet, which he believed would provide the basis of a sustainable information order.

> The global framework ... [should] be open enough so as to allow people to express their different cultures freely.

> It [should] contribute towards preserving cultural diversity and offer protection against the over-dominant control of new media by a small number of multinational distributors.

> The Information Society must become an open and multi-cultural society which will stimulate, rather than dilute, the expression of different cultures.[42]

The principles seek to order communications and information around communities, prioritising the needs of people over corporations and polities. There is a strong likelihood that online technologies will further divide the world into the information-rich and the information-poor. To meet the needs of the latter groups – and they will exist on every continent – new civil initiatives are necessary, not least to protect and facilitate a basic human right, the individual's right to communicate.

8
The (Re)construction of Reality: Local and Global Journalisms

The Internet is a potentially powerful vehicle to mitigate and ultimately change [social] dynamics. It is an empowering and
engaging means for personal exploration and expression. It is a
medium that enables one-to-one communications, communications 'up' and 'sideways', not just 'down', [and] it offers the
opportunity for an improved means for people to identify and
discuss amongst themselves the concerns of interest to them.[1]

History can be viewed, perhaps over-simplistically, as the story of
humanity's long struggle to escape social and political despotism. The
lasting protections from oppression won in the course of that struggle
tend to have been those embedded in and guaranteed by the social.
A by-product, or perhaps the main determinant, of humanity's innate
sociality is the protection afforded by the group. Accordingly, tyran-
nies of all sorts, including dictatorships and those based on
commodity forms, try to reorganise participation and association
away from the social and around themselves. The monopolies of the
age of mass media encouraged the atomisation of society and its
adjuncts, including the family, through ever-increasing layers of
mediation. A television in every room of the house became the guarantee of full (and spurious) sociability. The move from TV to
interactive media, perhaps web TV, appears to enable a reversal of
that trend and enables new relationships, implicitly political,
between groups and individuals. As media technologies converge on
the web the world, or at least those elements of it that can be appropriately mediated, reconfigures itself in a new set of relationships.

Communities of interest, often avowedly apolitical, organise around their town, their religion, their team, their sexuality and a thousand other factors including the commodity forms themselves (collectors of vinyl, dolls or books, *Star Wars* and *Star Trek* clubs). Their interest lies in what defines their world or significant elements of it. Life revolves around that significant object, whether it be the club, village, gang, church, sport or social club. This structuration of the everyday and the possibilities for subject identity that it opens is reorganised and extended by the web. Web users choose a portal organised around their interest which will colour their daily horoscope, weather, cartoons, stock indices, advertisements and news accordingly. Specialist search engines further limit association with the world at large, itself an increasingly problematised entity. While such virtual communities are hardly new – since communities brought together by the text or letter rather than by physical interaction have existed since the time of Saint Paul of Tarsus and before – Leigh Clayton emphasises that they are fundamentally different from face-to-face encounters.

> ... these forays into what may be considered alternate existences need have no implications for life extraneous to the web. In this way many virtual communities lack any real moral dimension. Morality too is virtual.[2]

Such communities, complete with their value systems and organising philosophies, can now readily seal themselves hermetically into small constellations of websites and media providers. Some communities and institutions, including the traditional news providers, carry a morality forged in the extraneous world into this imaginary place, others, such as Matt Drudge, create morality anew there. News, context, moral sense, search engines and links – in other words the machinery that informs our worlds – are organised around the community interest and can eventually begin to lose touch with society at large. The global news providers are not, however, about to lose their audiences so easily and many of them specifically tailor output to such affinity niches both on the web and in the world still served by traditional media.

A powerful grassroots political momentum on the Internet created 'new electronic networks, communities of shared *meanings*, rather than just those of shared interests or properties'.[3] Such 'shared meanings' make up the strands of identity and the fabric of community. News and information, immediate and apparently unmediated on the web, open to response and appropriately inflected by interest groups themselves is a powerful disseminator of the belief systems and ideologies which allow communities to amount to more than provisional associations geared around the exigencies of the present. The identity of news consumers is of course never as two-dimensional as some of the above might appear to claim. Any comprehension of the relationship between virtual and real communities has to take account of ' ... the shift in social theory from fixed accounts of self and agency, to ... conceiving of the self as having multiple and contradictory identities, community affiliations, and social interests'.[4] For most of us, identity is subject to a complex of sometimes contradictory affiliations. In some cases this makes particular communities less interesting to media producers as markets. Some are more likely to produce profit for the media than others, although any community organised around a commodified form, whether it be football, sex or gardening, seems to guarantee a healthy outcome.

Many local news providers making the transition from print to the web, such as Associated Newspapers' *West Britain* in Cornwall, have created determinedly open sites, gateways to their neighbourhoods – in this case *ThisisCornwall* – to act as a point of convergence for such communities and, where they already exist, to help them relocate or re-centre themselves on the web where as we have seen they become more amenable to further organisation and solicitation. Such sites, *Virtual Manchester*[5] for example, if they are operated as genuine partnerships with the involvement of local newspapers, TV and radio stations, local authorities and museums, etc., can become regional portals. By facilitating community interaction and discussion on news, community affairs and topics of local interest such as shopping and sport the kind of grassroots solidarity which was heavily discouraged by mass media forms and twentieth-century modes of consumption is fostered. *ThisisCornwall* provides a local web portal, as well as most of the news in the print edition (updated every few hours – the print edition is weekly), local discussion groups and access to the newspaper's electronic archives. The site also operates a directory of the websites of local businesses. Other local providers, the *Arizona Daily Star*, for instance, offer server space and technical assistance to non-profit organisations to publish newsletters. *Virtual Manchester* offers free email, server space, *Asian Manchester* and a virtual shopping mall. Many news organisations have gone even further and act as web consultants and designers to their advertisers. The ethical problems produced by some of these new relationships are far from being resolved.

John Pavlik, writing in the *Columbia Journalism Review*, offers a fairly typical example of community-focused journalism, here published by a national/global news provider in 1997. It brings together issue-driven journalism of general interest, interactivity and a focus on the local. The actual locus of the reporting could have been anywhere and the use of publicly accessible databases is equally applicable to issues from healthcare to wage levels.

> ... NBC's Dateline ran a piece about dangerous roads in America, zeroing in on three particularly treacherous thoroughfares. The program invited viewers to log onto the MSNBC site to learn about roads in their community. Those who did so could enter their zip code and, within seconds, based on federal data, find out how many fatal accidents had occurred in that community between 1992 and 1995 and on which roads. Within twelve hours MSNBC logged 68,000 visitors to that feature.[6]

Clearly local newspapers, radio stations, certain cable TV providers and associational groups such as clubs and sports teams have always involved themselves in similar community initiatives; however, the web brings new possibilities of interest to the community, particularly in terms of interactivity and the loss of distance. Such communities, chess players, gardeners and UFO enthusiasts, can now assemble from every corner of the planet as regularly and for as long as they wish. Interactive news media can be employed to connect them with the larger society or to isolate them. The potential of the web for the balkanisation of society must represent significant commercial opportunities for news producers.

Internet communities offer alternative modes for social interaction as it is increasingly foreclosed upon by contemporary urban and political structures. Internet communities, whether they are based upon news groups, news portals or other information centres, can offer individuals what appears to be a radically democratic polity, one in which she or he can communicate directly with political and cultural leaders, even the president of the United States. A limited power in these communities organises around those who speak, yet equal access makes hierarchy redundant, to the cost, as we have seen, of traditional political parties in many countries.

Distance and geography are also largely redundant conceptions. The Internet takes 'everything everywhere', including, for diasporic populations, the sense of place. Cornish Australians, whose grandparents were drawn to Australia by minerals and mines, have developed a powerful sense of roots that still signifies for them through access to the web. While there are important tributaries to this network, *ThisisCornwall* itself, for instance, as well as several Australian genealogy sites and various newsgroups, there is no hub, no determining power. It can hardly even be said to be democratic since, while there are some regular voices they have no more or less influence over its direction than others who drift in and out of the community. There is no marginalisation of those who merely 'lurk'; their identification with the community is just as viable as it is for those who speak. *Slashdot*'s 'anonymous cowards' are as integral to the reader community as those who post publicly and regularly to lead the discussion strands. Web communities can even transcend the barriers and prescriptions of totalitarian societies by allowing their subjects a platform to speak from, albeit, usually still with some degree of risk. If the problem of access, and it is significant even in the developed world, is resolvable then it seems likely that many of the discourses of society will take place with the web as their primary arena. In such an electronic public sphere a journalism capable of mapping those discourses is a necessity.

Al Gore argued, as part of his 'electronic superhighway' campaign during the first Clinton administration, that citizens, and by implication societies, without web access would find themselves at a serious social and economic disadvantage, eventually being bankrupted and marginalised as an information underclass. Accordingly, lower income social groups should be subsidised to get online. Gary Dempsey of the Republican think tank, the Cato Institute, criticised both Gore's presentation of the argument and his conclusion, claiming that, after 1996 in the USA one of the groups taking up the web most enthusiastically was people earning less than $15,000 a year, notably the group least interesting to advertisers. The impact on an informed democracy would be slight, however, since, by that time, the web was primarily being used for amusement. The 'information underclass is far from inevitable. Rather, information technology is on course to spread everywhere without government-mandated subsidies. The voluntary institutions of civil society ... are doing it on their own'.[7] The further suggestion that '*at the current rate of growth* [my italics] every man, woman, and child on the earth will be connected to the Internet by 2007' tendentiously ignores the plight of the information-poor of Africa and parts of Asia and South America.

In much of Europe and in America, while educational standards have risen, public engagement in politics and civic life has fallen dramatically since the Second World War. This is partly explained by a retreat into the private sphere driven and enabled by broadcast media technologies. One significant effect of the technologies of mass communication is to isolate citizens from each other. Telecommunications technologies, with the Internet, and a resurgence of political consciousness, albeit no longer revolving around the mass politics of the mid-twentieth century, are rapidly reversing such trends. Political debate, the canvassing of public opinion and political referenda will be mobilised around virtual communities with voting taking place over the web.

> ... electronic connections may become more important than the physical organisations and organisational units they connect. Societal and policy networks or configurations can effectively be represented in electronic networks. Cyberspace is the 'real' space.[8]

... perhaps the Habermassian Athenian space where citizens can set aside status differences to come together and debate matters of public concern. Most newspapers and the broadcast news forms of the mass media never constituted a public sphere as Habermas would have understood it since they are constrained to only represent private opinion. Many websites fail by the same standard.

The *UK Citizens Online Democracy (UKCOD)* site was set up in 1997 with high aspirations, the support of bodies and corporations such as the Joseph Rowntree Trust and Sun Microsystems and clients such as the UK Office of the European Parliament. In addition to political online services, the organisation proposed to offer a public discussion area, a wealth of political resources and a politicians' discussion area. Its aim was to 'promote informed discussion on matters of national and local importance by providing a forum for members of the public to discuss political issues'.[9] Two years later it had not been updated since April of its launch year and, amidst a maelstrom of political activity on the web, was fast on the way to becoming a classic if rather elegantly designed 'ghost site'. The problems with *UKCOD* were that, for all its claims, it was clearly constructed around a top-down paradigm which was firmly wedded to an anachronistic party politics. While it made strong claims about the public sphere it contrived to simulate one for purposes that were far from clear. Very few online democrats came.

The public sphere articulated by Habermas is specifically a space where the active process of opinion formation, through dialectic, takes place. The public sphere allows personal opinion to 'evolve through rational-critical debate of a public into public opinion'.[10] The news forms that are emerging on the web seem particularly suited to Habermas' 'subjectless' modes of communication and opinion formation. Clearly democracy cannot exist outside of the communities which practise it and hence we are unlikely to find it in global structures, whether they be social, economic or political. As we have seen it also tends to spill out from the official arenas that are constructed for it. It is, however, possible at the level of the local and the community and around the issues that are energising those communities.

The failure of *UKCOD* and mass politics generally seems to contradict one of the commonplaces about contemporary society. Community politics in particular and the web in general are forcing a re-evaluation of the much prophesied ...

> ... 'loss of community'. A shift [is] taking place ... from societies characterised primarily by community (*Gemeinschaft*) type relationships of kinship and face-to-face contact, to more associational (*Gesellschaft*) relations where contracts, and tokens such as money, hold people together.[11]

The distinction fails to take into account the implicitly contractual nature of community relationships. Relationships developed through the web problematise the distinction by foregrounding and articulating the social contracts, previously left implicit, which are the glue of community. Those 'associational relations' may well become the primary organising structures of the social. The change, in widening the definition of 'lived' communities, will not necessarily be construed as a net loss.

While virtual communities already form the basis of new forms of sociality and the web is used to advance and strengthen many disparate communities in the physical world, what is equally certain is that the global media cartels are expanding ways of controlling access to those new communities and will continue to control most of the media that most of us use, no matter where we consider our local to be. As Michael Schudson and many others have made clear, the sphere that news consumers have come to understand as community is constituted by commercial media as market. News itself is a commodity to be marketed for profit like any other. It is subject to the same vicissitudes, including the laws of supply and demand, as any other commercial product.

Global Journalisms

The local hubs which link the global networks are themselves part of the global; the fact that globality is, as Martin Albrow suggests, localised in them becomes a defining attribute of globality itself. There are several implications here, not least, as we saw during the Seattle round of the World Trade Organisation talks in November 1999, that 'resistance to globality may ... become a focus for local action'.[12] Even as it is resisted globality becomes localised in communities, companies and a range of other institutions with implicit globalist values such as journalism.

Albrow proposes that globality incurs 'an overall change in the basis of action and social organisation for individuals and groups'.[13] That change involves the discarding of assumptions about modernity, some recognition of the degradation of the environment, the loss of military security, the emergence of a world economy, 'the reflexivity of globalism, where people and groups of all kinds refer to the globe as the frame of their beliefs', and the implementation of global communications systems which saturate regions previously considered as peripheral, geographically, economically and socially with the influence of the economic and cultural centres. Importantly, globality by no means embraces everyone on the planet and its beliefs; information networks, economies, markets and culture, while they affect the whole population, remain completely inaccessible to most individuals. Those Internet prophets who anticipate an imminent wired world remain obdurately blind to those who have yet to see, much less use, their first telephone. Albrow emphasises that as industries such as finance move offshore their global centres can become entirely virtual places. 'International finance lives at the ends of telephone and video links.'[14] A further significance of the process is that as the world becomes one the nation state becomes an anachronism. Globalisation is not merely the 'intensification of global interconnectedness'[15] or the 'elimination of economic borders'. It represents fundamental systemic changes for the planet affecting both its polities and its economies.

> ... the system loses its coherence. It can no longer replicate itself by absorbing new lands and peasantries, and instead fractures into a whole variety of differing strategies for production, capital accumulation and the creation of new needs. It becomes what Lash and Urry (1987) call 'disorganized capitalism'.[16]

That capitalism, following the logic of Fordism to an inevitable and often draconian conclusion, entails the flexible production systems enabled by information technologies – lean and just-in-time production, zero-hour contracts and the flexible labour force, mobile capital and the focus on niche markets. One of the defining attributes of a disorganised capitalism is its capacity, since it can no longer expand into new markets, for falling back upon the old and appropriating any objects capable of turning a profit on its behalf, including its own discards and oppositional forms. George Soros, the speculator who took on whole economies in the 1980s and 1990s, fears a capitalism now voracious enough to devour even its own structural supports and ideology. '... The untrammeled intensification of laissez-faire capitalism and the spread of market values into all areas of life is endangering our open and democratic society. The main enemy of the open society, I believe, is no longer the communist but the capitalist threat.'[17]

The alternative press of the 1960s no less than the zines of the punk movement were enmeshed in the advertising machine almost as they emerged and their style and typography have been sold back to us in retro editions ever since. For all of the claims for independence of the press over the last century one has to return to the radical press of the early nineteenth century for a medium that stood outside of the then emerging advertising-based economy. At the time of writing it remains possible to imagine a web-based news media, amounting to something more than pamphleteering, which, if it is not fully autonomous, is at least still free to critique and possibly circumvent the global hegemony of capitalism if not its markets. This is not merely the radical fringe of journalism since as communities, corporations and institutions, including journalism, delink themselves from national definitions they also 'lose the animating and centralizing thrust of the nation-state'.[18] Journalism, along with the other institutions of modernity, thus has to relocate and reinvent itself in terms of the civic and the local as well as the global and develop new affiliations accordingly. At the same time news publishing on the web must remain a provisional enterprise until commercial models evolve which can more or less guarantee profits.

The Loss of the Peripheral

While global news providers and many Western media corporations can afford to experiment with the new media (indeed cannot afford not to) their competitors in the developing world and in countries such as Russia have to be more circumspect. Much online journalism away from the centres which still serve as the core markets for the media giants is conspicuously low-cost (and none the worse for that) or undertaken in partnership with online news providers based in the West. The *News Tribune* of Tacoma in Washington, for instance, has exchanged information and journalists with the *Vladivostok News* since the early 1990s. The papers' cooperation extends to their online services. The crucial question of access is also raised for providers beyond the reach of the dense networks of the West. In Russia for instance, outside of a few centres such as St Petersburg, Moscow and Nizhny Novgorod the telecommunications network would at present not be able to sustain intensive traffic even if computers were generally available. This should perhaps be unsurprising since, in 1999, even the countries of Southern Europe, Greece, Spain and Portugal did not have the infrastructure in place to enable the large-scale Internet development that was being so hastily undertaken by their Northern neighbours.

Nonetheless, there are many examples of partnerships between such countries and Western content providers willing to give their news organisations expertise and exposure abroad and, of course, the global news portal sites all have an interest in linking to local suppliers everywhere. While they bring many manifest benefits for publishers in Russia and Africa such relationships do come with a less benign edge. Many of the recipients of such aid view it as a kind of information colonialism, which, while it might well attract new global audiences for them, especially in times of local crisis, conspicuously does not attract extra advertising ... for them. To refuse it is, however, unthinkable. Peter Golding argues that the Internet as a whole merely widens an already entrenched technology gap between the North and the South.

> In many parts of the world, and especially in Africa, little movement has been evident over the past two decades. Africa has just 3% of the world's television sets, 2% of the world's daily newspapers, and 6% of the world's radio receivers. These proportions are scarcely changing as the world's richer countries pull further ahead in the technology race.[19]

The profit generated by the global media cartel rapidly finds its way back to the Northern hemisphere. Most of the world's data networks connect the countries of the North, fewer the North with the South and fewer still the countries of the Southern hemisphere. While progress is being made in bringing them online the process is proving much slower than the technological sprint that connected the cities and states of the North during the twentieth century. In an era of deregulated telecommunications it seems unlikely that a for-profit corporation is likely to wire the non-metropolitan areas east of the Urals or take on the even more commercially unpromising prospect of many African countries. In the longer term, except in those states which continue to deny web access to their subjects, extra local content clearly encourages greater readership, rises in commercial activity and a greater interest in subsequent online ventures, including news, which in turn will bring extended networks. The fear for those states which are not democracies but which are being drawn towards a liberal or liberalising economy must be that ...

> ... the globalising qualities of the Internet are ... responsible for producing new formulations of governance at the local level which are expressed through the notions of enhanced participatory democratic activity and economic regeneration on the one hand and the re-emergence of local cultural identities on the other.[20]

Such local cultural identities tend, paradoxically, to comprise consumers who have become decidedly global in orientation, accessing broadcast networks based on the other side of the planet and aspiring to alien lifestyles. The shrinking of the world through what David Harvey has described as the 'intensification of time-space compression in social life' tends to produce uncomfortable associations and juxtapositions for illiberal polities and, as Marx warned that it would, pressures on capitalism itself as it produces more commodities than there are consumers for. Globalisation, understood as a station on the upward cycle of economic growth and prosperity, signals a new level of saturation. With information itself as its consummate commodity the demands now placed on technology to bring it to market are exorbitant, hence the frantic bubble-like economy that surrounds the Internet. Since Caxton and Gutenburg new media and cultural forms have never arrived neatly packaged with either their enabling technologies or their social contexts. Rather they evolve from appropriations and hybridisations of earlier forms produced around other technologies and determined by the demands of other contexts.

> No significant cultural form springs into existence fully realized. There is always a gestation period, where the divisions between different genres, conventions, or media types are less defined. These transition points can be disorienting for the societies living through them, and some of the disorientation is of a taxonomic variety, the confusion of creating categories for – and perceiving relationships between – things that are not easily categorized.[21]

The implications for journalism, as its online forms develop, are momentous. Most journalisms are still discovering how to adapt their print forms to the very different capacities of the web. In the process value, style, meaning, function and the very structures that produce it must be rethought and risk being jettisoned as new factors are brought into play. One of those factors is the possibility of an authentic world journalism based on a local/global constituency. The Littleton killings in 1999 saw the world, for a day or two, take *InsideDenver.com* for its morning news. We can see a similar temporary elevation of the local to the global with every breaking news item. As most local papers which have gone online have discovered it does not take those headlining stories to produce global readerships. A century of diasporas and mass emigrations driven by economic and political crises has driven millions of us far from the places we still regard as home. For many the local paper remains the primary signifier of home.

For many others home is not even a place, it is a community based around an interest or an ideology. The failure of a white, colonial Rhodesia in the 1970s, for instance, left what was effectively a diasporic community of a few hundred thousand people scattered around the world. Until the arrival of the web they kept sporadically in touch with printed newsletters that became increasingly unrelated to their everyday lives. With the web they emigrated to the website *Rhodesians Worldwide*[22] and the community began to rebuild. The web takes the members of this global community to a notional, imaginary/historical locale to produce and reinforce a shared identity and a sense of place.

This global or globalised society should perhaps be approached with some caution since it is based on the assumption that the Internet will replace national identity, not with globality but with an almost infinite continuum of identity positions including the global. It implies the possibility of complete cultural dissolution for the offline world.

> ... the 'globalization of culture', ... partly refers to a trans-national or trans-ethnic set of attitudes and practices, and partly to the global cultural supermarket that is said to result from it. The thought is that, as a distinct global culture grows, the particular attitudes and practices that distinguish a culture become artifacts

to be self-consciously identified with rather than determinants of identity. Tibetan Buddhism, so the argument goes, is not different in kind to Coca-Cola, roller-blades, and the Spice Girls ... Cultural dissolution in an on-line world occurs when there are no longer inheritors of a culture, but only mere self-consciously willing possessors of lifestyle attitudes and practices.[23]

While such a cultural melting-pot reading of the globalised society might seem unlikely as a prospect for the near future it does contain elements, especially the economies of scale inherent in it, which must interest the global media providers and their advertisers.

The Global Information Society and the Media Cartel

Noting the decline in 'current affairs factual programming on international topics' in the UK since the beginning of the 1990s, the Third World and Environment Project's response to the EU's 'Green Paper on the Convergence of the Telecommunications, Media and Information Technology Sectors' opens with a statement to the effect that:

The convergence of media, telecommunications and information services is one part of the wider processes of globalisation; but will increasingly become a key economic 'driver' of those processes, creating a 'Global Information Society' ...[24]

The response proceeds to mount a sustained attack on the Green Paper for being 'tendentious' about regulation, accusing it even of 'misrepresentation' around the determining issue of 'economic competitiveness in the information era'. Rather than deregulating media services and abandoning them to the vicissitudes of the market the paper 'does not want to see a world in which information on global affairs is available to those who want it, but only on a niche, specialist, or self-select basis. Citizens of a global information society who, en masse, have little or no access to information that is global in nature, are citizens deprived of their rights and of the capacity to understand their world and to make choices within it'.[25] This is clearly deeply critical of the Green Paper's approach to media regulation and suggests that, far from impeding convergence, regulation can assist in determining a media that is inclusive, diverse and pluralistic, enabling and empowering of its citizens. A casual approach to deregulation or non-regulation 'underplays the dangers of concentration and monopolisation which are inherent in convergence'. The effects of a general gearing up of media companies, including expansion into other geographical markets, vertical and horizontal integration (including mergers) and joint ventures and alliances with other companies, does not augur well for an informed citizenry.

The fifth edition of Bagdikian's *The Media Monopoly* (1997) opens with a kind of grace note and demonstrandum to what has been his thesis since 1983, when he describes American media ownership as 'the new communication cartel'. The takeovers and partnerships that had by 1997 nearly completed the process of consolidating American media into a single mega-conglomerate scaled the process up to global levels in the succeeding years. Kaarle Nordenstreng's argument that even the largest media conglomerates are fairly small fish compared with the global manufacturing giants, debatable even when it was put forward by Robert Picard in 1998,[26] was placed in stark perspective by the proposed partnership between Time Warner, AOL and EMI in January 2000. It was a deal which guaranteed that the global corporate leviathans of the twenty-first century were going to be the telecommunications and media companies, with their online cohorts in the vanguard. The effect for most of the populations of the world seems likely to be one of alienation and disempowerment.

> ... if there has been a major epochal shift since the 1970s, it is not a major discontinuity in capitalism but, on the contrary, capitalism itself reaching maturity. This is indeed a major change – indeed a more substantial change than is encompassed by the idea of globalization. It may be that we are seeing the first real effects of capitalism as a comprehensive system. We are seeing the consequences of capitalism as a system not only without effective rivals but also with no escape routes.[27]

While it seems unlikely that the representation of the local will be lost as media ownership opts for a monolithic structure it will become ever more homogenised. The local media for most communities will be owned by the cartel. At risk, not through any political tyranny but, as George Soros has shown, through a totalitarianism of the market policed by the advertisers, are civil and political rights such as freedom of expression and association as well as the right to follow religions that oppose or are not themselves amenable to that commodification. Statutory rights around consumption will become paramount as consumption defines the subject and the conglomerates, accordingly, need close political allies in the states where they trade and tend to protect them as well as their business partners, stockholders and subsidiaries over the demands and rights of their consumers. Journalists taking the moral high ground over consumer issues and corporate and government crime are likely to find themselves even more personally exposed than their predecessors in the last century.

While local news is necessarily retained it will lose its particularity. Albrow sees the standardisation of media products, taking some elements from the local newsroom and others, such as the design template, from the global brand, as a kind of cultural 'karaoke effect'.

> The possibility of simultaneously providing and separating soundtrack, backing music, screened lyric, voice amplification and any volunteer singer to make a unique performance of a song which has become familiar worldwide makes the individual performance a global act.[28]

The metaphor effectively describes the homogenising effect produced by a global news industry whose values and agendas are set in the headquarters of a handful of global media companies. Those defining values are dictated by a universalisation of the human condition with a collateral flattening of cultural specificity.

For the moment, in most countries outside North America, while the component companies of AOL-Time Warner-EMI and their competitors have achieved the status of primary news providers (the BBC has used CNN footage since before the Gulf War) many citizens still get their daily news from national rather than global providers. In Italy in March 1999 the most visited sites included four Italian newspapers <www.republica.it>, <www.gazzetta.it>, <www.ilsole24ore.it> and <www.mondadori.it>, three Italian portals and Yahoo!, Lycos, Microsoft and Excite.[29] While the trends are as Bagdikian predicted the further one moves from the centres of global capitalism the more information comes from independent and often locally owned media. At the turn of the century the global media in Africa, Asia and South America was still largely independent, if not autonomous. In January 2000 CNN did not 'even rate as a source for news'[30] in South Africa where most online news sites connected to local providers in preference to the global ones. Until most African countries are wired many of their inhabitants will continue to get their news from local newspapers and radio, often still publicly owned since the deregulators have little or no interest in such markets.

For the future, while the consumers of many Southern hemisphere countries seem to prefer local programming, 'a great majority of programmes actually shown are US-made imports – small market diseconomies of scale allow the purchase of imports at 5 to 25 per cent of the cost of equal quality local productions, and local advertisers often prefer the foreign-made programmes anyway for political reasons'.[31] There is a direct impact on web use in these countries since media producers routinely use their output to point consumers to their own production in other media. Most Disney products now point to *Go* and the portal reciprocates by aggressively promoting those same products.

The Planetary News

In researching this book I came upon many examples of how online news has changed local and regional journalisms, usually through a kind of economically determined inevitability and occasionally for the better. Around the world we can now find many instances of a robust interventionist civic journalism which is successfully retaining its advertising and finding new roles in its communities, and while it must always remain at risk its owners seem willing to continue to support it as long as it remains popular and does not mount direct attacks on advertisers. The infinite bandwidth of the web presently also allows for an independent (in so far as it includes the full spectrum of opposition to the global liberal consensus), albeit less well-capitalised, online press to survive as well. As we might expect, on the web it is the popular and established press which continues to attract mass audiences, perhaps not quite at the levels anticipated in 1995, and the advertising revenues that follow them.

It was more difficult to find a continental or global journalism espousing the same standards and aspirations as the local or regional providers. Before the Kosovo crisis in 1999 forcibly changed their opinion many large national providers in the West were becoming increasingly convinced that they did not have to. There was strong evidence that, with the possible exception of the death of Princess Diana, their audiences had largely lost interest in world affairs with the end of the Cold War, since 'a world less threatening ... is less newsy'.[32] James F. Hoge, writing in the *Columbia Journalism Review* in 1997, lists a string of surveys and reports in North America tracing the contraction of foreign news.[33] Similar trends, while perhaps not so marked, were all too apparent in Western Europe. Where foreign news continued to appear it tended to be offered in short descriptive pieces based on events rather than in any depth. Hoge suggests that 'TV's emphasis on dramatic images and short narratives and the intense battle for audiences amid proliferating choices of outlets all work against foreign news. Crises do get covered but without context by correspondents who are parachuted in to report the inflammation.'[34] It may well be that the tendency to discount global news is increased as web-based news delivery systems give consumers the choice to limit their news to the *Daily Me*: lifestyle material, sports scores, listings and weather. Hoge does not omit the suggestion that the sheer expense of foreign news also contributes significantly to its decline. Seymour Topping, former managing editor of the *New York Times*, says, 'The great threat today to intelligent coverage of foreign news is not so much a lack of interest as it is a concentration of ownership that is profit-driven and a lack of inclination to meet responsibilities, except that of the bottom line.'[35] The intense global interest in events in Kosovo in 1999 proved the point and forced national and global news providers to confront their full responsibilities and the demands for a meaningful international news.

If we discount the news portals, which are developing a role for which there is no real equivalent in the traditional media, there are clearly a group of news providers, including, once it has arrived at a sustainable method of underwriting its ambition, *BBC News Online* and some of the news titles now locked into the major media conglomerates such as CNN and *MSNBC*, which are jockeying to be the world's first global consumer news providers. Both *CNN* and *BBC News Online* come to this with something of a head start; however, it is still an open competition for those with the resources to stay in the race.

As the contenders battle it out they have produced news forms offering a depth that was largely absent in the traditional media. The capabilities of hypertext and multimedia forms, and the web's panoramic bandwidth enable the coverage of stories in full context for the first time (books possibly excepted), with their histories, the social and technological forces that determine them and the economic trends and cultural tensions that drive them and emerge from them all represented. The complexity of globality and its stories, for example the Pacific economic crisis of 1998, demand such depth and more if news consumers are to have any real hope of understanding them and their implications. With the web, information about such issues can, for the first time, be offered in organised and accessible structures.

The *Asian Crisis Homepage*,[36] created and maintained by Nouriel Roubini at New York University, while it looks not unlike the *Drudge Report*, indexes every newspaper item, academic report or paper, policy analysis and commentary that Professor Roubini and his assistants can find on the subject. The thousand or so links make it the key global resource on the crisis facing the Pacific Rim economies and one which is regularly used by more than 50,000 users.

Sites such as the *Asian Crisis Homepage* extend the reach of serious journalism dramatically. While they make no claims to be journalism *per se*, they are used by journalists as resources in the production of stories on complex, equivocal subjects and are also likely to be offered to readers as links or sources. Journalism employs the layers that hypertext makes available to enable readers to drill through the news into its contexts and primary sources. This radical approach produces informed and critical readers able to draw out the implications of the news for themselves and to use sophisticated information structures.

Databases, no matter how sophisticated and easily accessible, do not, however, constitute news. For that, perversely as it may seem, the global information society will direct consumers back to their local provider, often owned by a subsidiary of one of the media giants. For global events that provider will direct them in turn to *Tanjug.co.yu*, *DenverPost.com*, *Belfasttelegraph.co.uk* or the appropriate national or regional title. The selection and checking of the day's links have already become a central task of effective journalism. The general sources of news and information which proliferated as mass media forms have been rendered obsolete by the sheer ubiquity and volume of information. From that mass of detail consumers only really need to know about the local – that the fabric of their particular corner of society is still holding together, that the shopkeepers on the High Street are still resisting the planning application for the new out-of-town mall and that there are still a few tickets for the school pantomime which started its run on Tuesday. For the rest, unless it is something they are personally interested in, in which case their local source will deliver the appropriate links accordingly, the broadest outlines are adequate.

Conclusion

The press was the first media sector to test the possibilities of the web as a medium for business. Hesitantly at first but with the coalescing certainty of the gambler on a roll it poured money into a virtual future. With a proven and apparently secure business model that had been developed over 200 years supporting them and an infrastructure geared to producing the content which the web, if it was to succeed, so desperately needed, in 1994 the global press seemed to be standing on the cusp of a golden age. The expensive and, in terms of distribution, intractable wood pulp that blocked the optimisation of profits would soon be a thing of the past and they could focus on the twin goals of reporting the news and selling advertising.

In the event, few newspapers were able to make that smooth transition to online news. In the new medium it soon became clear that their advertising base was not nearly as secure as it had seemed. They opened a war of attrition with web start-ups to defend advertising share, not always successfully. The newspapers had forgotten perhaps that they were themselves a kind of omnibus business with elements accumulated from every corner of the cultural sphere including news of all sorts, from business to sports, weather forecasting, astrology, listings, display and classified advertising and general entertainment. They tried to shovel this unwieldy package wholesale on to the web and were shocked when it started to unravel. Parts of what they saw as their core business were taken up by specialists in the new medium able to handle them rather better than the newspapers had. Valuable assets such as classified and recruitment advertising were stripped away by start-up specialists in the use of online databases. The attrition even stretched as far as the newspapers' primary product, the news itself, as portals, commentators and freebooters such as Matt Drudge began to appropriate it in one way or another.

The most successful online newspapers were those which were able to defend a niche which they had already dominated in print, such as the financial heavyweights of many countries or papers like the *Guardian* in the UK or the *Boston Globe* in North America. Those titles conspicuously reinvented themselves and their role for their online readerships. They developed new ways of telling the news and held their own against the larger resources of the broadcast news corporations who were also reinventing themselves for the web and were now their direct competitors. In 1999 the first Wireless Application Protocol (WAP) telephones included a web browser that provided the news from broadcasters (ITN in the UK) rather than newspaper websites. The *BBC News Online* and *CNN Interactive* had their eyes on even larger fish which were rapidly evolving, to take advantage of the opportunities presented by the first really global medium.

In 1996, with Microsoft already making the move from software to media, Bill Gates wrote that the press 'will change fundamentally' as consumers adopt the Internet. He saw the change as being largely economically determined as first newspapers and then broadcast media lost their advertising base to the web. Just as during the nineteenth century journalism was transformed from a necessarily partisan discourse of conviction to the 'independent' journalism of commerce based on the symbiotic relationship between advertising and the news, so we are now seeing the emergence of an interventionist civic form, in which that relationship is partly disconnected, on the web. Online journalism has not, however, reverted to the partisan medium that existed before the emergence of objectivity. Nor is its agenda, however interventionist, a political one in any conventional sense. Albrow suggests that another process is at play.

> Global citizens are not ruling the global state as Aristotle's citizens did, nor do they have a contractual relationship with it in the manner of modern nation-state citizens. In an important sense

they are actually *performing the state,* creating it through practices which they have learned as the colonized and skilful citizens of the nation-state.[37]

Journalism articulates or scripts that performance of the global polity. As Albrow recognises, the relationship between subject and polity (his notion of the global state is something of an oxymoron) changes the nature of ideology itself, which, instead of organising its apparatuses around the state must find a new object. There are several possibilities, not least the subject, but it seems more likely that, as new sets of power relations emerge they will serve either globality, or, more probably, the global media cartel itself and the corporations that comprise it. Mark Poster proposes that the 'great ideological fiction of liberalism is to reduce the public sphere to existing democratic institutions'.[38] Globality exposes the greater fiction of the relationship between liberalism, at least that liberalism which is articulated through the idea of the liberal democracy, and a capitalism which has outgrown it.

While online editions in English are available for most national news brands and English as *lingua franca* permeates more and more areas of the lives of those who do not have it as their first language, even for those readers with the skills to employ search engines successfully the 'performance' of the global is by no means a simple exercise. The effect of news on the web can be overpowering, like a news-stand confronting the browser with a display of every edition of every newspaper and magazine that the world's media companies have ever published. Tim Berners-Lee himself has described it as being unusably complex, like a huge, unindexed book. It is for journalism and the recognised and read news brands, whether they come from the traditional news sector or are web start-ups, to help consumers to navigate that chaos. The survival of a credible and sustainable global society not entirely based in and preyed upon by the world's largest corporations depends on that informed citizenry.

Notes

Introduction

1. Philip E. Agre, 'Yesterday's tomorrow: the advance of law and order in to the utopian wilderness of cyberspace', *Times Literary Supplement*, 3 July 1998, no. 4970, p. 4.
2. Forrester Research, <www.news.com/News/Item/0,4,24119,00.html>
3. Cheryl Arvidson, 'Is online journalism "different"? A wide divergence of views', *The Freedom Forum Online*, 20 June 1997, <www.freedomforum.org/technology/1998/1/9conffinal.asp>
4. David Randall, *The Universal Journalist*, London: Pluto Press, 1996, p. 2.
5. Bob Steele and Roy Peter Clarke, 'Coverage of the Kennedy Crash: the Crisis of Celebrity Journalism', *Poynter Online*, 29 July 1999, <www.poynter.org/special/point/kennedy.html>
6. Tim Berners-Lee interviewed in 'Visions of the Future', *CNN Interactive*, 1996, <cnn.com/EVENTS/1996/anniversary/visions.future/index.html>
7. Peter Golding, 'Global Village or Cultural Pillage? The Unequal Inheritance of the Communications Revolution', in McChesney, R.W., Ellen Meiksins Wood and John Bellamy Foster (eds), *Capitalism and the Information Age: The Political Economy of the Global Communication Revolution*, New York: Monthly Review Press, 1998, p. 79.
8. Zakon R. Hobbes, *Hobbes' Internet Timeline*, <www.isoc.org/guest/zakon/Internet/History/HIT.html>

Chapter 1

1.   Michael Marien, 'Some Questions for the Information Society', in Tom Forester (ed.), *The Information Technology Revolution*, Oxford: Basil Blackwell, 1985, p. 658.

2.   Walter B. Wriston, 'Dumb Networks and Smart Capital', *The Cato Journal*, Vol. 17, no. 3, October 1997, <www.cato.org/pubs/journal/cj17n3-12.html>

3.   McKenzie Wark, *Virtual Geography: Living with Global Media Events*, Bloomington and Indianapolis: Indiana University Press, 1994.

4.   Robert W. McChesney and Ed Herman, *The Global Media: The New Missionaries of Corporate Capitalism*, New York: Cassell, 1997.

5.   'Pew Research Center Biennial News Consumption Survey', Pew Research Center, 1998, <www.people-press.org/med98rpt.htm>

6.   Carolyn Marvin, *When Old Technologies Were New*, New York: Oxford University Press, 1988.

7.   Nicholas Negroponte, *Being Digital*, London: Hodder & Stoughton, 1995, p. 71.

8.   Negroponte, p. 152. Steve Outing notes that the phrase is to be found in Stewart Brand's 1987 book, *The Media Lab*, in the section about Walter Bender's work at MIT.

9.   Ibid, p.152.

10. Steve Outing, 'Web Community News Finds Its Way to Print', <www.ephome/news/newshtm/stop/stop.htm>

11. Jonathan Steuer, (1992), 'Defining Virtual Reality: Dimensions Determining Telepresence', *Journal of Communication*, vol. 42, no. 4, p. 76.

12. Outing, 'Web Community News'.

13. Walter Bender, *Communicating Business*, London: Forward Publishing, Winter 1994–95.

14. Ibid.

15. Al Gore, 'Networking the future we need a national "Superhighway" for computer information', *Washington Post*, Outlook Section, 15 July 1990, p. B03.

16. Robert H. Reid, *Architects of the Web: 1,000 Days that Built the Future of Business*, New York: John Wiley & Sons, 1997, p. 310.

17. Ian Katz, 'Final Edition', *newsUnlimited*, 13 December 1999, <www.newsunlimited.co.uk/media/story/0,3650,113757,00.htm>

18. 'The Editorial Process', *The Online Newshour*, Media Watch, 26 April 1999 <www.pbs.org/newshour/bb/media/jan-june99/yahoo_qa.html>

19. Pew Research Center, 'Pew Research Center Biennial News Consumption Survey'.

20.   Ibid.
21.   James Fallows with John McChesney, 'The Net as Media Saviour', *HotWired*, September 1997, <www.hotwired.com/synapse/hotseat/9//36/transcript2a.html>
22.   Steven Clift, 'Democracy is Online', *OnTheInternet Magazine*, March–April 1998, from Democracies Online, <www.e-democracy.org/do>. Clift observes that the SangKancil is a small deer capable of routing tigers with its sheer ferocity.
23.   Douglas Jehl, 'Riyadh Journal; The Internet's "Open Sesame" is Answered Warily', *New York Times*, 18 March 1999.
24.   Michael Whine, 'The Far Right on the Internet', in Loader, D. B. (ed.) *The Governance of Cyberspace*, London: Routledge, 1997, pp. 209–27.
25.   <www.almurabeton.org>

Chapter 2

1.   Douglas Rushkoff, *Cyberia: Life in the Trenches of Hyperspace*, London: Flamingo, 1994.
2.   Ben H. Bagdikian, *The Media Monopoly*, Boston: Beacon Press, 1983, p. 182.
3.   John Naughton, 'Internet: Economists reaching a conclusion? Don't be silly', *Observer*, 5 July 1998, p. 9.
4.   <www.stern.nyu.edu/nroubini/asia/AsiaHomepage.html>
5.   Alan Rosenthal, *The New Documentary in Action: A Casebook in Filmmaking*, Berkeley: University of California Press, 1971, p. 103.
6.   Bagdikian, *The Media Monopoly*, p. 132.
7.   John C. Merrill, *Existential Journalism*, New York: Hastings House, 1977, p. 121.
8.   Phillip Knightley, *The First Casualty*, London: Pan, 1989, p. 434.
9.   <www.rawa.org>
10.   I am indebted here to a thread on the *Online News* (online-news@planetarynews.com) list, moderated by Steve Outing, which took place during December 1998.
11.   Jonathan Steuer, 'Defining Virtual Reality: Dimensions Determining Telepresence', *Journal of Communication*, vol. 42, no. 4, Autumn 1992, p. 84.
12.   James Fallows with John McChesney, 'The Net as Media Saviour', *HotWired*, September 1997, <www.hotwired.com/synapse/hotseat/9//36/transcript2a.html>
13.   Steuer, 'Defining Virtual Reality', p. 88.
14.   Ibid., p. 86.
15.   Ibid., p. 86.

16.   Ibid., p. 87.

17.   Department of Trade and Industry, Future Unit, 'Converging Technologies: Consequences for the New Knowledge-Driven Economy', September 1988, <www.dti.gov.uk/future-unit>, p. 18.

18.   Steve Case cited in Sheila Owens, 'Value of journalism rising in info age, AOL's Steve Case says', *The Freedom Forum Online*, 24 September 1998, <www.freedomforum.org/technology/1998/9/24case.asp>

19.   George Gerbner, 'Persian Gulf War: The Movie', in Mowlana, H., G. Gerbner and H. Schiller (eds), *Triumph of the Image: The Media's War in the Persian Gulf – A Global Perspective*, Boulder, CO: Westview Press, 1992, p. 247.

20.   McKenzie Wark, *Virtual Geography*, Bloomington: Indiana University Press, 1994, p. 22.

21.   Linton Weeks, 'The Tangled Web of Libel Law', *Washington Post*, 30 August 1997.

22.   Jon Katz, 'The Browser: Report from Hell High', *Brill's Content*, July–August 1999,
<www.brillscontent.com/columns/browser_0899.html>

23.   Don Aucoin, 'Denver Stations Provide Lens and Voice for Tragedy', *Boston Globe*, 21 April 1999,
<https://commerce.boston.com/bg_archives/newarch.cgi>

24.   Kevin Flynn, 'AOL freezes shooter's Web site', *InsideDenver.com*, 22 April 1999,
<www.insidedenver.com/news/aa/shooting/0422net16/shtml>

25.   <news.excite.com/news> 12 May 1999.

26.   Steve Outing, 'Post-Mortem: Web Coverage of the Columbine Tragedy', *Editor & Publisher Interactive: The Media Info Source*, 3 May 1999.

27.   Ibid.

28.   Peter M. Zollman, 'Community Disaster Coverage: is your news Web site ready?', *Mediainfo.com*, September 1997,
<www.mediainfo.com/ephome/news>

29.   Danny Schechter, 'Covering Wars at Home and Abroad: The Kosovo-Columbine Connection', *Common Dreams News Center*, 29 April 1999,
<www.commondreams.org/kosovo/views/schechter2.htm>

Chapter 3

1.   Don Middleberg and Steven S. Ross, 'Media in Cyberspace', 2 March 1999, *mediasource.com*. The study addressed 3,400 US daily and Sunday newspapers.

2.   Michael Kinsley, editor of *Slate* interviewed in 'Visions of the Future', *CNN Interactive*, 1966, <cnn.com/EVENTS/1996/anniversary/visions.future/index.html>

3.   George Landow, *Hypertext: The Convergence of Contemporary Critical Theory and Technology*, Baltimore: The John Hopkins University Press, 1992, pp. 52–3.

4.   Janet H. Murray, *Hamlet on the Holodeck: The Future of Narrative in Cyberspace*, New York: The Free Press, 1997.

5.   Ibid., p. 137.

6.   Ibid., p. 160.

7.   Thom Lieb, 'Editing for the Web', 1998, <www.towson.edu/~lieb/updates/chapter12/ch12open.html>. The web document is a supplement to Thom Lieb's *Editing for Clear Communication*, New York: McGraw Hill, 1997.

8.   Ibid.

9.   The News Industry Text Format is administered by the International Press Telecommunications Council in the UK, <www.iptc.org/iptc>

10. Brewster Kahle, 'Archiving the Internet', *Scientific American*, March 1997.

11. J.D. Lasica, 'Keeping Online Staffers in Exile', *AJR Newslink*, May 1998. <www.newslink.org/ajrjdmay98.html>

12. Steve Lawrence and C. Lee Giles, 'Accessibility and Distribution of Information on the Web', *Nature*, 400, 8 July 1999, pp. 107–9.

13. Jacob Nielsen interviewed by Amy Gahran, 'Content is a service' and 'Other content considerations', *Contentious*, 14 August 1998, <www.contentious.com/articles/1-5/qal-5b.html>

14. Jeremy Iggers, *Good News, Bad News: Journalism Ethics and the Public Interest*, Boulder, CO: Westview Press, 1999, p. 83.

15. Ibid., p. 83.

16. Akiba A. Cohen, Mark R. Levy, Itzhak Roeh and Michael Gurevich, *Global Newsrooms, Local Audiences: A Study of the Eurovision News Exchange*, London: John Libbey, 1995, p. 144.

17. Eric Meyer, 'Re online-only reporters', Online-News mailing list, Monday 28 June 1999, 17:11:34.

18. Ibid

19. Department of Trade and Industry, Future Unit, 'Converging Technologies: Consequences for the New Knowledge-Driven Economy', September 1998, <www.dti.gov.uk/future-unit>, p. 19.

20. Jacob Nielsen, 'How Users Read on the Web', *Alertbox*, 1 October 1997, <www.useit.com/alertbox/9/10a.html>

Chapter 4

1. Quoted in Derrick Mercer, Geoff Mungham and Kevin Williams, *The Fog of War: The Media on the Battlefield*, London: Heinemann, 1987, p. 10.
2. Matt Welch, 'Beyond B92: 24 Online Sources of Kosovo News', *Online Journalism Review*, 30 March 1999, <www.ojr.usc.edu/sections/features/99stories/storieskosovo 033099.htm>
3. Veran Matic, 'Authoritarian Society and Information Guerilla: Discovering the Values of Civil Society with the Help of the Net (The case of *B92*)', International Studies Association Conference, 17–19 February 1999, Washington DC, <www.nyu/globalbeat/index.html>
4. Adam Clayton Powell, 'Balkans-related Sites Offer Images, Analysis Online', *The Freedom Forum Online*, 2 April 1999, <www.freedomforum.org/technology/1999/4/2radiob92/asp>
5. J.D. Lasica, 'Conveying the War in Human Terms: The Internet Has Been a Major Player in Kosovo Coverage', *AJR*, June 1999, <ajr.newslink.org/ajrjdjune99.html>
6. Tom Standage, *The Victorian Internet*, London: Weidenfeld & Nicolson, 1998, p. 144.
7. Paul Frissen, 'The Virtual State: Postmodernisation, Information and Public Administration', in Loader, B.D. (ed.), *The Governance of Cyberspace: Politics, Technology and Global Restructuring*, London: Routledge, 1997, p. 124.
8. Matic, 'Authoritarian Society and Information Guerilla'.
9. Don North, 'Kosovo: Website War and Cyber Warriors', *Pressroom.com*, June 1999, <dirckhalstead.org/isse9903/north.htm>
10. Jeffrey Benner, 'The China Syndrome?', *Mother Jones*, 13 May 1999, <www.motherjones.com/totalcoverage/kosovo/china.html>
11. North, 'Kosovo'.
12. Declan McCullagh, 'Banning Iran', *HotWired – The Netizen*, 28 August 1996, <www.netizen.com/netizen/96/35/special13a.html>
13. John C. Merrill, *Existential Journalism*, New York: Hastings House, 1977.
14. McKenzie Wark, *Virtual Geography: Living with Global Media Events*, Bloomington and Indianapolis: Indiana University Press, 1994, p. vii.
15. 'Balkan File', *Time.com*, 20 July 1999, <cgi.pathfinder.com/time/daily/special/kosovo/index.html>
16. Frederick M. Dolan, 'Crisis in the Gulf, by George Bush, Saddam Hussein, Et Alia. As Told to the *New York Times*', *Postmodern Culture*, 1991, 1.2, <muse.jhu.edu/journals/postmodern_culture/v001/1.2dolan.html>
17. Ibid.
18. Ibid.

19. 'Reality Check: Genocide', *Mother Jones*, 14 May 1999,
     <www.motherjones.com/total coverage/kosovo/reality check.html>
20. Dolan, 'Crisis in the Gulf'.
21. Ibid.
22. Quoted in David Mercer, Geoff Mungham and Kevin Williams, *The Fog of War: The Media on the Battlefield*, London: Heinemann, 1987, p. 260.
23. Lasica, 'Conveying the War in Human Terms'.
24. This episode was posted to the *Online-News* list by Bonnie Scott on 17 May 1999 under the strand heading, 'Covering your mistakes'.
25. Don North, 'Kosovo Reporting: Website Wars and Cyberwarriors', *General Journalism Discussion*, SPJ–L@LISTS.PSU.EDU, 18 January 1999.
26. Matt Welch, 'Kosovo Highlights Journalism's Failings', *Online Journalism Review*, 9 April 1999,
     <ojr.usc.edu/sections/features/99 stories/stories kosovo 040999.htm>
27. Ibid.
28. Kevin McAuliffe, 'How Correspondents are Dealing with the Hazards, Harassments and Hassles of Getting the News out of the Balkans', *Columbia Journalism Review*, July 1999.
29. Lasica, 'Conveying the War in Human Terms'.
30. Paul Goble, 'World: Analysis from Washington – A War on the Web', *Radio Free Europe/Radio Liberty*, 6 April 1999, <www.referl.org>
31. Lasica, 'Conveying the War in Human Terms'.
32. A.G., 'The War Diaries', 24 March 1999.
33. Ibid.
34. Lasica, 'Conveying the War in Human Terms'.
35. Puay Tang, 'Multimedia Information Products and Services: A Need for "Cybercops"?', in Loader, p. 199.
36. 'Psychological Operations', *US Army Field Manual* 33-1, in Whitaker, R. (ed.), 'Glossary: The Convoluted Terminology of Information Warfare', 24 May 1998,
     <www.informatik.umu.se/~rwhit/IWGlossary.html>
37. Tom Regan, 'Wars of the Future ... Today: The Stealth Battlefields of Information Warfare', *Christian Science Monitor*, 24 June 1999,
     <www.csmonitor.com/durable/1999/06/24/fp13sl-csm.shtml>
38. William Drozdiak, 'Allies Target Yugoslav Phones, Computers', *Washington Post*, 27 May 1999,
     <www.washingtonpost.com/wpssrv/inatl/longterm/balkans/stories/brussels052799.htm>
39. Whitaker proposes a range of synonyms for Netwar which all carry slightly different inflections, including cyberwar and third-wave war.
40. Michael Satchell, 'Captain Dragan's Serbian Cybercorps: How Milosevic Took the Internet Battlefield', *US News.com*, 10 May 1999,
     <www.usnews.com/usnews/issue/990510/10info.htm>

41.   'Serb Hackers Declare Computer War', *Associated Press*, 22 October 1999,
      <search.washingtonpost.com/wp-srv/WAPO/19981022/
      V000405-102298-idx.html>
42.   Edward Stourton, 'Spinning for Victory', *Daily Telegraph*, 16 October 1999, pp. w1 and w2.
43.   Gary Webb, 'Censored: The News that Didn't Make the News', June 1999,
      <www.informinc.co.uk/itn-vs-lm/press/coverage/jun99/
      06-censored-1999.html>
44.   Spomenka Lazic, 'War with Information', AIM Podgorica, 18 May 1999,
      <www.aimpress.org/dyn/trae/archive/data/199905/
      90521-001-trae-pod.htm>
45.   Reporters Sans Frontières, 'War in Yugoslavia – Nato's media blunders', June 1999,
      <www.medienhilfe.ch/News/Archiv/1999/KosoWar/r-s-f1.htm>
46.   Jamie Shea cited in Reporters Sans Frontières.
47.   Reporters Sans Frontières, 'War in Yugoslavia'.
48.   Philip Hammond, 'Nato's Propaganda War', *LM On-line Magazine*, 1 June 1999,
      <www.informinc.co.uk/LM/documentary/kosovo/docu2.html>
49.   Kerrin Roberts cited in Carol Guensburg , 'Online Access to the War Zone', *AJR*, May 1999, <Ajr.newslink.org/ajrcarolmay99.html>
50.   Kerrin Roberts cited in Guensburg.
51.   Matic, 'Authoritarian Society and Information Guerilla'.
52.   Ibid.

Chapter 5

1.   John Naughton, 'Arts Review of the Year: Internet: What the Coronation Did for Television, Bill and Monica Did it for the Net', *Observer*, 27 December 1998, p. 7.
2.   <starr-report.altavista.com>. The site carries the warning, 'The translation of these pages was done without human intervention. The quality of these translations may not fully capture the precision of the original legal text.'
3.   J.D. Lasica, 'A Cybersleaze Timeline: from the Fringes to the Mainstream', *Online Journalism Review*, 7 January 1999,
      <olj.usc.edu/sections/departments/99_stories/watch-_drudgeline.htm>
4.   *Brill's Content*, November 1998, <www.brillscontent.com>
5.   Daniel Dayan and Elihu Katz, *Media Events: The Live Broadcasting of History*, Cambridge, MA.: Harvard University Press, 1996, p. 64.

6.   J.D. Lasica, 'Drudge and Flynt: Two of a Kind', *Online Journalism Review*, 7 January 1999, <olj.usc.edu/sections/departments/99_stories/watch-_010799.htm>

7.   ibid.

8.   Peter Robinson, Robert Zelnick and James Risser, 'Media Circus: The State of the Media', *Uncommon Knowledge*, 1998, <www-hoover.stanford.edu/main/uncommon/fall98/305.html>

9.   Tom Rosenstiel and Bill Kovach, *Warp Speed*, New York: Century Foundation Press, 1999.

10.   BBC SouthWest, 'Regional News', 9 p.m., 21 October 1999.

11.   'Drudge at the National Press Club', *Drudgewatch*, October 1998, <www.intrepidnetreporter.com/drudgewatch.com>

12.   Jonathan Wallace, 'No Gatekeepers', *Ethical Spectacle*, March 1998, <www.spectacle.org/398/hillary.html>

13.   Matt Drudge, *Montreal Gazette*, 23 August 1998.

14.   Jared Sandberg, 'Call it the Drudgegate Affair : the Internet's Intrepid Reporter Finds he Can't Adapt to TV', *Newsweek*, 29 November 1999, <www.newsweek.com/nw-srv/printed/us/na/a21906-1999nov21.htm>

15.   David McClintick, 'The Big Extract: Drudge's Report Card', *Guardian*, 31 October 1998, p. 12.

16.   Ibid.

17.   B.G. Yovovich, 'Journalists Shouldn't Make News Entertaining', *Editor & Publisher Interactive*, 12 April 1999, <www.mediainfo.com/ephome/news/newshtm/stories/041299h2.htm>

18.   Guy Debord, *The Society of the Spectacle*, thesis 193, <www.nothingness.org/SI/debord/SOTS/sotscontents.html>

19.   J. Habermas, *The Structural Transformation of the Public Sphere: an Inquiry into a Category of Bourgeois Society*, Thomas Burger, trans., Cambridge, MA: MIT Press, 1991, p. 193.

20.   Steven Johnson, *Interface Culture: How Technology Transforms the Way We Create and Communicate*, San Francisco: Harper Edge, 1997, p. 102.

21.   <leary.com/mainline.html>

22.   Dayan and Katz, *Media Events*, p. 120.

23.   <whitehouse.gov/WH/New/html/senatebrief.html>

24.   Jean Baudrillard, *Selected Writings*, Mark Poster (ed.), Stanford: Stanford University Press, 1988, pp. 166–84.

25.   Ilham Sadeq, 'Window on Jordan: "Monicagate" gets Jordanians talking', 17 September 1998, <star.arabia.com/9809217/jo3.html>

26.   Joann Byrd, 'Online Journalism Ethics: A New Frontier', *American Editor*, November 1996, p. 6.

27.   Sadeq, 'Window on Jordan'.

28. Gaye Tuchman, 'Objectivity as Strategic Ritual: an Examination of Newsmen's Notions of Objectivity', *American Journal of Sociology*, 77, no. 4, January 1972.
29. Everette E. Dennis, *Reshaping the Media: Mass Communications in an Information Age*, Newbury Park, CA: Sage Publications, 1989, p. 83.
30. Dayan and Katz, *Media Events*.
31. Jeremy Iggers, *Good News, Bad News: Journalism Ethics and the Public Interest*, Boulder, CO: Westview Press, 1999, p. 63.
32. Ibid., p. 75.
33. David McClintick, 'Town Crier for the New Age', *Brill's Content*, November 1998, <brillscontent.com/features/cryer 1198.html>
34. Iggers, *Good News, Bad News*, p. 91.
35. Mark Fishman, *Manufacturing the News*, Austin: University of Texas Press, 1980, p. 88.
36. Jonathan Miller, 'Tangled Web', *Guardian*, 28 July 1998, p. 2.
37. Dayan and Katz, *Media Events*, p. 97.
38. Ibid., p. 216.
39. Iggers, *Good News, Bad News*, p. 120.
40. Ibid., p. 120.
41. Ibid., p. 136.
42. Ibid., p. 137.

Chapter 6

1. Michael Rogers, editor *Newsweek.com*, quoted in Lasica, J.D. 'A Late, Impressive Web Debut', *AJR NewsLink*, January/February 1999, <ajr.newslink.org/ajrlasicajan99.html>
2. Edward Chancellor, *Devil Take the Hindmost: A History of Financial Speculation*, London: Macmillan, 1999, p. 72.
3. Dan Roberts, 'Fishy Ideas Resurface in Rich Waters of the Internet', *Daily Telegraph*, 4 September 1999, p. 28.
4. 'The Emerging Digital Economy', April 1998, US Department of Commerce, reproduced on *Public Agenda Online*, February 1999, <publicagenda.org/issues...ail.cfm?issuetype=internet&list=5>
5. Joshua Cooper Ramo, 'Winner Take All', *Time Magazine*, 16 September 1996, p. 57.
6. Chip Brown, 'Vanity and Panic: Going with the Flow: Money Rushes to Online but, at Least for Now, Doesn't Seem to Come Back', *American Journalism Review, AJR Newslink*, 1999. Based on a 1998 Dataquest report, <ajr.newslink.org/special/12-2.html>
7. Department of Trade and Industry, Future Unit, 'Converging Technologies: Consequences for the New Knowledge-Driven Economy', September 1988, p. 5, <www.dti.gov.uk/future-unit>

8. Department of Trade and Industry, Future Unit, 'Mapping the Future: a Study of Future Thinking within the Department of Trade and Industry', November 1998, p. 4, <www.dti.gov.uk/future-uni>

9. Dan Okrent, 'The Death of Print?', The Hearst New Media Lecture, Graduate School of Journalism, Columbia University, 14 December 1999, <indigo.ie/~liztai/elizabeth/deathofprint.htm>

10. Brown, 'Vanity and Panic'.

11. Ben H. Bagdikian, *The Media Monopoly*, Boston: Beacon Press, 1983 [1992], p. 123.

12. Rosalind Resnick, 'Newspapers on the Net', *Internet World*, July/August 1994, pp. 69–73.

13. Ibid., p. 70.

14. Ibid., p. 71.

15. Steve Outing, 'Get Ready to Sell Innovative, Unique Content Online', *Editor & Publisher Interactive*, 1 March 1999, <mediainfo.com/ephome/news/newshtm/stop/stop.htm>

16. Brown, 'Vanity and Panic'.

17. Mark Toner, 'Extended New Media Index', *Presstime*, Newspaper Association of America, 3 March 1999, <www.naa.org/presstime/9903/htm.html>

18. DTI, Future Unit, 'Mapping the Future', p. 19.

19. Trish Barker, 'Banners Still Dominate', *Spike*, 1999, <www.comm.uiuc.edu/spike/tlbarker/>

20. Henk Rijks, 'Non-local Interest in Local Content ...' posted to *Online News* list, 7 January 1999.

21. Clifford Stoll, *Silicon Snake Oil: Second Thoughts on the Information Highway*, London: Macmillan, 1995, pp. 51–2.

22. Cited in Neda Raouf, 'Editorial or Advertorial: What's the Difference?', *Online Journalism Review*, May 1988, <olj.usc.edu/sections/features/98_stories/stories_advertorial.htm>

23. Bagdikian, *The Media Monopoly*, p. 5.

24. Ibid., pp. ix–x.

25. DTI, Future Unit, 'Mapping the Future', p. 6.

26. Dan Kennedy, 'Merger Mania', *Boston Phoenix*, 1998, <www.igc.apc.org/an/book/merger1.html>

27. Jesse Drew, 'Who Owns the Internet?: an Investigation into the Privatization and Corporate Control of the National Information Infrastructure', *The Committee on Democratic Communications of the National Lawyers Guild*, <www.nlgcdc.org/articles/internet_drew.html>

28. Heather Menzies, 'Challenging Capitalism in Cyberspace: The Information Highway, the Postindustrial Economy, and People', in McChesney, Robert W., Ellen Meiksins Wood and John Bellamy Foster

(eds), *Capitalism and the Information Age: The Political Economy of the Global Communication Revolution*, New York: Monthly Review Press, 1998, p. 89.

29.   Nicholas Baran, 'The Privatization of Telecommunications', in *Capitalism in the Information Age*, pp. 123–34.
30.   Drew, 'Who Owns the Internet?'
31.   Ibid.
32.   <www.igc.org/igc/pn/hg/projectc.html>
33.   Drew, 'Who Owns the Internet?'
34.   Graham Murdoch, 'Large Corporations and the Control of Communications Industries', in Gurevitch *et al.* (eds), *Culture, Society and the Media*, London: Methuen, 1982.
35.   Ibid., p. 133.
36.   DTI, Future Unit, 'Mapping the Future', p. 7.
37.   Baran in McChesney *et al.*, 'The Privatization of Telecommunications', p. 132.
38.   Menzies in McChesney *et al.*, 'Challenging Capitalism in Cyberspace', pp. 87–8.
39.   Robert Reich in an interview with David Bennahum, *Meme 2.02*, 1996, <memex.org/meme2-02.html>
40.   Ibid.
41.   Chatham House Forum, 'Unsettled Times: Three Stony Pathways to the Future', Royal Institute of International Affairs, 1996.
42.   Edward S. Herman and Noam Chomsky, *Manufacturing Consent: The Political Economy of the Mass Media*, New York: Pantheon, 1988.
43.   Edward S. Herman, 'The Propaganda Model Revisited', in McChesney *et al.*, p. 201.

Chapter 7

1.   Hillary Clinton cited in Michael Ronde 'Drudge at the Press Club', <www.intrepidnetreporter.com/drudgewatch.htm>
2.   Adrian Levy and Ian Burrell, 'Anarchists Use Computer Highway for Subversion', *Sunday Times*, 12 March 1995.
3.   Jeffrey A. Perlman, 'Net Censors: The New Control Freaks', *Online Journalism Review*, 6 May 1998, <ojr.usc.edu/sections/features/98_stories/mainbar_censorship_main.htm>
4.   'Trial Possible on Web Porn Law', *CNN Interactive*, 2 February 1999.
5.   'Anti-Abortion Site on Web has Ignited Free Speech Debate', *New York Times*, 13 January 1998.
6.   Alan Travis, 'Watchdog Moves to Curb Racist Websites', *newsUnlimited*, 26 January 2000, <www.newsunlimited.co.uk/racism/Story/0,2763,128931,00.html>

7.   Brian D. Loader, *The Governance of Cyberspace: Politics, Technology and Global Restructuring*, London: Routledge, 1997, p. 6.

8.   'Censored Internet Access in Utah Public Schools and Libraries', *Censorware Project*, March 1999. Cited in <www.publicagenda.org/issues/news.cfm?issue_type=internet>

9.   Steve Lawrence and Lee Giles, 'Accessibility and Distribution of Information on the Web', *Nature*, no. 400, 1999, pp. 107–9.

10. Deja News CEO Guy Hoffman cited in 'Cyber Patrol and Deja News: Censorware Product Blocks an Important Research Resource', *Censorware Project*, 17 February 1998, <www.censorware.org/reports/dejanews/>

11. Kathy Chen, 'China Bans Access to as Many as 100 Web Sites', *Wall Street Journal*, 5 September 1996.

12. John Gittings and Patrick Barkham, 'China Blocks Internet Explosion', *Guardian*, 27 January 2000.

13. James Ryan, 'China's Internet: Boon to Reform or Just a Quick Buck?', *Online Journalism Review*, 11 February 1999, <ojr.usc.edu/sections/features/99_stories/stories_china_021199.html>

14. Posting to 'Internet Licensing' strand SPJ-L@lists.psu, 2 February 1999.

15. <www.eff.org/pub/Publications/John_Perry_Barlow/HTML/porn_and_responsibility.html>

16. <www.amin.org>

17. Brian Whittaker, 'Computing and the Net: Holes in the Censors' Net', *Guardian*, 11 March 1999, p. 6.

18. 'Internet Speech and Privacy: Story Angles', *Public Agenda Online*, 1999, <www.publicagenda.org/issues/angles.cfm?issue_type=internet>

19. Whittaker, 'Computing and the Net'.

20. 'Global Internet Liberty Campaign Member Statement', Electronic Frontier Foundation, 9 September 1999, <www.eff.org/pub/censorship/rating...9990907_gilc_intl_ratings_statement.html>

21. James Kynge, 'Singapore Cracks Down on Internet', *Financial Times*, 12 July 1996.

22. 'Singapore Safeguards Community Interest through Internet Regulation', *Singapore Broadcasting Authority*, news release, 12 July 1996, <www.eff.org/pub/global/singapore/censorship/regulations.071196/txt>

23. Loader, *The Governance of Cyberspace*, p. 15.

24. Dorothy E. Denning, 'The Future of Cryptography', in Loader, *The Governance of Cyberspace*, p. 176.

25. Goh Mui, 'The War is On. It's Official', February 1995, <www.eff.org/pub/censorship/foreig...Hong_Kong/hk_isp_shutdown_022895.article>

26.   Ferdinand David Schoeman, *Privacy and Social Freedom*, Cambridge: Cambridge University Press, 1992, p. 1.

27.   Ibid., p. 13.

28.   Paul Frissen, 'The Virtual State: Postmodernisation, Information and Public Administration', in Loader, Brian D., *The Governance of Cyberspace: Politics, Technology and Global Restructuring*, London: Routledge, 1997, p. 114.

29.   'Beyond Concern: Understanding Net Users' Attitudes about Online Privacy', *AT&T Labs*, 14 April 1999.

30.   Tim Berners-Lee, 'Web Founder Admits Concern about Internet Privacy', *CNN Interactive*, 15 April 1998, <www.cnn.com/TECH/computing/9804/15/aust-internet.ap/index.html>

31.   'The Perspectives in Detail', *PublicAgenda Online*, 1999, <www.publicagenda.org/issues/debate_detail2.cfm?issue_type=internet>

32.   Cited in Frank Beacham, 'The Internet: Can it Become the Next Mass Medium?', April 1996, <www.beacham.com/mediadem.html>

33.   Marty Rimm, 'Marketing Pornography on the Information Superhighway', *Georgetown Law Journal*, no. 83, 1995, pp. 1839–934.

34.   DTI, Future Unit, 'Converging Technologies', p. 27.

35.   <www.shetland-news.co.uk/headline/97nov/settled/settled.html>

36.   Declan McCullagh, 'Plague of Freedom: the Internet's Being Disinfected for your Protection', *Internet Underground*, August 1996, no. 9, pp. 28–33.

37.   John Peryy Barlow, 'Thinking Locally, Acting Globally', *Cyber-Rights Electronic List*, 15 January 1996, <pathfinder.com/time/magazine/archive/1996/dom/960115/essay.html>

38.   Norman Solomon, 'Reporting the News on a "Need to Know" Basis', *Media Beat*, July 1997, <www.zmag.org/zmag/articles/solomonjuly97.html>

39.   Philip Hammond and Ed Herman, *Degraded Capability: The Media and the Kosovo Crisis*, London: Pluto Press, 2000.

40.   Martin Bangemann, 'A New World Order for Global Communications: the Need for an International Charter', *Telecom Inter@ctive*, 8 September 1997, Geneva: International Telecommunications Union.

41.   Ibid.

42.   Martin Bangemann, 'Europe and the Information Society – the Policy Response to Globalisation and Convergence', *Telecom Inter@ctive*, 18 September 1997, Geneva: International Telecommunications Union.

Chapter 8

1.   Steve Case cited in Cheryl Arvidson, 'AOL's Case: Net Could Provide the Ties that Bind Democracy', *The Freedom Forum Online*, 9 January 1998, <www.freedomforum.org/technology/1998/1/9case.asp>
2.   Leigh Clayton, 'Are There Virtual Communities?', *Ends and Means*, vol. 2, no. 1, Autumn 1997, <www.abdn.ac.uk/cpts/clayt.htm>
3.   David Lyon, 'Cyberspace Sociality: Controversies Over Computer-mediated Relationships', in Loader, Brian D. (ed.), *The Governance of Cyberspace: Politics, Technology and Global Restructuring*, London: Routledge, 1997, p. 37.
4.   Loader, *The Governance of Cyberspace*, p. 34.
5.   <www.manchester.com/java/home.shtml>
6.   John V. Pavlik, 'The Future of Online Journalism', *Columbia Journalism Review*, July/August 1997, <www.cjr.org/year/97/4/online.asp>
7.   Gary, T. Dempsey, 'The Myth of an Emerging Information Underclass', *CATO This Just In*, 20 November 1997, <www.cato.org/danys/11-20-97/html>
8.   Loader, *The Governance of Cyberspace*, p. 113.
9.
10. Jurgen Habermas, *The Structural Transformation of the Public Sphere: an Inquiry into a Category of Bourgeois Society*, Thomas Burger, trans., Cambridge, MA: MIT Press, 1991, p. 219.
11. David Lyon, 'Cyberspace sociality: Controversies over computer-mediated relationships' in Loader (ed.), p. 25.
12. Martin Albrow, *The Global Age*, Cambridge: Polity Press, 1996, p. 110.
13. Ibid., p. 4.
14. Ibid., p. 73.
15. Anthony G. McGrew, 'A Global Society?', in Hall, S., D. Held and A. McGrew (eds), *Modernity and its Futures*, Cambridge: Polity Press, 1992, p. 63.
16. Albrow, *The Global Age*, p. 112.
17. George Soros, 'The Capitalist Threat', *Atlantic Monthly*, February 1997, <www.theatlantic.com/issues/97feb/capital/capital.htm>
18. Albrow, *The Global Age*, p. 112.
19. Peter Golding, 'Global Village or Cultural Pillage? The Unequal Inheritance of the Communications Revolution', in McChesney, R.W., Ellen Meiksins Wood and John Bellamy Foster (eds), *Capitalism and the Information Age: The Political Economy of the Global Communication Revolution*, New York: Monthly Review Press, 1998, pp. 75–6.
20. Loader, *The Governance of Cyberspace*, p. 9.

21. Steven Johnson, *Interface Culture: How Technology Transforms the Way We Create and Communicate*, San Francisco: Harper Edge, 1997, p. 37.

22. <bluering.cowan.edu.au/rwebb/>

23. Jonathan Friday, 'Who's Afraid of an On-Line Society?', *Ends and Means*, vol. 3, no. 2, Spring 1999, <www.abdn.ac.uk/cpts/Friday1.htm>

24. <www.ispo.cec.be/convergencegp/3we.html>

25. <www.ispo.cec.be/convergencegp/3we.html>

26. Kaarle Nordenstreng, 'Mass Communication', Gary Browning, Abigail Halcli and Frank Webster (eds), *Understanding Contemporary Society: Theories of the Present*, London: Sage Publications, 2000, pp. 328–42.

27. Ellen Meiksins Wood, 'Modernity, Postmodernity, or Capitalism?', in McChesney, R.W., Ellen Meiksins Wood and John Bellamy Foster (eds), p. 47.

28. Albrow, *The Global Age*, p. 147.

29. Osservatorio Internet Italia, 21 March 1999, <www.sda.uni-bocconi.it/oii>

30. Megan Knight, posting to the thread 'AOL-Time Warner – worldwide domination?', *Online-News List*, 17 January 2000.

31. Edward Herman and Robert W. McChesney, *The Global Media: the New Missionaries of Global Capitalism*, London and Washington: Cassell, 1997, p. 191.

32. James F. Hoge, 'Foreign News: Who Gives a Damn?', *Columbia Journalism Review*, November/December 1997, <www.cjr.org/year/97/6/foreign.asp>

33. Ibid.

34. Ibid.

35. Ibid.

36. <www.stern.nyu.edu/nroubini/asia/AsiaHomepage.html>

37. Albrow, *The Global Age*, p. 177.

38. Mark Poster, 'CyberDemocracy: Internet and the Public Sphere', in Porter, D. (ed.), *Internet Culture*, London: Routledge, 1996, pp. 201–17, <humanities.uci.edu/mposter/writings/democ.html>

Glossary

accessibility The degree to which social, cultural and other resources including information are available to users. The exclusion of large fractions of the world's populations from such resources because of their economic or social status is one of the major challenges that now faces providers.

aggregator A website whose main function, rather than producing news stories and other information, is to link, perhaps with brief synopses, to sites that do, allowing users to gain access to the maximum number of stories with minimal searching.

bandwidth The amount of data, measured in bits per second, that can be sent through a connection. A page of text usually comprises about 15,000 bits and can be processed by a fast modem in a second or so. Fully featured multi-media with audio and video demands about 10,000,000 bits per second depending on how it has been compressed.

[ro]bots Any type of automated software; however, the word specifically refers to programs (also known as spiders and crawlers) that trawl the web for specific targets and return information to their originators. Large web directories such as AltaVista and Lycos are largely built and maintained on information from bots. Another type of bot, specialising in cocktail party chat lines, is employed to draw people (and presumably other bots) into IRCs.

browser Client software enabling consumers to take information from the web. At the time of writing the market is evenly split between two products, Netscape Communicator and Microsoft's Internet Explorer.

CERN (Conseil Européen Pour La Recherche Nucléaire) The European Particle Physics Laboratory in Switzerland. The place where Tim Berners-Lee devised the WWW software.

click-stream The footprints that web users leave behind them as they link from page to page and website to website. This trajectory is evident both from within the user's own browser, where it is recorded as a 'history', and from external tracking software.

client A device (usually software) that accesses the information and services provided by a server (another piece of software). For the most part clients are the web browsers or search engines used to access information on the web.

cookies Small files which seek information about user registration and preferences. They are sent by web servers to browsers to be saved and returned when the user revisits the server. Browsers can be configured by users to accept or reject cookies and are usually set anyway to expire after a predetermined time. Cookies are not malign and usually speed up the process of web browsing as well as supplying the information that ultimately pays for so much apparently free content on the web.

CPM (cost per thousand) Websites selling advertising set rates at their CPM rate multiplied by a guaranteed number of page impressions (number of times ads are downloaded).

cryptography Encryption changes the form of data so that it can only be read by someone with knowledge – the decryption key – of those changes, usually the intended receiver. Public-key encryption employs a public key coupled with a private key for decryption. PGP (Pretty Good Privacy) is a public-key encryption system. Many of the debates around state regulation of the web are around the level of encryption that should be legal for private individuals and organisations.

disintermediation The tendency of information systems to short-circuit the machinery of the industrial age. Traditional retailing loses its central role in commerce with the emergence of e-commerce and journalists and political party machines are no longer required to mediate between politicians and their constituencies.

Domain Name System The hierarchical and universal system of naming servers or websites (such as *newsUnlimited.co.uk*)

email (electronic mail) Messages – usually text but other media forms can also be mailed – sent from one person to another via a computer or other devices. Email can also be bulk mailed which makes it a useful news medium.

filtering The reduction of a stream of information to more or less impoverished strands through the use of criteria such as news value or the public good (*see* information overload).

flame Derogatory comment often articulated with some crudity; also employed as a verb.

form and content Markup languages for news now insist on the separation of form and content. The basic text of documents is structured separately from stylistic and design elements. The principle allows for the greater portability of content across a whole range of applications from print to WAP.

GIF (Graphics Interchange Format) A file format employed to transmit images pixel by pixel over the Internet. Other formats in current use are JPEG and PNG.

globalisation A catch-all concept used to describe the interpenetration of national markets determined by systems of capital that remain unattached to nation states and technologies of production which easily and rapidly leapfrog themselves (and hence can be redeployed in new locations on a regular basis). Contemporary models of consumption, seemingly encouraging violent cultural and social fragmentation, give a cultural inflection to a process that might otherwise appear to be largely economic.

graphics Two- or three-dimensional images such as illustrations or photographs. The convention of small graphics (icons) used to symbolise complex computing functions led to the development of the 'graphical browser' or icon-driven web server and similar interfaces for most popular software packages.

hacker (more correctly **cracker**) A (usually malicious) user who tries to access sensitive information. The term 'hacker' also applies to those who enjoy exploring software systems with a view to extending their capabilities.

home page The main (entry) web page for a business, organisation, person or simply the main page out of a collection of web pages. The word originally referred to the page that a browser was defaulted to open to.

host (server) A web host or server stores web pages and allows clients (browsers and search engines) to read them and to write to them.

HTML (Hypertext Markup Language) A set of instructions (tags) which render text and images browser-readable and enable hyperlinks. Most web pages are still constructed in HTML.

HTTP (Hypertext Transfer Protocol) The computer protocols (or handshake) which enable the movement of data (rendered as hypertext) around the Internet.

hyperlink A gateway from a particular point in a document which opens on to another location either in the same document or another one hosted in the same or another server. Hyperlinks can call up appropriately tagged documents anywhere on the Internet and are thus the basic building blocks for connectivity.

hypertext (hypermedia) Text that contains multiple more-text cues or links instead of, or in addition to, the implicit one that lies at the foot of the page or column and which hence produces narratives that are non-linear and which refuse accepted notions of closure.

information overload The state of confusion and inertia that arises when searchers after information aspire to everything on their subject rather than appropriate information. The sense of vertigo that new web users experience on receipt of 698,436 hits from a search engine query is a typical response to information overload.

information society The notion of a post-industrial global economy which employs information as its primary currency. The defining characteristics of the information society seem to include the development of information (and knowledge work) as the primary strategic resource for economic development, the introduction of the global information networks upon which the structure is based and a globalisation of capitalism which is enabled by, and exists within, those networks.

information space Cyberspace, the dimension where everything reducible to information (communication, media, money, identity) is transacted and deposited.

intelligent agent Software programmed to scour the Internet for specified kinds of information. Such agents are intelligent in so far as they can remember what they have already found, refine search patterns in the light of the success or failure of previous results and extrapolate new kinds of information that the user is likely to wish to access.

interactivity - The real-time production or adaptation of texts (form and content) by users in a mediated environment.

interface Also user interface (UI). The space in which users and computers communicate. A command-driven interface requires the user to type in instructions for the computer to follow while a graphical user interface (GUI) offers sets of commands represented by icons, windows, menus and dialog boxes.

Internet (Net) An electronic network of networks linking many, although not all, parts of the world. Information is broken into small packets and passed between computers linked to these networks to be reconstituted at its destination.

inverted pyramid - Journalistic form based on the hierarchical arrangements of facts in order of importance (as established by a suitably qualified professional). Model of news writing associated with the cult of objectivity.

IP (Internet Protocol) The rules that govern the transmission of information over the Internet.

IRC (Internet Relay Chatline) A multi-user live text-based chat facility. Users create a channel to attract interventions from others which are shared by everyone in the channel. Also used for multi-person conference calls.

ISP (Internet Service Provider) An organisation which provides users with connection to the Internet by cable, phone or wireless. In most cases the ISP acts as a gateway for information pulled and pushed by the user.

Java Originally designed to drive small devices, this programming language was taken up to expand radically the functionality of browsers. Java programs called applets (little applications) run inside browsers to produce effects and interactivity.

JPEG (Joint Photographic Experts Group) A more economic format for encoding images than GIFs or PNGs.

lexia Self-contained unit of signification capable of producing meaning on its own and comprising the basic element of hypertext.

micropayment Conventions enabling the purchase, integral to the process of browsing, of very low-priced access to web-based documents.

mobile devices Phones and other hand-held communications devices which are increasingly configured as web clients. Adaptations of markup languages such as WAP are specifically geared to serving such devices.

Mosaic Developed by Marc Andreessen and others, the first graphical web browser to gain a mass currency and the model that defined most contemporary browsers.

newsgroup Discussion groups on the Usenet.

NITF (News Industry Text Format) Also NewsML. Developments of markup languages geared to the creation, transfer and delivery of news forms and the data they carry.

NNTP (Network News Transfer Protocol) The rules that govern the transfer of news articles around the network. Items are posted to computers that do not yet have them.

node The object or point where links meet. For hyperlinks the node is the web page and for data networks it is the computer.

open source Programs whose source code is in the public domain and freely distributed. Anyone can modify or repurpose such programs, or extend them through the development of other software that will operate in conjunction with them. The operating system LINUX is open source.

PGP (Pretty Good Privacy) A security system mainly for email that employs public key cryptography. It is based on the notion that users should be able to choose who they can trust.

plug-in An applications program used in a browser to view or play multimedia downloaded from the web.

PNG (Portable Network Graphics) A browser-readable file format which encodes images pixel by pixel.

portal A website designed as a main point of entry to the web usually offering a combination of news, an index of other sites and a search engine. Users can set a favourite portal as the default site that their browser will load up to.

push/pull Push technologies send data to clients without the client requesting it. Pull data is requested by clients. The web is based on a pull technology with web pages only being transmitted at the request of clients. Broadcast media are push media in that they send information out regardless of whether they even have an audience. While they remain the exception there are now many examples of push media systems (such as *Pointcast*) on the web. Email is a good example of push media.

search engine Web-based software which allows users to search web resources by keyword.

server (*see* host)

SGML (Standard Generalized Markup Language) The international standard for markup languages.

Shockwave A Macromedia technology which enables web pages to include multimedia objects. Most current web editors include the possibility of adding 'shocked' files to web pages. For Shockwave objects to work the client needs the Shockwave plug-in.

shovelware The inappropriate and direct transfer of text from one medium to another against the dictates of convention and genre. Early television drama might be considered to have been shovelled from the stage (*see* form and content).

style sheet The instructions that enable a browser to produce a web page, with its component layout, colours, fonts, etc., from a marked-up document.

telepresence The subjective experience of presence in a technologically mediated environment such as an IRC (*see* virtuality).

Telnet A mechanism for remote log-in. Enables users to access resources on remote computers using the Internet.

URI (Universal Resource Identifier) The string which identifies web objects or pages, <www.ordinalia.com/glasney>

URL (Uniform Resource Locator) A descriptor which allows some URIs, such as those attached to some news articles, to be subject to change.

Usenet A decentralised global network of over 10,000 discussion groups on subjects from online journalism to geranium growing. The network extends beyond the web and the Internet.

virtual hypertext Hypertext that is produced by a program rather than through the retrieval of a stored file.

virtual reality (virtuality) An artificial environment in which all sensory information is generated by computer hardware and software. Virtuality systems complete the illusion of a total environment by monitoring users' actions and responding to them.

virus An application designed to infect and affect – sometimes destroy – other programs, data and even computer equipment.

WAP (Wireless Applications Protocol) The specification, including WML (Wireless Markup Language, based on XML), that standardises the way in which wireless devices, such as telephones and radio transceivers, can be used for Internet access, including email, the web, newsgroups and chat lines.

website A set of web pages (usually connected by hyperlinks and stylistic conventions) constructed around a specific organisation, person or interest group.

WWW (World Wide Web, abbreviated to the web) All the information, identifiable through URIs, which is available to networked computers. The popular face of the Internet.

XML (Extensible Markup Language) The generic language, developed from SGML, for creating new markup languages. XML takes account of the separation of form and content in web documents.

Bibliography

Agre, Philip E., 'Yesterday's Tomorrow: the Advance of Law and Order into the Utopian Wilderness of Cyberspace', *Times Literary Supplement*, 3 July 1998, no. 4970, pp. 3–4.

Albrow, M., *The Global Age*, Cambridge: Polity Press, 1996.

Arvidson, Cheryl, 'Is Online Journalism "Different"? A Wide Divergence of Views', *The Freedom Forum Online*, 20 June 1997, <www.freedomforum.org/technology/1998/1/9conffinal.asp>

Bagdikian, B., *The Media Monopoly*, Boston: Beacon Press, 1983.

Baudrillard, Jean, *The Gulf War Did Not Take Place*, Paul Patton, trans., Bloomington and Indianapolis: Indiana University Press, 1995.

Bender, W., *Communicating Business*, London: Forward Publishing, 1994.

Benedikt, M. (ed.), *Cyberspace: First Steps*, Cambridge, MA: MIT, 1992.

Blumler, J.G. and Michael Gurevitch, *The Crisis of Public Communication*, London: Routledge, 1995.

Bourdieu, P., *Outline of a Theory of Practice*, Cambridge: Cambridge University Press, 1972, 1977.

Britton, J., *Language and Learning*, London: Penguin, 1970.

Browning, G., Abigail Halcli and Frank Webster (eds), *Understanding Contemporary Society: Theories of the Present*, London: Sage Publications, 2000.

Burnstein, M.R., 'Conflicts on the Net: Choice of Law in Transnational Cyberspace', *Vanderbilt Journal of Transnational Law*, 29(75), 1996, pp. 77–116.

Byrd, J., 'Online Journalism Ethics: A New Frontier', *American Editor*, November 1996, pp. 6–7.

Chancellor, E., *Devil Take the Hindmost: A History of Financial Speculation*, London: Macmillan, 1999.

Chartier, R., *Forms and Meanings: Texts, Performances, and Audiences from Codex to Computer*, Philadelphia: University of Pennsylvania Press, 1995.

Chomsky, Noam, *Necessary Illusions: Thought Control in Democratic Societies*, London: Pluto Press, 1989.

Cohen, A.A., Mark R. Levy, Itzhak Roeh and Michael Gurevich, *Global Newsrooms, Local Audiences: A Study of the Eurovision News Exchange*, London: John Libbey, 1995.

Curran, J. and Jean Seaton, *Power Without Responsibility: The Press and Broadcasting in Britain*, 4th edn, London: Routledge, 1991.

Dayan, D. and Elihu Katz, *Media Events: The Live Broadcasting of History*, Cambridge, MA: Harvard University Press, 1996.

Dennis, Everette E., *Reshaping the Media: Mass Communications in an Information Age*, Newbury Park CA: Sage Publications, 1989.

Duncombe, S., *Notes from the Underground: Zines and Politics of Alternative Culture*, London and New York: Verso, 1997.

Featherly, Kevin, *Guide to Building a Newsroom Web Site*, Radio and Television News Directors Foundation, 1998.

Ferrarotti, Franco, *The Myth of Inevitable Progress*, Westport, CT: Greenwood, 1985.

Fishman, Mark, *Manufacturing the News*, Austin: University of Texas Press, 1980.

Forester, T. (ed.), *The Information Technology Revolution*, Oxford: Basil Blackwell, 1985.

Habermas, J., *The Theory of Communicative Action*, vol. 1, *Reason and the Rationalization of Society*, Thomas McCarthy, trans., Boston: Beacon Press, 1984.

Habermas, J., *The Structural Transformation of the Public Sphere: An Inquiry into a Category of Bourgeois Society*, Thomas Burger, trans., Cambridge, MA: MIT Press, 1991.

Hall, S., D. Held and A. McGrew (eds), *Modernity and its futures*, Cambridge: Polity Press, 1992.

Hamilton, A., *The Financial Revolution*, New York: The Free Press, 1986.

Harvey, D., *The Condition of Postmodernity*, Cambridge and Oxford: Blackwell, 1989.

Hawkins, R., John M. Wiemann and Suzanne Pingree (eds), *Advancing Communication Science: Merging Mass and Interpersonal Processes*, Newbury Park, CA: Sage, 1988.

Hellin, Daniel C., *We Keep America on Top of the World: Television Journalism and the Public Sphere*, London: Routledge, 1994.

Herman, E. and Noam Chomsky, *Manufacturing Consent: The Political Economy of the Mass Media*, New York: Pantheon, 1988.

Herman, E. and Robert W. McChesney, *The Global Media: The New Missionaries of Global Capitalism*, London and Washington: Cassell, 1997.

Hohendahl, P., 'Jurgen Habermas: "The Public Sphere" 1964', *New German Critique*, no. 3, Fall 1974, pp. 45–55.

Iggers, Jeremy, *Good News, Bad News: Journalism Ethics and the Public Interest*, Boulder, CO: Westview Press, 1999.

Johnson, S., *Interface Culture: How Technology Transforms the Way We Create and Communicate*, San Francisco: Harper Edge, 1997.

Jonscher, C., *Wired Life: Who Are We in the Digital Age?*, London: Bantam Press, 1999.

Jussawalla, M., Tadayuki Okumaa and Toshihiro Araki (eds), *Information Technology and Global Interdependence*, New York: Greenwood Press, 1989.

Kahle, B., 'Archiving the Internet', *Scientific American*, March 1997.

Kellner, Douglas, *The Persian Gulf TV War*, Boulder, CO: Westview, 1992.

Kleiner, K., 'Sweet Sound of Cash Registers on the Internet', *New Scientist*, 3 June 1995, p. 7.

Knightley, P., *The First Casualty*, London: Pan, 1989.

Landow, G., *Hypertext: The Convergence of Contemporary Critical Theory and Technology*, Baltimore: The John Hopkins University Press, 1992.

Landow, G. (ed.), *Hyper/Text/Theory*, Baltimore: The John Hopkins University Press, 1994.

Lawrence, S. and Lee Giles, 'Accessibility and Distribution of Information on the Web', *Nature*, no. 400, 1999, pp. 107–9.

Levinson, P., *Digital McLuhan: A Guide to the Information Millennium*, London: Routledge, 1999.

Loader, D.B. (ed.), *The Governance of Cyberspace*, London: Routledge, 1997.

Lull, J. and Stephen Hinerman, *Media Scandals: Morality and Desire in the Popular Culture Marketplace*, Cambridge: Polity Press, 1997.

Markley, R., *Virtual Realities and their Discontents*, Baltimore: John Hopkins University Press, 1996.

Marvin, C., *When Old Technologies Were New*, New York: Oxford University Press, 1988.

Mattelart, Armand, *Mapping World Communication: War, Progress and Culture*, Susan Emmanuel and James A. Cohen, trans., University of Minnesota Press, 1994.

May, T., 'Crypto Anarchy and Virtual Communities', *Internet Security*, April 1995, pp. 4–12.

McChesney, R.W. and Ed Herman, *The Global Media: The New Missionaries of Corporate Capitalism*, New York: Cassell, 1997.

McChesney, R.W., Ellen Meiksins Wood and John Bellamy Foster (eds), *Capitalism and the Information Age: The Political Economy of the Global Communication Revolution*, New York: Monthly Review Press, 1998.

Mercer, D., Geoff Mungham and Kevin Williams, *The Fog of War: The Media on the Battlefield*, London: Heinemann, 1987.

Merrill, J., *Existential Journalism*, New York: Hastings House, 1977.

Morrison, David E. and Howard Tumber, *Journalists at War: The Dynamics of News Reporting during the Falklands Conflict*, London: Sage Publications, 1988.

Moulthrop, S., 'Containing Multitudes: The Problem of Closure in Interactive Fiction', *Association for Computers and the Humanities Newsletter*, 10 (1988) 1, 7.

Mowlana, H., G. Gerbner and H. Schiller, *Triumph of the Image: The Media's War in the Persian Gulf – A Global Perspective*, Boulder, CO: Westview Press, 1992.

Murray, J.H., *Hamlet on the Holodeck: The Future of Narrative in Cyberspace*, New York: The Free Press, 1997.

Negroponte, N., *Being Digital*, London: Hodder & Stoughton, 1995.

Noelle-Neumann, E., *The Spiral of Silence. Public Opinion – Our Social Skin*, 2nd edn, Chicago: University of Chicago Press, 1993.

Porter, D. (ed.), *Internet Culture*, London: Routledge, 1996.

Randall, D., *The Universal Journalist*, London: Pluto Press, 1996.

Reddick, R. and E. King, *The On-line Journalist: Using the Internet and Other Electronic Resources*, Fort Worth, TX: Harcourt Brace College, 1995.

Reid, R.H., *Architects of the Web: 1,000 Days that Built the Future of Business*, New York: John Wiley & Sons, 1997.

Resnick, Rosalind, 'Newspapers on the Net', *Internet World*, July/August 1994, pp. 69–73.

Rheingold, H., *The Virtual Community: Finding Connection in a Computerized World*, London: Minerva, 1994.

Rimm, Marty, 'Marketing Pornography on the Information Superhighway', *Georgetown Law Journal*, no. 83, 1995, pp. 1839–934.

Rosenstiel, Tom and Bill Kovach, *Warp Speed*, New York: Century Foundation Press, 1999.

Rosenthal, A., *The New Documentary: A Casebook in Film-making*, Berkley: University of California Press, 1971.

Rushkoff, D., *Cyberia: Life in the Trenches of Hyperspace*, London: Flamingo, 1994.

Schoeman, F.D., *Privacy and Social Freedom*, Cambridge: Cambridge University Press, 1992.

Schofield, J., 'Portal combat', *Guardian*, 15 April 1999, p. 2.

Schudson, Michael, *The Power of News*, Cambridge, MA: Harvard University Press, 1995.

Servaes, J. and Rico Lie (eds), *Media and Politics in Transition: Cultural Identity in the Age of Globalisation*, Leuven, Belgium and Amersfoort, NL: Uitgeverij Acco, 1997.

Shenk, David, *Data Smog*, San Francisco, CA: Harper Edge, 1997.

Slouvka, Mark, *War of the Worlds: The Assault on Reality*, London: Abacus, 1996.

Sofos, S., 'Mass Communication and the "Nationalisation" of the Public Sphere in Former Yugoslavia', *Res Publica, Belgian Journal of Political Science*, 2, 1997.

Solomon, N., 'Virtual History and Virtual Mendacity', *The Columbus Free Press*, 23 May 1997, <www.freepress.org/solomon/virtual.html>

Standage, T., *The Victorian Internet*, London: Weidenfeld & Nicolson, 1998.

Steuer, J. (1992), 'Defining Virtual Reality: Dimensions Determining Telepresence,' *Journal of Communication*, vol. 42, no. 4, 1992, pp. 73–93.

Stoll, Clifford, *Silicon Snake Oil: Second Thoughts on the Information Highway*, London: Macmillan, 1995.

Taylor, J.A. and H. Williams, 'Public Administration and the Information Polity', *Public Administration*, 69, 1991, pp. 171–90.

Tsagarousianou, R., D. Tambini and C. Bryer, *Cyberdemocracy: Technology, Cities and Civic Networks*, London: Routledge, 1998.

Tuchman, Gaye, *Making News*, New York: The Free Press, 1978.

Turkle, S., *Life on the Screen: Identity in the Age of the Internet*, London: Weidenfield and Nicolson, 1996.

Wark, M., *Virtual Geography: Living with Global Media Events*, Bloomington and Indianapolis: Indiana University Press, 1994.

Whittaker, B., 'Computing and the Net: Holes in the Censors' Net', *Guardian*, 11 March 1999, p. 6.

Web

Benner, Jeffrey, 'The China Syndrome?' *Mother Jones*, 13 May, 1999, <www.motherjones.com/total coverage/kosovo/china.html>

Berners-Lee, T. and others interviewed in 'Visions of the Future', *CNN Interactive*, 1996, <cnn.com/EVENTS/1996/anniversary/visions.future/index.html>

Chomsky, N., *Comment on Iraq Bombing*, <www.zmag.org/chomiraq>

Clift, S., 'Democracy is Online', *OnTheInternet Magazine*, March/April 1998. Article downloaded from Democracies Online: <www.e-democracy.org/do>

Dolan, F.M., 'Crisis in the Gulf, by George Bush, Saddam Hussein, Et Alia. As Told to the *New York Times*', *Postmodern Culture*, 1991, 1.2, <muse.jhu.edu/journals/postmodern_culture/v001/1.2dolan.html>

Fallows, J. with John McChesney, 'The Net as Media Saviour', *HotWired*, September 1997, <www.hotwired.com/synapse/hotseat/9//36/transcript2a.html>

Hoffman, D. and Thomas Novak, 'Marketing in Hypermedia Computer-Mediated Environments: Conceptual Foundations', <www2000.ogsm.vanderbilt.edu/cme.conceptual.foundations.html>

Katz, J., 'The Browser: Report from Hell High', *Brill's Content*, July/August 1999, <www.brillscontent.com/columns/browser_0899.html>

Lasica, J.D., 'Keeping Online Staffers in Exile', *AJR Newslink*, May 1998, <www.newslink.org/ajrjdmay98.html>

Lasica, J.D., 'Conveying the War in Human Terms: the Internet Has Been a Major Player in Kosovo Coverage', *AJR Newslink*, June 1999, <ajr.newslink.org/ajrjdjune99.html>

Lieb, T., 'Editing for the Web', 1998, <www.towson.edu/~lieb/updates/chapter12/ch12open.html>

Middleberg, D. and Ross, S. S., 'Media in Cyberspace', 2 March 1999, <mediasource.com>

Nielsen. J., interviewed by Amy Gahran, 'Content is a service' and 'Other content considerations', *Contentious*, 14 August 1998, <www.contentious.com/articles/1-5/qal-5b.html>

Outing, S., 'Web Community News Finds Its Way to Print', <www.ephome/news/newshtm/stop/stop.htm>

Poster, M., 'CyberDemocracy: Internet and the Public Sphere', 1995, <humanities.uci.edu/mposter/writings/democ.html>

Steele, B. and Roy Peter Clarke, 'Coverage of the Kennedy Crash: The Crisis of Celebrity Journalism', *Poynter Online*, 29 July 1999, <www.poynter.org/special/point/kennedy.html>

Welsh, Matt, 'Beyond B92: 24 Online Sources of Kosovo News', *Online Journalism Review*, 30 March 1999, <ojr.usc.edu/sections/features/99_stories/stories_kosovo_033099.htm>

Whitaker, Randall (ed.), 'Glossary: The Convoluted Terminology of Information Warfare', 24 May 1998, <www.informatik.umu.se/~rwhit/IWGlossary.html>

Zollman, P.M., 'Community Disaster Coverage: is your news Web site ready?' September 1997, *Mediainfo.com*, <www.mediainfo.com/ephome/news>

Index